# William Roscoe

*Commerce and Culture*

# William Roscoe
## *Commerce and Culture*

ARLINE WILSON

LIVERPOOL UNIVERSITY PRESS

First published 2008 by
Liverpool University Press
4 Cambridge Street
Liverpool L69 7ZU

British Library Cataloguing-in-Publication data
A British Library CIP record is available


ISBN 978-1-84631-130-7 cased




Typeset by XL Publishing Services, Tiverton
Printed and bound by Bell and Bain Ltd, Glasgow

For Michael, David, Alice and Rory

# Contents

# Acknowledgements

My thanks for help in the preparation and writing of this book are innumerable and inevitably there will be omissions for which I sincerely apologize. Particular mention must be made of David Stoker and his team at Liverpool Record Office, based at Central Library (special thanks to Roger Hull for help with picture research) and of the staff at Special Collections, Sydney Jones Library, University of Liverpool.

My interest in Liverpool history (apart from it being my native city) was stimulated by Professor John Belchem, the late Dr Michael Power and Dr Jenny Kermode and I owe a considerable debt of gratitude to all three. The comments of Professor Belchem have proved particularly helpful and thought-provoking. Anthony Cond of Liverpool University Press has also been a constant source of support, encouragement and advice.

Among the many other individuals who have offered some form of help I would like to make special mention of the following: Chris Williams, Stephen Williams and Helen Paver for reading and commenting on draft chapters and for suggesting changes and improvements; Dr Di Ascott and fellow members of the Historic Society of Lancashire and Cheshire who have been instrumental in providing valuable advice at key moments; and Dr Diana Newton for continued friendship and moral support throughout.

Lastly, I would like to thank the members of my family, who have required great patience to live with someone whose main interest and constant preoccupation has been William Roscoe rather than them. I hope they will think the wait was worth it.

# List of Abbreviations

| | |
|---|---|
| LVRO | Liverpool Record Office |
| SJL | Sydney Jones Library, University of Liverpool |
| *RI Arch* | Royal Institution Archives |
| *RP* | Roscoe Letter and Papers |
| *THSLC* | *Transactions of the Historic Society of Lancashire and Cheshire* |

# Introduction

The Man of letters, who speaks of Liverpool, speaks of it
as the residence of Roscoe. The intelligent traveller who
visits it inquires where Roscoe is to be seen.

Washington Irving[1]

Historian, writer, poet, art patron and collector, botanist, MP
and anti-slavery campaigner, William Roscoe has been widely
acclaimed as the founding father of Liverpool culture. From
humble beginnings he rose to become an historian of international repute. For Horace Walpole, Roscoe was 'by far the
best of our historians both for beauty and style and for deep
reflections'.[2] He corresponded with and in many cases became
a personal friend of many of the leading literary and political
figures of the day including Lord Lansdowne, Lord Holland,
Thomas Jefferson, Sir Joshua Reynolds and Robert Burns.
Lord Henry Brougham, the Whig lawyer, founder of the
*Edinburgh Review* and one of the leading radicals in Parliament, judged Roscoe to be 'in some respects one of the most
remarkable persons that have of late years appeared in either
the political or literary world'.[3] From the poet Samuel Taylor
Coleridge came praise for Roscoe's personal as well as literary
qualities: 'a man of the most fascinating manners... good
sense, sweetness, simplicity, hilarity, joining in a literary man
who is a good Husband and the Father of nine children'.[4]
Roscoe, however, was also a man embroiled in the world of
commerce. As lawyer, banker and businessman, he was

involved in and concerned for the commercial success of the port, and as such lauded as living proof that culture and commerce were not, and are not, mutually exclusive.

Subsequent historians of Liverpool, equally lavish in their praise, have cemented this image. On his election to the chair of modern history at the University of Liverpool in 1906, Professor Ramsay Muir chose William Roscoe as the subject of his inaugural lecture. In his *History of Liverpool*, Roscoe is portrayed as the antidote to the 'fierce roar of commercial competition' and 'vulgar lust for money' that Muir felt was so characteristic of late eighteenth-century Liverpool.[5] In 1953 George Chandler, the city librarian, was commissioned by the city council to write a biography to commemorate the bicentenary of Roscoe's birth, the second part of the book being dedicated to Roscoe's poetry. Chandler not only confirmed Roscoe's position as Liverpool's cultural icon but also designated him the 'leader of the movement for the abolition of the slave trade'. Twenty years later Francis Hyde, a noted historian of Liverpool, concurred and went so far as to state that 'If a description of the spirit of Liverpool between 1790 and 1820 were to be sought, it could not be better described than by the term "Roscoe's Liverpool"'. More recently Liverpool John Moores University's Foundation for Citizenship, which is committed to promoting active citizenship within the university and the wider community, entitled its lecture programme the 'Roscoe Lectures'. The Prince of Wales, when delivering the Roscoe Lecture in April 2007, hailed Roscoe as a poet and a scholar, a passionate educationalist and a vigorous patron of the arts, and praised him for having the courage to challenge the 'status quo' by campaigning for the abolition of slavery. Lord David Alton, who holds a chair in citizenship at the university, insists that Liverpudlians should 'look back with pride to this cultured man of deep integrity' and claims that 'today's city leaders could do worse than imitate Roscoe'.[6] Endorsements indeed, but this book will look at whether it was Roscoe's personal achievements alone that served to ensure his elevation to iconic status or whether factors such as the town's need for a cultural hero at that time played their part.

In his book *Liverpool 800*, John Belchem claims that the Capital of Culture year in 2008 offers Liverpool a great opportunity to finally disassociate the city from the negative image which, although more media myth than reality, has nonetheless been pervasive. However, as Belchem points out, there is an historical irony here in that the late eighteenth and early nineteenth centuries witnessed a similar attempt to utilize culture to initiate a sea change in external perceptions of the town,[7] and a major player in this earlier exercise in rebranding was William Roscoe.

Despite Roscoe's multifarious talents, his choice as Liverpool's cultural icon and the support he received was surprising. A supporter of the abolition of the slave trade, a reformer in politics and a religious dissenter, Roscoe was not the most likely candidate of an elite characterized by its loyalty to King, the constitution and the established church. Yet in 1815 he was presented with the freedom of the town 'in testimony of the high sense entertained by the Council not only of his great literary talents but of his private worth and value as a member of society, so justly appreciated by his fellow townsmen'.[8] Although there is ample attestation as to Roscoe's personal qualities, it seems doubtful that these would have been sufficient to overcome the merchants' prejudices and the historiography on Roscoe does little to explain their support. In the absence of any other explanation, it has been wryly suggested that Roscoe stood out because there were not many other likeable men in early nineteenth-century Liverpool![9]

The following chapters begin by examining the circumstances that led to this unlikely choice of William Roscoe as Liverpool's cultural leader. Liverpool's rise during the

eighteenth century might be described as meteoric: it grew
from an insignificant seaport into Britain's second city. For
most of this period the newly rich merchants tended to define
themselves through material possessions, conspicuous
consumption and spatial separation from their fellow
townsmen; nevertheless, it will be argued that Liverpool
shared some of the features of Peter Borsay's urban renaissance in eighteenth-century provincial towns. The rebuilding
of the town hall, venues for theatrical entertainment, a music
hall, pleasure gardens and the laying out of residential squares
are just a few indications of the desire of the town's merchants
to acquire some of the characteristic features of cultured
urban life. However, efforts to found societies and institutions
devoted expressly to learning and the arts were short-lived and
Jon Stobart argues that by the 1770s cultural development
was slowing down if not grinding to a halt, as commerce
increasingly dominated the town's identity and landscape.[10]
The outside world saw Liverpool as a town dedicated solely
to commerce and profit-making, its merchants noted more for
their love of rum than reading. The turn of the century,
however, witnessed Liverpool apparently experience a second
cultural renaissance, inspired in part by the censure and negative stereotypes resulting from the town's association with the
slave trade. With culture seen as the medium through which
this redefinition of the merchants' and the town's identity
would hopefully be achieved, who better than William
Roscoe, a man of national and international status, to spear-
head a transformation.

When looking at Roscoe's life and achievements it is
crucial to give due consideration to the influences and events
in his early and middle years that helped to shape his life.
Friendships were always of great importance to him, and we
look at the close companions in his adolescence and in matu-
rity whose advice and support he valued most highly. From a
young age religion was a guiding factor in Roscoe's life, and

the vital role it played in fashioning and defining his moral code – a code he applied to both his personal and his public life – is explored in some depth.

Roscoe's national and international reputation was earned as an historian; his Italian writings were particularly significant. His contribution in this field was recognized when he was elected an honorary associate of the Royal Society of Literature in 1827 and received the society's gold medal. This volume does not attempt a detailed textual analysis of his writings, but considers the ways in which his admiration (bordering on adulation) for his hero Lorenzo de Medici and for Medici Florence informed his thinking in relation to his cultural aspirations for his native town. Finding his inspiration in the glories of Renaissance Florence, Roscoe sought to remake post-slavery Liverpool in its image, as a city-state dedicated to culture, commerce and civilization. His rewriting of history in a way that allowed the merchants to celebrate themselves was instrumental in confirming his selection as Liverpool's cultural leader.

Roscoe's interpretation of the significance of the cultural institutions and societies of Lorenzo de Medici convinced him that the creation of a similar infrastructure in Liverpool was vital. The seminal role that Roscoe played in the founding of learned societies and institutions in the town and their lasting influence is explored. Similarly, Roscoe's admiration for Lorenzo coloured his attitude to the cause of art in Liverpool, and he played a formative role in establishing the Academy of Art in the town. He was influential not only in establishing art societies but also as an art patron and collector. Some have argued that his collection of art was his greatest gift to Liverpool.

Roscoe's twin roles as an opponent of the slave trade and a politician both deserve a full discussion. His contribution to the movement for the abolition of slavery has been the subject of considerable controversy, and it is sometimes overlooked that it took courage for Roscoe and his circle to oppose fellow citizens who were their friends and neighbours and who fervently believed abolition would result in the town's economic ruin. Roscoe was never happy away from his home and family, and preferred to express his ideas through his writings rather than public speaking. However, as MP for Liverpool he cast his vote in favour of abolition, which incurred the wrath of his electors and resulted in the loss of his seat. He continued to work to end slavery and espoused the cause of reform until the end of his life.

Roscoe's career as a businessman is an aspect of his life that is generally minimized, not least because there is little of relevance in his papers and his son Henry tended to ignore it, preferring to concentrate on the aesthetic characteristics of his father. For Roscoe the law was an occupation rather than a vocation and he often spoke of his dissatisfaction with the profession. This should not detract from the fact that Roscoe was a highly successful lawyer who was able to retire at the age of 43 despite his heavy family commitments. Similarly, his bankruptcy illustrates less his failure as a banker but more the stresses and strains placed on the economy by the long years of war. To ignore Roscoe's immersion in business is to negate his success in combining the worlds of commerce and culture, and does not do justice to his memory.

The last years of Roscoe's life were far from unproductive. In his late sixties, despite his straitened circumstances and uncertain health, he produced his famous book on Monandrian plants, edited the works of Alexander Pope, catalogued the Holkham manuscripts and entertained many distinguished visitors at his home in Lodge Lane.

Roscoe left behind a voluminous correspondence as well as his printed historical works and poems. His son Henry penned a detailed two-volume biography of his father, which has proved an invaluable source, albeit as a loving tribute rather than a dispassionate account. Much has been written about Roscoe and the archives have been well trawled. The most recent account of his life and work by a member of the Roscoe family, Donald Macnaughton, published in 1996, is a judicious and sympathetic account that pays most attention to Roscoe the littérateur and astutely analyses Roscoe's two great biographies. Numerous articles have paid tribute to different aspects of Roscoe's talents, but – as with Macnaughton's account – most centre on Roscoe the man of letters rather than Roscoe the businessman and politician. Roscoe still excites interest today and it is not only in his native town that he is still remembered. Roscoe the self-made man was particularly admired in the USA, with Caldersburgh, Ohio being renamed Roscoe in his honour in 1830.

Despite the enormous amount of paper that has already been expended on William Roscoe, hopefully the perspective adopted by this account – which focuses not only on his life and the importance of his achievements but also on his deeply held belief in the conjunction of commerce and culture – offers something new. This, it is argued, was his greatest legacy to Liverpool and to the wider world.

# CHAPTER 1

# Cometh the Hour, Cometh the Man

On the floating wings of commerce, the inhabitants have
extended their intercourse with the world, which has enlightened their ideas and given them not only the pride of
imitation, but the ambition of equality.[1]

In 1753, the year of William Roscoe's birth, Liverpool was a
town of recent and remarkable growth. Although granted
borough status by King John in 1207, in recognition of its
strategic importance in relation to Ireland,[2] Liverpool had
remained a small and relatively unimportant outport until about
1660. Up to the beginning of the reign of Elizabeth I in 1558,
the chief occupations of the inhabitants of Liverpool (estimated
to number 500) were agriculture and fishing, and only a small
number of ships could be described as merchant ships. In 1558
the town's inhabitants owned 13 vessels; in 1572 the number
had increased to 16; by 1586 it had probably not increased any
further.[3] Its geographical position, poor communications and an
undeveloped hinterland all conspired to hamper Liverpool's
economic growth. What trade there was in the north-west tended
to be concentrated at Chester, which was the principal head-port
of the region. Not only were the havens and creeks of Lancashire
and Cheshire subordinated to Chester but also those along the
whole coast of North Wales.[4] However, from the fifteenth
century onwards, Chester was faced with the problem of the
silting of the River Dee, which made it difficult for vessels to
reach the port. Chester's ill-luck was Liverpool's good fortune,

for despite attempts to improve the navigation of the river, much of Chester's trade, particularly its Irish trade, was diverted to Liverpool.[5] The relatively settled state of Ireland in the sixteenth century, the lower dues payable at Liverpool and the demands of the growing Lancashire textile industry all combined to further increase Liverpool's share of this trade. Ireland remained Liverpool's main trading partner throughout the sixteenth century, but Liverpool's merchants also traded coastwise (especially with ports in north-west England and North Wales) and with Europe, Scotland and the Isle of Man.

Liverpool exported coal, salt, cloth, ironware, soap, leather goods and haberdashery in exchange for barley, rye, wheat, herrings, linen cloth, linen yarn, wool, hides and tallow.[6] Although the volume of this trade was modest, by the end of the century Liverpool had overtaken Chester and by 1626, according to the Liverpool historian C. Northcote Parkinson, 'Liverpool's superiority to Chester, in shipping, was beyond question; and its superiority in trade was probably still more manifest'.[7] However, he goes on to point out that while Liverpool had outstripped Chester 'in point of commerce', it was 'still greatly inferior to that venerable city in point of wealth, reputation and dignity'.[8] Nationally, Liverpool still remained a relatively insignificant seaport and during the whole of the period Liverpool continued to be contained mainly within the framework of the original streets laid out by King John in 1207.[9]

Liverpool's entry into trans-oceanic commerce during the last decades of the seventeenth century marked the beginning of the rapid transformation of the town. Visitors to the town were impressed with the physical evidence of this growing prosperity. Daniel Defoe marvelled at the speed with which these changes were taking place:

> Liverpoole is one of the wonders of Britain ... the town was, at my first visiting it, about the year 1680, a large, handsome, well-built and encreasing or thriving town; at my second visit,

anno 1690, it was much bigger than my first seeing it ... but
at this my third seeing it ... it was more than double what it
was at the second ... what it may grow to in time, I know
not.[10]

Despite his enthusiasm, in Defoe's estimation Liverpool still did
not compare with Bristol, which he cited as 'the greatest, the
richest, and the best port of trade in Great Britain, London only
excepted'.[11] However, as the century wore on there was a
growing awareness that Bristol's trading position was being
challenged, and by the end of the century Bristol had been forced
to surrender its status.[12] Liverpool was now proclaiming itself to
be 'the first town in the kingdom in point of size and commercial importance, the Metropolis excepted'.[13] Although Bristol's
commerce had continued to grow during the eighteenth century,
this expansion had been far less rapid than that of her northern
rival. The shipping entering Liverpool increased from 14,600
tons in 1709 to 450,000 tons in 1800, a thirty-fold increase in
the course of the century.[14] This was closely allied to a quick
growth in population, from fewer than 7,000 in 1709 to 77,653
in 1801. The diverse base of Liverpool's trading economy, the
implementation of an innovative dock-building programme,
improved communications with a rapidly industrializing hinterland, a major raw material for export in the form of the rock salt
that was discovered in Cheshire in 1670 (labelled by one contemporary observer as 'the nursing mother' of the port[15]), and entry
into, and domination of, the slave trade all helped to ensure that
by the early 1790s 'Liverpool had gained, beyond question, the
status of England's largest outport in foreign and foreign
coasting trade... Its rise had to that extent been accomplished.
The way for its further rise had been prepared.'[16]

There is general agreement amongst Liverpool's historians
that the enterprise and foresight of Liverpool merchants were
dynamic elements in this economic success story, yet – despite
valuable recent research – our knowledge of them is still disap-

pointingly patchy.[17] When such men left records, these generally concerned their business affairs; evidence, even of their numbers, is limited. In 1766, *Gore's Liverpool Directory* gave 'an alphabetical list of the merchants, tradesmen and principal inhabitants' but with no indication of the criteria used to make this selection. A total of 1,134 names appear, less than one-fifth of the estimated number of householders, with 188 men listed as merchants. By 1790 this had risen to 619 merchants out of a total entry of over 7,000 names from a population of about 55,000.[18] While a few can be traced to families of long-standing in the town – descendants of 'the nest of rogues' referred to in Sir Edward Moore's rental of 1670: for example, the Tarleton, Clayton and Williamson families – the majority appear to have been lured by the town's increasing prosperity. They migrated to Liverpool from Lancashire, Yorkshire, Derbyshire, Staffordshire, Cheshire and North Wales and were said to include 'many gentlemen's sons'.[19] Some (such as the Gladstones and Ewarts) came from Scotland; others (such as William Brown) came from Ireland; and the appearance of names such as Becken, Busch, Wilckens, Zuill and Zinck in the 1790 directory indicates the increasingly cosmopolitan nature of the merchant community.[20]

The formal route to the position of merchant was through apprenticeship, in which bonds of consanguinity and membership of a particular religious body often played an important part. Thomas Fletcher, for example, was apprenticed to James France, a Jamaica merchant, on the recommendation of his minister at Key Street Chapel, Reverend John Yates. He later obtained a share in the firm with money loaned in part by a fellow Unitarian, Matthew Nicholson.[21] However, other merchants came from adjacent occupations, such as shipbuilding, retailing and seafaring. It was said of Liverpool that 'no town in England had so many merchants in it who rose from Saylors'.[22] Large fortunes could be made by captains in the slave trade; a survey of a group of ship's captains from 1785 to 1807 identified at least 45 Liverpool slave-ship captains who became Liverpool merchants. However, it should be noted that not all were as fortunate. It was not only among the ordinary seamen that mortality rates were high. Of the captains in the Liverpool and Bristol slave trade during the same period, at least 27 per cent died on slave voyages.[23] Tales of 'rags to riches' can be recounted: an example is the story of William Boat(e)s (c.1730–1794), so named because he was reputed to have been a waif who was found in a boat and reared by the person who found him. He was placed in the Bluecoat School and later apprenticed to the merchant service. He carefully invested any prize money he received and bought a ship, later becoming a merchant trader and entering the slave trade. One of his ships was said to have captured a Spanish ship with a large prize, and Boates was claimed to have run around Liverpool shouting 'born a beggar, die a lord'.[24] However, such tales were the exception, not the rule. In general those in the best position to make a fortune were men in possession of at least a modest amount of capital rather than those with none.

The interests of these increasingly prosperous men directed the politics of the town. In the late seventeenth century the town secured its independence from the local landed interest and (with the granting of the 1695 Charter) the reins of political power were securely in the hands of its leading merchants. Through the self-elected and self-perpetuating 'common council' a narrow oligarchy of well-established merchant families demonstrated their single-minded devotion to furthering commerce. They confirmed their entrepreneurial flair by promoting ambitious dock-building schemes (the first commercial wet dock in the world was constructed in Liverpool between 1709 and 1715) and by investing in improved transport links. In 1793 the council supported the town's merchants and economy during depressed trading conditions brought about by the Napoleonic wars. When commercial panic led to a run on the banks, the council obtained a unique Act of Parliament empowering it to mint £300,000 to restore confidence.[25] In the period 1780–1800, 57 of the 73 men who served on the council were merchants. Although the common council was castigated by its opponents as a 'family compact' and newcomers might be resentful of their exclusion from the charmed circle that controlled the corporation, in essence, it can be argued, they were the same sort of people: sharing the same economic and political objectives, firmly supporting the principles of the established church, prominent in Liverpool society and associated with local charities and good works.[26] Of course, not all Liverpool's merchants conformed neatly to this pattern. However, on occasion even some of those merchants (mainly dissenters of the Unitarian and Quaker persuasion) who did wish for change – a more liberal economic policy and a measure of social and political reform – judged the economic issues that confronted them 'by the law of the survival of their House'.[27] It was only in times of crisis, when feelings ran high in the town, that the more radical reformers were abused and ostracized.[28]

A 'typical' Liverpool merchant of the last quarter of the seventeenth century has been described by Checkland as a 'mercantilist, a materialist and an empiricist', and both contemporary and more recent accounts depict an elite characterized 'by the philistinism of self-made men'. Wealth was regarded as 'unabashedly the overwhelming concern and the principal source of self-esteem'.[29] However, this preoccupation with money-making, although often subjected to criticism, is not surprising. From the outset, Liverpool trade, based on the West Indies and West Africa, was highly speculative, bringing riches or ruin on an enormous scale.[30]As one contemporary observed, albeit with some exaggeration:

> As commercial pursuits are in their nature hazardous, the annals of a town of such extensive commercial dealings as Liverpool may be naturally expected to exhibit most striking instances of the vicissitudes of fortune. It often happens that

the servant rises while the master falls. Today a man is a merchant, all spirit and enterprise, and living in splendour and luxury – tomorrow he is bankrupt, humbly requesting the signature of his certificate, or soliciting for some scantily salaried situation in the customs or excise. Families, which twenty or thirty years ago took the lead in the circles of Liverpool fashion, are now reduced, forgotten and unknown... In Liverpool, the prophesy may at any given time be safely pronounced – 'Many that are first shall be last, and the last shall be first'. In this town, few families can count three opulent generations.[31]

Thus before a merchant could invest his time and energy in less material pursuits it was first necessary to acquire the security and surplus wealth that would allow him do so. Even then, investment in dock-building schemes, transport links and new industrial undertakings all had claims on capital before investment in 'the more refined pursuits of a leisured class'.[32]

In the middle of the eighteenth century, however, selective improvements in the physical fabric of the town began to indicate a developing sense of civic pride. In common with other provincial towns, growing prosperity resulted in a number of initiatives which, it is argued, to some extent locate Liverpool within Peter Borsay's description of an 'urban renaissance' in provincial towns between 1660 and 1770.[33] Although Jane Longmore suggests that the town's preoccupation with commerce impeded any pursuit of a polite culture,[34] the choice of John Wood, the architect of Bath, to design a new exchange and town hall reflects a growing awareness of life outside the confines of Liverpool and its immediate environs. The building, not surprisingly, celebrated the fount of the town's prosperity and was ornamented with heads and emblems of commerce. 'The Genius of Commerce is the proper representation of the prosperity and importance of this town, and of which the erection of this magnificent pile is a memorable instance', enthused one of

Liverpool's early historians.[35] The opening in 1754 was accompanied by a week-long extravaganza which demonstrated the merchants' clear recognition of the importance of overt display and ceremony in establishing the image and reputation of their burgeoning town. The new building quickly became central to Liverpool's social life. When Samuel Derrick, master of ceremonies at Bath, visited the town in 1760 he reported that the assembly room in the town hall was 'grand, spacious and finely illuminated, here is a meeting once a fortnight to dance and play cards; where you will find some women elegantly accomplished and perfectly well dressed'.[36] From the mid-1760s onwards, the town's wealthier residents could also mingle at the Ranelagh Gardens (which took its name from the fashionable pleasure gardens at Chelsea) while they listened to music, watched the occasional firework display or enjoyed a strawberry tea-party. The more active could enjoy archery, tennis, bowls or horse-racing at nearby Crosby.[37]

From the 1760s the town's domestic as well as public architecture began to concern the mercantile community as they sought to live in a style commensurate with their influence. The Unitarian minister William Enfield declared:

> The extension of commerce, and the consequent increase of its wealth, have introduced a taste for ornament and splendor, which has of late appeared in a variety of forms, and particularly in its buildings both public and private.[38]

In the first half of the century, even the most well-off merchants usually lived near the centre of the town, either above or adjacent to their business premises. Now, however, the wealthier residents of the town began separating themselves from their less prosperous fellows and distinct new middle-class areas began to emerge.[39] Duke Street was described by William Moss, the author of the Liverpool guide books, as 'the first attempt at embellished extension the town experienced; and was considered

an airy retreat from the busy and confined parts of the town'.[40]
In the 1790 directory, Duke Street, Hanover Street, Bold Street,
Church Street and Clayton Square accounted for the names and
addresses of 103 merchants or one-sixth of those listed, with 43
merchants residing in Duke Street alone.[41] Some wealthy
merchants retreated outside the town, building mansions in
Everton, Wavertree and Toxteth Park.[42] As early as 1768 the
Yates and Perry map shows 32 'country seats' within a four-mile
radius of Liverpool,[43] and by 1795 John Aikin was claiming that
'all the villages in the vicinity of Liverpool are filled with the
country seats and places of retirement of the merchants and other
inhabitants of Liverpool'.[44] The township of Everton proved to
be particularly popular: 'The village of Everton has of late years
become a very favourite residence and several excellent houses
are built along the western declivity of the hill.'[45] The directory
of 1790 includes the names of 13 merchants with addresses in
Everton.

According to Ramsay Muir, it was 'the pleasures of the table'
that provided the chief relaxation of Liverpool's eighteenth-
century merchants, in contrast to 'the exacting labours of
commerce'. This conclusion owed much to the frequently-
quoted opinion of Samuel Derrick:

> Though few of the merchants have more education than
> befits a counting-house, they are genteel in their address, very
> friendly to strangers, even those of whom they have the least
> knowledge. Their tables are plenteously furnished, and their
> viands are well served up; their rum is excellent, of which they
> consume large quantities.[46]

If a merchant joined a club, it was of the convivial rather than
cultural variety. Drinking, dining and gossip appear to have been
the main activities. One of the earliest of these – the Ugly Face
Club, founded in January 1743 – left a record of the physical
characteristics of 55 of its members, a large proportion of whom

were merchants. As the most favoured qualifications for membership were 'a large Mouth, thin Jaws, Blubber Lips, little goggling or squinting eyes', with a 'large carbuncle Potatoe Nose being esteemed the most honourable of any', one suspects that exaggeration was the order of the day; it is to be hoped that these accounts were caricatures of the merchant community.[47]

In 1753 a dining club was founded for 'gentlemen of the first families of the town; many of them were members of the Council, and several afterwards served the offices of mayor and bailiff of Liverpool'. The Unanimous Club met every Saturday evening, from the first Saturday in September to the last Saturday in April, at a local coffee house, on occasion venturing further afield to dine at inns in Prescot, Ormskirk and Warrington.[48]

Another popular club, the Mock Corporation of Sefton, which existed from 1753 to 1829, attracted more than 300 Liverpool citizens during its lifetime, nearly two-thirds of whom appear in *Gore's Directory* listed as merchants, tradesmen and gentlemen.[49] Unlike mock corporations in other towns, its programme was social rather than political.[50] The first session was held at the Sefton Inn (later demolished) in the grounds of Sefton Church; later sessions were held at the Punch Bowl Inn in Sefton. It is unclear why Sefton was chosen as a venue: possibly the Liverpool men saw it as a day out in the country. They travelled on horseback, in gigs or by carriage. An alternative venue was Baxter's Coffee House in Bootle, probably chosen because it was more accessible in the winter months. The numbers attending the Sunday meetings varied from three to forty. It had a pew in church (although this religious commitment was tempered by the members' custom of timing the sermon with a stopwatch), elaborate rituals and a distaste for party disputes; in March 1784 Pitt and Fox were simultaneously voted the freedom of the corporation. The involvement of many of the members in the slave trade explains the 'Corporation's indignant sense of the ridiculous notion for abolishing the slave trade proposed by fanatic Wilberforce', as noted in the minutes of 7 June 1789.[51]

However, on occasion these clubs were also organs for phil-anthropic enterprise: in 1760, for example, the Noble Order of the Bucks, a social club which met at the Golden Fleece Inn in Dale Street from 1756, was recorded as having subscribed £70 towards the clothing of 'our brave troops abroad and the relief of the widows and orphans who fell nobly in their country's and liberty's cause', and later 50 guineas to the Marine Society.[52] Many merchants were leading contributors to charities and char-itable institutions despite being mainly preoccupied with their business affairs and materialistic in outlook. The Liverpool Bluecoat School for the education of orphans and fatherless chil-dren, which opened in 1718, was founded by the sea captain and merchant Bryan Blundell, whose family remained closely connected to it throughout the century. An infirmary was opened in 1749, the money for the building and annual costs being raised by subscription; merchants were conspicuous contributors and filled posts such as treasurer, deputy treasurer and auditor. In all but three of the years between 1783 and 1793 the president of the infirmary was a local merchant. Merchants also contributed generously to the Liverpool Dispensary, which opened in 1778 with the aim of supplying the poor with free medicines and medical advice. During the harsh winter of 1788–1789, local merchants were instrumental in organizing help for the poor, occupying seven of the nine places on the committee appointed to oversee the relief. There are many other instances of the char-itable efforts of the merchant elite, making generalizations about the aggressive commercial nature of the Liverpool elite diffi-cult.[53]

Not surprisingly, the branches of the arts that held most appeal for Liverpool's merchants were also the most public and the most social, notably the theatre:

Encouragement to theatrical exhibitions is not confined solely to the metropolis. The inhabitants of the town of Liverpool showed an early partiality, and as their notions

refined a more splendid exhibition of these favourite amuse-
ments was liberally patronized.[54]

The need for a well-built theatre in Liverpool – a prerequisite for
every town of any pretension – was met in the middle of the
century.[55] Although the site of the earliest theatrical performances in the town is a matter of some dispute among historians,
there seems to be general agreement that around 1742 a theatre
was built in Old Ropery by Alderman Thomas Steers, the
constructor of the first dock. This building proving too small, a
new theatre was opened in 1749. In common with other provincial towns, Liverpool began to 'put on London airs', naming the
theatre Drury Lane and an adjoining thoroughfare Covent
Garden.[56] The house had a pit and a gallery, priced at two
shillings and one shilling respectively, but no boxes. In 1759 the
theatre was reconstructed and renamed the New Theatre in
Drury Lane. It was described as a 'handsome structure …
elegantly furnished, with the scenes extremely well painted by
London artists'.[57] Boxes, priced at three shillings, were now
added to the auditorium and placed around the pit. From here
the wealthy could hope to comfortably display themselves to
their fellow citizens while avoiding any direct contact.

> A just partition for the better sort to withdraw from the
> near contact of drunken sailors and their female associates,
> who by paying two shillings, which many could and would
> afford, for the honour of mixing with their employers and
> their families.[58]

London artistes were engaged and Shakespearean tragedies vied
with farces to entertain the mixed audience of theatregoers. On
the evening of 13 June 1766 the programme included *Romeo
and Juliet*, an interval of various dramatic readings and dance,
and a farce, *The Contrivances*.[59] In the early 1760s the manager
of the theatre, Mr Gibson, drew up a petition to the corporation

asking for support for his application to Parliament to build a theatre 'more worthy of the town' to which Royal Letters Patent would be granted. The corporation agreed and Parliamentary approval was finally gained in 1771. The cost was estimated at about £6,000, which was raised in shares of £200. The amount necessary for the venture was achieved less than an hour after the list was opened, an indication that dedication to the arts was allied with a keen interest in investment potential: the share-holders drew a regular 5 per cent interest and the capital value of the shares rose steadily.[60] The foundation stone was laid by Mayor John Sparling in 1771 and on 5 June 1772 the Theatre Royal, on the north side of Williamson Square, was opened 'with great *éclat*. All the elite of the town were present on this very auspicious occasion and the initial performance was a great success.'[61] The prologue, written by George Colman (the play-wright and later manager of the Covent Garden and Haymarket theatres) began by paying tribute to the connection between culture and commerce ('Whenever commerce spreads her swelling gale, Letters and arts attend the prosperous gale'), an early intimation in verse of the motif that was to become central to the development of Liverpool's intellectual life in the early nineteenth century.

As with the theatre, so with music, which attracted the patronage of the wealthy (and on occasion the town council) from early in the century. In 1766 the opening of a new organ in St Peter's church was the occasion for a performance of the first grand oratorio to be performed in Liverpool (*Messiah*) in front of 'a crowded and genteel audience consisting of the prin-cipal nobility and gentry in the neighbourhood, the Mayor and the Magistrates'.[62] In 1784 came the first of the great triennial music festivals held in aid of local charities. These quickly estab-lished themselves as major social occasions for the leaders of fashion in the town. Handel's oratorios dominated the programme, although the festivals were by no means devoted to music alone; among the attractions of the 1784 festival were horse-racing, a theatrical play, and a grand fancy-dress ball and supper.[63] However, with tickets priced at one-and-a-half guineas for five performances, they cannot be said to have done much for the diffusion of music in the town at large. In 1785 the success of the growing number of musical ventures in the town prompted a scheme to give Liverpool its own purpose-built concert hall in Bold Street. The cost of the building was to be met by public subscription, with the initial issue of shares set at ten guineas each. This proved so successful that the scheme was doubled in size, and the hall opened on 12 June 1786. Although externally it was unprepossessing, internally it was described as being 'in extent and elegance, perhaps superior to any room, which is employed merely as a concert room, in the kingdom'.[64]

Anecdotes can certainly be cited to support Samuel Derrick's criticisms of the narrowness of the merchants' educational attainments. A leading merchant, Joseph Leigh, was reputed to be 'marvellously at home in arithmetic, compound addition, the rule of three, multiplication and so forth', but subjects such as history and literature were considered 'the exotics of education'. Leigh was said to buy his books as he bought his cloth, 'by the foot'.[65] However, for some merchants at least rising affluence did encourage a desire for self-improvement. The second half of the century witnessed the beginning of public lecturing in Liverpool, a phenomenon that became common in provincial towns in the eighteenth century; 'knowledge is become a fashionable thing', claimed one top lecturer.[66] Natural philosophy was the most usual subject of these lectures. The first course known to be held in Liverpool was given by Adam Walker, a self-educated Yorkshire schoolmaster, in 1771. It consisted of twelve two-hour lectures delivered on consecutive days for a fee of one guinea. Walker was careful to stress the entertainment value of his course: it 'consists of all the most curious, useful, new and entertaining parts of Philosophy; 'tis an Epitome of the whole Æconomy of the Universe'. Such lecture courses were often accompanied by spectacular experiments and demonstrations, and they appear to have been attended mainly by the well-to-do merchants and professional men of Liverpool and their wives.[67] Debates in local coffee houses also attracted a good response in the town. Although commercial topics were discussed at Banner's Great Room Debates at the Fleece Inn in Dale Street, the agenda also included debates on less material matters: for example, 'Has the cultivation of a taste for the beauties of nature and of the Fine Arts, an influence favourable to morality?' This heralded, perhaps, a broadening cultural and intellectual awareness on the part of the town's wealthier residents. Other early debating societies included the Conversation Club, which met at George's Coffee House on Castle Street; the Free Debating Society, which met at a hotel in Lord Street in the 1780s; and the Debating Society, attended by William Roscoe and Dr James Currie, which lasted from 1795 to 1797 and met at the Large Room in Marble Street, off Williamson Square. Although there is no evidence as to the composition of the audience and the debates were free, the considerable sums raised for charity on these occasions suggested that in the main the participants were drawn from the wealthier stratum of society.[68]

An increasing demand in Liverpool for the 'amenities of civilised life' was also reflected by a growing demand for books, newspapers and periodicals. The first Liverpool newspaper, the *Leverpool Courant*, had appeared in 1712, but it was short-lived. The first edition of Williamson's *Liverpool Advertiser and Mercantile Register* appeared on 28 May 1756, and it continued under a number of different names until 1856. In 1758 the Liverpool (later referred to as the Lyceum) Library was founded; it survived until 1941. This was the first of the English gentlemen's subscription libraries (the first subscription library in Britain was founded in Scotland in 1741) and was widely imitated in other provincial towns, including Warrington (1760), Manchester (1765), Lancaster, Carlisle, Leeds and Halifax (1768), Rochdale and Settle (1770), Sheffield (1771) and Bradford (1774). Others founded before the close of the century included Birmingham (1779), Newcastle (1787) and York (1794).[69] The library emerged from the amalgamation of three informal discussion groups, the foremost of which had been meeting at the home of William Everard, a schoolteacher and mathematician, since about 1756. The three groups decided to pool their resources and to launch the library in Princes Street, moving in 1759 to (North) John Street and in 1787 to a new building in Lord Street. In 1803, a new building was opened in Bold Street, designed by Thomas Harrison in the classical tradition, incorporating the library, a newsroom and a coffee room under one roof.

In November 1758 the library published its first catalogue, which listed 450 volumes and pamphlets. The collections of most subscription libraries were fairly similar, consisting of a little fiction and many books on history, travel, belles-lettres, philosophy, theology, natural history and jurisprudence. However, as in other provincial towns, the civic preoccupations and commercial interests of the Liverpool members were reflected; the library held many books about the slave trade. The subscriber list, which was said to include 'most of the chief persons of the town',[70] gave the names of 109 members, 47 of whom were merchants.[71] By 1760 this number had risen to 140, and the preface to the catalogue for that year enumerated the benefits to be gained from membership, neatly combining an appeal to both the commercial and the cultural instincts of prospective members:

> As many kinds of useful and polite knowledge cannot otherwise be acquired than by Reading, an attempt to furnish the public with an ample fund of amusement and improvement of this kind at the easiest Expense, can hardly fail of general approbation ... the terms are moderate; and prospects of Advantage are obvious and extensive.[72]

The increase in members to 950 by the end of the century suggests that these dual advantages had been recognized by those of Liverpool's citizens who could afford the privilege. Despite the proviso in the catalogue, entry fees did ensure a certain exclusivity. Initially set at one guinea with an annual subscription of five shillings, it steadily rose as the century progressed. Exclusivity remained a feature in the nineteenth century. When the American novelist and poet Herman Melville arrived in Liverpool in 1839 as a nineteen-year-old sailor and looked for a congenial place to read, he was forcibly ejected from the library by a 'terribly cross man' who 'took me by my innocent shoulders, and then putting his foot against the broad part of my pantaloons, wheeled me right out into the street, and dropped me on the walk'.[73]

It is interesting to note that from the beginning the library, unlike the dining clubs and the early learned societies, was not a men-only organization. On 3 February 1758 the first advertisement for the scheme in the *Liverpool Chronicle and Marine Gazeteer* was addressed 'To all Gentlemen and Ladies, who desire to encourage the progress of useful Knowledge', and the names of four women – including Sarah Clayton, a noted figure on the Liverpool business scene – appeared in the first list of subscribers.[74] From 1774 until 1828, when the custom was allowed to lapse, the president of the library was allowed to nominate a lady patroness (invariably single) for the duration of his year of office. However, although the lady concerned was granted all the rights and privileges of a member and presented with a handsomely bound catalogue for her pains, the position was purely decorative and women do not appear to have played an active role in the library's affairs.[75]

Towards the end of the eighteenth century the library acted to some extent as an informal literary club. The committee meetings of the library generally took place in the Star and Garter Hotel in Paradise Street. Here, men such as William Roscoe, Dr James Currie, the fourth William Rathbone and Dr John Rutter met together for business, dinner and conversation. These became celebrated occasions as much for the brilliance of their literary and intellectual content as for the business transacted.[76]

Although, as has been shown, Liverpool's involvement in commerce did not preclude some cultural beginnings, efforts to establish formal literary and scientific societies were not successful. In 1779 a society calling itself the Liverpool Philosophical and Literary Society was inaugurated. The members included Dr James Currie, William Rathbone, Reverend John Yates, William Clarke Jr and Matthew Gregson. It met at a number of different venues and a variety of papers were read.[77] However, it proved short-lived, and was dissolved in 1783: 'This conclusion was submitted to with regret by some of the members, but the almost total want of zeal and attention in the larger number seemed to leave no alternative'.[78] This early society is interesting in that it preceded the Manchester Literary and Philosophical Society, which was founded at the house of Dr Thomas Percival in 1781 and became the prototype for similar middle-class societies throughout the provinces. In 1784 a new society was founded which eventually became known as the Literary Society. Members met at each other's houses to discuss literary and scientific subjects. Among these were William Roscoe, Reverend William Shepherd, Dr James Currie, Reverend John Yates, William Rathbone, William Smyth (afterwards Regius Professor of Modern History at Cambridge) and probably also the blind poet Edward Rushton, who was said to have belonged to a group of this kind in 1790. These men were to take the lead in the cultural advancement of Liverpool. In politics they were reformers; in religion they were predominantly Unitarian or Quaker.[79] The Literary Society, however, came to an end in the early 1790s, when the atmosphere of suspicion engendered by the French Revolution meant that such meetings were open to the charge of sedition. However, when the Liverpool Literary and Philosophical Society was formed in 1812, its first members included the Reverends John Yates and Joseph Smith, and six other members (W.W. Currie, William Rathbone, Richard Rathbone, Joseph B. Yates, J.A. Yates and

Thomas Binns) were the sons of gentlemen who had belonged to the earlier society.[80] Other efforts to institute societies devoted expressly to art were unsuccessful, despite the fact that many of Liverpool's merchants were now actively seeking to commemorate themselves and their families on canvas, attracting artists such as Joseph Wright of Derby to seek patrons in the town.[81]

It was the failure of these cultural initiatives that led one commentator in the early 1790s to conclude that:

> Arts and sciences are inimical to the spot, absorbed in the nautical vortex, the only pursuit of the inhabitants is COMMERCE... Liverpool is the only town in England of any pre-eminency that has not one single erection or endowment, for the advancement of science, the cultivation of the arts, or promotion of useful knowledge; they have been proved truly exotic, and so little deserving cultivation when attempts have been made to fertilize them, that they have been suffered to wither and decay, and finally to be neglected and forgotten ... the liberal arts are a species of merchandize in which few of the inhabitants are desirous to deal, unless for exportation.[82]

Yet within a few years, plans for the first of the institutions that were to underpin Liverpool's nineteenth-century cultural infrastructure (and which were mostly the initiatives of socially marginal men) gained enthusiastic support from both the merchant community and the council. By the middle of the century J.W. Hudson was making a very different assessment of Liverpool's cultural development:

> There is no town in the Kingdom in which there are so many temples dedicated to the improvement of mankind as in Liverpool, nor can any city provide equal evidence of the zeal of its Merchant Princes in raising mansions for the advancement of civilisation.[83]

Although hyperbole played its part in both these judgements, they nevertheless are indicative of a dramatic sea change in external perceptions of Liverpool's civic and cultural identity. The motivation for this redefinition can, in part, be explained by Liverpool's evolution into a metropolitan centre and cosmopolitan crossroads towards the close of the eighteenth century, but it can also be argued that the depth of this commitment may well have been influenced by the association of Liverpool's prosperity with the slave trade.[84]

For much of the century Liverpool's share of the slave trade had been something to be envied, the legitimate reward of enterprise in which everyone would have been delighted to share. In 1773, William Enfield's analysis of the slave trade showed no trace of self-consciousness; his comparisons with other trades were quantitative, not qualitative.[85] However, the inauguration of the national abolitionist movement in 1787 saw public opinion change and Liverpool now found itself becoming increasingly isolated and facing threats not just to its economic base but to its cultural identity.[86] As early as 1788, a London correspondent of Matthew Gregson (an upholsterer and later antiquary) categorized the pro-slave-trade Gregson as 'a proper Liverpool man', while dubbing himself a 'humanity man'. The inference was that to the outside world the two terms were incompatible.[87] The town found itself subjected to vociferous criticism in Parliament, branded 'the metropolis of slavery', and visitors to the town expressed similar moral distaste. When the artist Fuseli visited Liverpool in 1804 and was shown the sights, he declared: 'I viewed them with interest, but methinks I smell everywhere the blood of slaves'.[88] Similarly, an actor hissed and booed for appearing drunk on a Liverpool stage answered his audience by declaring that he refused to be insulted 'by a pack of men every brick in whose detestable town was cemented by the blood of a negro'.[89] Liverpool's merchants, of course, had no intention of letting such a lucrative source of wealth disappear without a fight, and the twenty years before abolition saw them unceasingly petition Parliament against abolition, while their involvement in the trade increased rather than diminished. At formal dinners and civic occasions toasts were drunk to the 'African trade', and when the first abolition bill was defeated in 1791, church bells were rung. However, Seymour Drescher draws on contemporary descriptions and local guides to suggest a growing unease at this 'stain' on Liverpool's reputation. In the *Liverpool Guide* of 1796, for example, William Moss had few qualms about justifying the trade, yet by 1799 the *Guide* had discovered that the trade was conducted mainly by outsiders, and Moss took care to emphasize that only a few Liverpool merchants were involved: 'Much illiberal and ungenerous reflection has been indiscriminately cast upon the town on account of this trade, which must have arisen from ignorance, since it is limited to a very few of the merchants'. This was an obvious manipulation of the truth. A new Liverpool guide that appeared in 1805 reflected even greater eagerness for disassociation.[90] If 'humanity man' and 'Liverpool man' could not be reconciled, it might have seemed much more important to Liverpool's merchants to legitimize their status as 'Liverpool gentlemen', and polite culture could well have seemed a tempting avenue to explore.

The eighteenth century saw the foresight and entrepreneurship of Liverpool merchants steering the town to economic prominence. Now these merchants brought the same gifts to bear in their efforts to establish a matching cultural profile. Nowhere is this more evident than in the apparent willingness of these men, whose creed was 'Church and State, King and Constitution', to adopt the cultural formulae laid down by the small group of radicals, dissenters and abolitionists who had been at the forefront of previously unsuccessful cultural societies. Liverpool now needed a cultural leader, preferably someone who had already earned himself a reputation on a wider stage. William Roscoe was essentially an outsider – a Unitarian by religion, a radical in politics and a staunch opponent of the slave trade – but he was admired nationally and internationally for his historical writings. He was also a successful self-made businessman who, inspired by his interpretation of Medici Florence, steadfastly believed that culture and commerce were not incompatible. Moreover, Roscoe had a deep love for, and commitment to, his native town. Ever pragmatic, Liverpool's merchants apparently felt that in the circumstances of the times, Roscoe was simply the best man to develop a cultural profile for Liverpool commensurate with its economic status. They were thus prepared to adopt Roscoe as their cultural icon despite his political and religious credentials.

# CHAPTER 2

# The Shaping of the Scholar

The childhood shows the man, as Morning shows the day.

Milton, *Paradise Regained*

Born on 8 March 1753 at the Old Bowling Green Inn, Mount Pleasant, Liverpool, William Roscoe was the son of innkeeper William Roscoe and his wife Elizabeth. The following year the family moved to the neighbouring New Bowling Green Inn, which William Roscoe senior had been building at the time of his son's birth. He also ran a market garden that was attached to the inn. The senior William Roscoe was a man of great bodily strength, given to field sports and athletics.[1] The fact that his name is not listed in the town's first directory (1766) is indicative of how distant from the town centre Mount Pleasant was at the time.

In his biography of his father, Henry Roscoe suggests that Roscoe's early years were largely responsible for shaping the principles and interests that came to dominate his mature life.[2] This is confirmed by a draft letter written by William Roscoe junior to his sister-in-law, Mrs Moss, shortly before his death in 1831.[3] He claims to have little recollection of his earliest years but does recall that he had 'a decided aversion to compulsion and restraint' and describes how he had to be carried to school, struggling violently, by a servant armed with a rod. At the age of six the young William went to a school in Paradise Street run by a Mr Martin, and it was to this schoolmaster and the influence of his mother that Roscoe credits much of his future conduct. His mother encouraged his love of reading by providing him 'with such books as she thought would contribute to my literary improvement'. Roscoe claimed that 'It is to her I owe the inculcation of those sentiments of humanity which became a principle in my mind', and in a poem written in his youth soon after her death, he pays tribute to her care.

> O! best of Mothers! Thou, whose guardian care
> Sustain'd my infant life, when weak and faint,
> I pour'd the feeble cry! Thou, whose kind hand
> Through scenes of childhood led my devious steps
> Towards Virtue's arduous way, and bade my soul
> With ceaseless assiduity attempt
> The glorious road! Thou, whose preserving hand
> With friendly aid restrain'd my boisterous speed
> When maddening passions ruled! To thee I owe
> Health and existence![4]

After two years with Mr Martin he moved to a school in the same premises run by a Mr Sykes, where he studied arithmetic, writing and English grammar, the latter not being to the juvenile Roscoe's liking. Although deploring 'the shameful and indecent method of flogging prevalent in England' which was the vogue in many educational establishments at the time, he appears to distinguish it from caning, and viewed Mr Sykes' wielding of a small stick with a degree of equanimity, receiving this punishment on at least one occasion. Unlike his peers, who tried to lighten the punishment by issuing loud shrieks of pain after the first few strokes, Roscoe recalls that he obstinately (some would say foolishly) refused to show any emotion, resulting in marks on his back that remained for 'a considerable period'.

Leaving school at the age of twelve, 'my master having reported that I had learned all that he was capable of teaching

me', and happily consigning his English grammar book to the
fire, Roscoe spent three contented years helping in his father's
market garden. He cultivated vegetables and early potatoes,
carrying the produce to the Liverpool market – then situated
at the top of Lord Street – in a basket on his head. He observed:
'In that and other laborious occupations, particularly in the
care of a garden, I passed several years of my life, devoting
my hours of relaxation to reading my books. This mode of
life gave health and vigour to my frame and amusement and
instruction to my mind.' At the close of his life he declared:
'If I was asked who I considered the happiest of the human
race, I should answer those who cultivate the earth by their
own hands'.[5]

Despite the early end to his formal schooling, Roscoe came
to value education highly, a trait shared by many of the self-
taught. Henry Roscoe believed that the lack of educational
constraints allowed his father's mind to 'remain unshackled
by the prejudices or the interests of those around him'.[6] The
young William Roscoe was wide-ranging in his search for
knowledge. His life-long interest in botany began during the
three years he spent labouring on the land. He visited a neighbouring china manufactory, taking lessons in painting and
engraving from the workers, in particular Hugh Mulligan, an
engraver and painter. Roscoe never lost touch with Mulligan
despite the former's later fame and fortune; 'my acquaintance
with him continued under different circumstances, till his
death, at an advanced period of my life'.[7] Any leisure time
Roscoe had was devoted to reading. He claimed to have developed into 'a tolerable joiner', building himself a bookcase with
folding doors, which served him for many years and which he
filled with 'several volumes of Shakespeare, a great part of
whose historical plays, I committed to memory ... and other
valuable works, which I perused with great pleasure'. He
describes himself at this age as of 'a wild, rambling and unso-
ciable disposition', enjoying solitary walks along the shores

of the River Mersey or practising outdoor pursuits such as fishing. During one of his strolls he was fortunate not to lose his life when he lingered so long that he was in danger of being marooned by the incoming tide. As he was unable to swim, it was only with considerable difficulty that he managed to struggle back. It was during these years that he developed his abhorrence of all forms of cruelty. On a shooting expedition he killed a thrush, and he was so appalled by the sufferings of the dying bird that he vowed never to go shooting again.[8] At a time when cock-fighting, dog-fighting and bull-baiting still appealed to all classes, Roscoe's views on the treatment of animals were unusual. He argued that 'mankind are no less, in proportion, accountable for the ill-use of their dominion over creatures of the lower rank of beings, than for the exercise of tyranny over their own species. The more entirely the inferior creature is submitted to our power, the more answerable we should seem for our mismanagement of it.'[9]

Perceiving his son's love of reading, Roscoe senior agreed to apprentice him to a local bookseller, John Gore (publisher of the first *Liverpool Directory* of 1766). The young William apparently found this uncongenial for he remained there for only a month, although even in this brief period he may have learned something about the variety of texts available and the workings of the market. He would have been introduced to such concepts as travelling booksellers, London publishers, catalogues, early editions, specific imprints and so on. This might have been useful in later years when building up his library.[10] In 1769, aged sixteen, he became an articled clerk of Mr John Eyes, a local attorney (solicitor). After living at home during the first year of his clerkship, he was sent to board at the house of his employer's sister and her husband, who were intended, one assumes, to act as mentors to the young man. However, the husband, a retired sea captain from the Africa trade, appears to have been an alcoholic. Roscoe received little advice or help from this man: however, he was often called upon to deal with the captain's drunken delusions. Roscoe remained in the house for several months, watching the captain's mental and physical deterioration and on one occasion having to forcibly restrain the captain from cutting his own throat. Roscoe claimed that the appalling effects of alcoholism made a lasting impression on him. In his small amount of leisure time he read, in particular the poet and essayist William Shenstone (1714–1763), and he admitted that he endeavoured to imitate Shenstone in his own work. The captain's death from the effects of drinking was closely followed by that of Roscoe's employer, John Eyes, who was only thirty years of age: 'an unfortunate victim of intemperance, no less a martyr to his own misconduct as his unhappy relative'.[11] Roscoe was transferred to Mr Peter Ellames, a well-respected attorney, and he returned to live in his family home with his father and sister until his marriage in 1781.

Early mornings found Roscoe and a few like-minded friends – including Francis Holden, a young schoolmaster – gathering before work to study literature, the classics and modern languages. Holden appears to have been a particular influence on Roscoe. At an early age, he was appointed an assistant at a school in Liverpool run by his uncle, Richard Holden, where he taught mathematics and languages (Greek, Latin, French and Italian). It was Holden who encouraged Roscoe to study languages, and a close bond seems to have developed between the two men. Holden left Liverpool to attend lectures at the university in Glasgow but he corresponded regularly with Roscoe. It is clear from these letters that he enjoyed the 'French fencing lessons, dancing, broadsword classes' and the charms of the Scottish girls. He wrote of having met someone who seemed 'to be of our friend Rousseau's sentiment', showing that by 1772–1773 Roscoe was familiar with this vein of French thought.[12] Holden moved on to France, but the two men continued to correspond and on his return the friendship was resumed. During his absence Roscoe continued to study Latin and Greek, and he was joined in his classical studies by William Clarke (the son of a banker) and Richard Lowndes. The study circle continued to attract other members. On their evening walks, Holden had often recited passages from famous Italian poems; this appeared to have made a great impression on Roscoe and led him to study Italian. Roscoe described his command of the language as 'having [been] acquired rather by slow degrees, and by gradual application, than by any sudden and laborious effort'.[13] It seems likely that it was from this period that Roscoe's interest in the Italian Renaissance and the Medici developed, helping to shape his belief in the potentialities of the individual, and the power of education to produce the complete man: a man of action who was also the master of all the culture of his age. If the businessmen of medieval Florence could use their wealth to promote and stimulate art and learning, did Roscoe begin to wonder whether a latter-day Medici could emulate this feat in his native town?

Holden left Liverpool to qualify for the bar in London often asking Roscoe for advice on his legal studies, but later moved to Chesterton where he earned his living tutoring. His death in 1782 at the age of thirty from consumption was a great blow to Roscoe. This sadness was compounded the following year when another member of the group, Robert Rigby, aged twenty, was drowned in the Irish Channel. Roscoe turned to writing poetry, including two poems in commemoration of Rigby. Roscoe's early friends also included three sisters who lived in Westmoreland. He seems to have had a love affair with the youngest sister, Maria Done. They exchanged correspondence, and typically Roscoe turned to poetry to express his feelings. Henry Roscoe claimed that his father's first published work, *Mount Pleasant*, was originally inscribed to Maria Done, but the inscription did not appear when the volume was published. The poem celebrates the rise of the town:

> How numerous now her thronging buildings rise!
> What varied objects strike the wondering eye!
> Where rise yon masts her crowded navies ride,
> And the broad rampire checks the beating tide;
> Along the beach her spacious streets extend
> Her area open, and her spires ascend

In the same poem he attacks the seemingly insatiable appetite of Liverpool's merchants for money:

> Ah! Why, ye sons of wealth, with ceaseless toil,
> Add gold to gold, and swell the shining pile?
> Your general course to happiness ye bend:
> Why then to gain the means, neglect the end?
> – O spurn the grovelling wish that pants for more![14]

A letter from Holden to Roscoe in July 1793 congratulating him on his approaching happiness with Miss Done[15] suggests that the affair was serious, at least on the part of Roscoe. Maria Done, however, seems to have had other ideas, and Roscoe's hopes were dashed when he received a letter from her announcing her engagement. She married John Barton, who later became a friend and associate of Roscoe in the campaign against slavery. Roscoe appears to have recovered from his disappointment quite quickly; Holden wrote to congratulate him on his success in falling out of love with Miss Done.[16]

His family's attendance at the dissenting chapel at Benn's Garden (which moved to Renshaw Street in 1811) was another formative influence on the young Roscoe. The congregation was 'said to have been one of the most numerous and respectable of the Liverpool Dissenters',[17] and included some of the leading families of the town. Here he would have listened to the sermons of William Enfield (1741–1797), minister at the chapel from 1763–1770 before his removal to the post of rector and tutor in belles-lettres at Warrington Academy, an institution which had from its outset enjoyed links with Liverpool dissent. Morality was the central theme of Enfield's sermons: 'It is indeed my opinion that morality, as it includes all the duties we owe to our Maker, our fellow creatures and ourselves, should be the principal subject of preaching'.[18] It is possible that Enfield was a mentor to the young Roscoe, as the association of cultural endeavour with moral improvement was an essential part of Roscoe's thinking. Throughout his life, his Christianity played a central role in guiding his actions. His faith, rooted in Unitarianism, was profound, with humility and humanitarianism being its outstanding features.[19] In common with other Unitarians Roscoe disliked proselytising, and blind adherence to any religious creed was anathema to him: 'there is one truth, paramount to all the rest, which is the very basis of religious enquiry, without which all discussion is absurd, viz that every person, in his spiritual concerns, has a right to adopt such opinions as appear to him to be right'.[20]

One of Roscoe's earliest writings was a manuscript entitled 'Christian Morality as contained in the Precepts of the New Testament'. Roscoe explained in his introduction that the work was to 'collect in one uniform and regular system the moral duties which are inculcated in various of parts of the New Testament, by the direct and immediate words of our Saviour'. Dr Enfield read it and made a few corrections and comments. Roscoe treasured the volume all his life, although shortly before his death he added a note: 'done when I was very young, erroneous and imperfect'.[21] Roscoe continued to maintain contact with Dr Enfield after the latter's removal to Warrington, and submitted his poem *Mount Pleasant* to the 'cultivated judgement of Dr Enfield'.[22] As the poem was published in Warrington, Roscoe would probably have combined visits to the academy with visits to his publisher.[23] Warrington Academy was one of the most distinguished of the eighteenth-century dissenting academies. It was renowned for the eminence of its tutors (of whom the scientist and political and theological writer Joseph Priestley (1733–1804) was perhaps the most famous) and for the spirit of companionship and rational inquiry that prevailed there.[24] Although classical learning always stood at the centre of the curriculum, something firmly defended by William Roscoe in his *A Vindication of Classical Learning*,[25] Warrington Academy introduced a business course in line with the commercial spirit of the age.[26] One-third of students went on to become merchants, bankers or manufacturers, although one-third went on to become 'gentlemen'.[27] The gentlemanly ethos of the academy is suggested by the fact that some of the students kept their own horses; fencing classes were part of the curriculum. At Warrington, Roscoe came into contact with John Aikin MD, and a life-long friendship developed between the two men. In a letter to John Aikin's daughter Lucy after her father's death, Roscoe acknowledged Aikin's influence on his intellectual development. Roscoe wrote that it was Aikin who had first directed him to 'the perusal of the modern writers of Latin poetry'.[28] From a letter to Dr James Currie in 1794, it is clear that Aikin placed an equal value on his links with Liverpool: 'There are few of my old acquaintances to whom I look with more affection than the knot of select men at Liverpool'.[29]

It was with like-minded men, mainly from the dissenting congregations, that Roscoe joined in discussion circles and early cultural initiatives: men such as James Currie, William Rathbone IV, the blind poet and bookseller Edward Rushton, the Unitarian ministers John Yates and William Shepherd, and William Smyth (an Anglican and later Regius Professor of Modern History at Cambridge). These early institutions served as common forums for intellectual improvement, observation and debate.

William Roscoe and James Currie became close friends and political allies. Currie (1756–1805) was a physician who studied at Edinburgh and settled in Liverpool in 1780, where in time he was able to establish a wealthy practice. An admirer of Voltaire and a friend of Joseph Priestley, Currie has been called the 'genuine philosopher' of the group.[30] In Edinburgh he had been a noted member of the Speculative Society, and it was Currie, not Roscoe, who did most to make explicit in Liverpool the current trends in Scottish thought on social and economic matters. He was well-read in the philosophy of Berkeley, Locke, Hume and Adam Smith. Cut off from Edinburgh intellectuals, Currie took some comfort in the company of Roscoe and his friends: 'I lived in a small circle of friends in Liverpool remarkable for their prompt discussion and open declaration of their opinion on public questions'.[31] According to Checkland, he was to Roscoe and his circle as Dugald Stewart was to the Whig Party: its philosophic light and sage. His influence had a lasting effect.[32] Although a radical, Currie was conservative by temperament, claiming: 'I was by disposition and education a monarchist in opposition to a republican'.[33] He may well have been a moderating influence on his companions, possibly contributing to the fact that reform politics in Liverpool did not achieve the same notoriety of those in neighbouring Manchester.[34] He preached caution before any course of action, preferring to work in the background. His medical rather than his political writings secured him national recognition; in 1788 he was made a member of the Medical Society of London, and in 1793 he became a Fellow of the Royal Society. He was interested in mental illness, and was instrumental in the opening of a lunatic asylum in Liverpool in 1792. He also worked hard to establish a fever hospital, which finally opened in 1806, the year after his death. He contracted tuberculosis not long after his marriage in 1783 and although he managed to keep the disease under control, he was often in pain and suffered long periods of depression during which he admitted longing for death. His political views did not discourage the common council from electing him a freeman of the borough in January 1802 in recognition of his services to the town.[35]

William Rathbone IV (1757–1809) was the eldest son of the principal of William Rathbone and Sons, a firm of shippers and merchants founded in 1746. Although originally a Quaker, Rathbone became a member of Benn's Garden Chapel and was to become greatly influential in the political and economic affairs of the town. Despite his busy business life, he rose early to study Latin before breakfast and went to bed late after spending an hour or so studying French or reading Malthus, keeping himself awake by adopting a kneeling position and wrapping a wet towel around his head.[36] This quest for self-improvement was characteristic of the religious sect to which he belonged. A committed abolitionist, he nonetheless was happy to boast that his business had been the first to import American (slave-cultivated) cotton into the country in 1784.[37] John Yates (1755–1826) became the minister of Kaye Street Chapel and then, in 1791, of the newly built Paradise Street Chapel. He married a wealthy heiress, the daughter of John Ashton of Woolton (who unsuccessfully opposed the match), and became extremely wealthy himself. He has been described as a 'speculative parson' and it was rumoured that he obtained the money to establish his son Joseph as a West India merchant by a fortunate deal in tobacco. In 1843, his third son Richard Vaughan Yates (1785–1856) paid £50,000 for 44 acres of ground, most of which he threw open to the public to become Princes Park. William Shepherd (1768–1847) was educated at the dissenting academy at Daventry and at New College Hackney, where Joseph Priestley was trained. In 1790 he was appointed tutor to the sons of John Yates and was introduced to William Roscoe. The following year he became minister of the Unitarian chapel at Gateacre, where he opened a school. He was a strict disciplinarian; in a letter to his mother, Roscoe's eldest son wrote that Mr Shepherd had been poorly but 'it made very little difference to the fagging of the lads, for as he could not use his hands he used his horsewhip ... poor Arthur Heywood has dined two days together on bread and water'.[38] He took an active part in radical politics and wrote witty satirical squibs. In 1803 he published *The Life of Poggio Bracciolini*, the Italian humanist and calligrapher, which bears all the hallmarks of Roscoe's influence. It was well received and was translated into French, German and Italian. Edward Rushton (1756–1814), the blind poet, was also reputed to have attended the literary meetings although he was not a fully fledged member of the Roscoe circle. Born in Liverpool, the son of a small tradesman, he became a seaman in the African trade, rising to the position of mate on a slaving ship, before an epidemic of opthalmia on board resulted in blindness and forced him to settle on shore. In the 1780s Rushton ran a tavern in Liverpool. His experiences led him to become a committed abolitionist, and in his poems the *West Indian Eclogues* (published in 1787) he castigated the slavers and the trade. He was a little cut off from the circle by his poverty and blindness, but also by the fact that he was more forthright in airing his opinions than Roscoe and Currie.[39]

Despite Roscoe's protestations that 'the object of our meeting was merely literary',[40] it seems inconceivable that political questions were not discussed. Some argue that the group was the nearest thing to a corporate identity that the Liverpool radicals had. Although the fears engendered by the French Revolution led to these meetings being abandoned, when the Literary and Philosophical Society resurfaced in 1812 many of the same men were among its members. William Roscoe was president from 1817 until his death in 1831 and presented several papers in which, characteristically, morality was a dominant theme, notably an eloquent plea for the principles of morality to be as applicable to the public dealings between nations as to private dealings between individuals.

Roscoe's lack of private means ensured that he did not

neglect his legal career. In January 1775 he was admitted as an attorney of the Court of King's Bench. He entered into partnerships successively with Mr Bannister, Samuel Aspinall (sometimes spelt Aspinwall) and Joshua Lace. He seems to have been reasonably contented with his profession at this time, writing in 1779 that 'I am extremely happy in my present connection' and that Aspinall is 'one of the most friendly hearted, sincere men I have ever met with'.[41] It was now that he had met his future wife, Jane Griffies, the second daughter of William Griffies, a linen draper and barber of Castle Street. In the love poems that Roscoe composed for her she is given the poetic name Julia, and he continued to write poetry to her throughout his life.

> Come then my Julia to thy lover's arms
> Nor let the voice of friendship hold thee long:
> O let me once more gaze upon thy charms
> And hear once more the music of thy tongue.[42]

Although living in the same town, the couple entered into a regular correspondence which illustrates the highs and lows of their extended courtship. Roscoe suggested rather pompously that they should each keep a journal and communicate its contents to the other: 'I cannot help pleasing myself with the reflection, what an infinite variety of subjects this intercourse would give rise'.

Despite the need to save for the future, Roscoe purchased numerous books and prints. Happily Jane shared his literary interests and helped him with his book collection. When she went to London in the spring of 1778 she visited bookshops and sent Roscoe a list of books she thought might be suitable for his collection. She continued to be supportive and to forgive him even when she felt that his extravagance might threaten the security of their children. On occasion she did endeavour to check him, once suggesting that they would need a 'Fortunatus's purse' to support his love of the arts. Here Jane was referring to Fortunatus Wright, one of Liverpool's most famous and wealthy privateers.

Roscoe worked for three years in the law partnership before becoming engaged, and a further four years elapsed before he felt sufficiently financially secure to marry. His letters to Jane reveal how despondent he sometimes was about having to delay their wedding, but he reminded himself that his duty to support his father and sister had to come before his personal feelings. 'It is with no common degree of satisfaction that I reflect, I have been enabled, so far, to screen a hapless parent, and a deserving sister, from the hardships of an unfeeling world; and whilst I make that reflection I never can be wholly unhappy.'[43] The pair were finally married in St Anne's Church, Liverpool, on 22 February 1781. They enjoyed forty years of happiness together, rearing a family of seven sons and two daughters.[44]

The Roscoes remained in Liverpool after their marriage while William established himself as a successful lawyer. In 1790 they moved to Toxteth Park, which at that time was about two miles outside Liverpool. One of the attractions of his new home was its proximity to a small but beautiful dingle leading to the shores of the Mersey. It was here that he wrote his poem *The Dingle* in which he extols the beauty of Dingle Point.

> Stranger, that with careless feet,
> Wanderest near this green retreat,
> Where, through gently bending slopes,
> Soft the distant prospect opes;
>
> Where the fern in fringed pride
> Decks the lonely valley's side
> Where the linnet chirps his song,
> Flitting as thou treadst along[45]

This is a description that few modern-day residents of Liverpool would recognize! Toxteth Park was close enough for Roscoe to continue his professional engagements and to enjoy the company of his friends. The Roscoes often visited Greenbank, the home of William Rathbone, and enjoyed dinner parties with friends such as the Clarkes, the Yates, Shepherd and the Earles. It was at Greenbank that Roscoe met John Dalton (1766–1844), the great Manchester chemist. Dalton was impressed by the discussions he had with Roscoe, Yates and Rathbone, and visited Roscoe's home, admiring his library. The austere Quaker was less impressed with their 'stilish manner of living'. He wrote to his brother that 'Breakfasting at nine, getting little till after three, and then eating and drinking almost incessantly to ten, without going out further than to the door, does not suit my constitution.'[46] It was while living at Toxteth Park that Roscoe composed many of the political poems that earned him a national reputation.

Roscoe's family soon outgrew its Toxteth Park home, and within three years the Roscoes moved again. In 1793 Roscoe purchased some land at Birchfield, Folly Lane, Islington, on which he built a house where he remained for six years. It was while living here that his father died, having lived with the Roscoes for many years. Much of the work on his magnum opus, a biography of his hero Lorenzo de Medici, was undertaken at Birchfield, and he laid the foundations for his great book collection there. In 1793 the Liverpool printer John McCreery started printing the Lorenzo book at Roscoe's expense.

Shortly after the publication of his *Life of Lorenzo*, Roscoe decided to retire from the legal profession at the age of 43 (the same age chosen by his hero). Roscoe had never found fulfilment in the practice of law and had always looked forward to the day when 'he would be free to enjoy a few tranquil years of leisure and retirement to pursue his own interests and to be free to avoid crowds, noise and contention in the company of a few chosen friends'. In a letter to his friend Ralph Eddowes in Philadelphia, Roscoe explained that he had invested in a scheme to drain Chat and Trafford Mosses, which he was certain would be a financial success. His involvement in the project meant that he would not have sufficient time to undertake his legal work satisfactorily.[47]

However, even if not to his taste, the legal profession must have been remarkably munificent to him, given that he had a large family to support. His friend William Rathbone questioned the wisdom of the decision, but Roscoe remained unmoved and criticized those who were prepared to sacrifice health, wisdom, peace of mind and conscience for 'the absurd purpose of heaping up, for the use of life, more than life can employ'.[48] An unconvinced Rathbone teased his moralistic (and, in his view, somewhat hypocritical) friend: 'I told my wife last night how pleasantly you argue on the folly of toiling for wealth and yet how happily you indulge yourself in all that wealth can purchase... I cannot help but smile that you should so earnestly contend for avoiding the toil of wealth and yet cultivate the relish in yourself.'[49]

That Roscoe may have had second thoughts about his decision is evidenced by his visit to London in 1797 in order to enter Gray's Inn, with a view to becoming a barrister. However, he spent only Hilary term there and soon returned home. Whether this was for personal reasons (he was never happy when away from his family for any period) or because of the demands of his agricultural undertaking at the Mosses is not clear. His son Henry felt that it was a great pity that his father did not become a barrister, as he believed that he possessed all the qualities that would have made him very successful.[50] Deciding that his career in law was at an end, an agreement was drawn up with his partner Joshua Lace. Lace agreed to pay him a £200 annuity for seven years on condition of his not engaging in the business of law within twenty miles of Liverpool. It was also agreed that Lace would accept Roscoe's eldest son as an apprentice, if the boy so wished. Roscoe stated that he wanted his son brought up 'in a regular system'. Thus although he protested that he, himself, found little satisfaction in the practice of law, it appears that he felt it a suitable and safe career for his progeny.[51]

In 1799 Roscoe sold Birchfield to William Ewart, a close friend and associate of John Gladstone (the father of William Gladstone, the future Prime Minister) for 4,000 guineas and moved to Allerton Hall, five miles south-east of Liverpool. Roscoe knew the property well and its rural location suited him. He bought the hall, 153 acres of land and half of the manorial rights and immediately set about making improvements. Although the manor was held by the Lathoms in the fourteenth century, the Palladian house that is seen today was almost certainly begun by John Hardman, a merchant from Rochdale, who purchased the estate in 1736 with his brother James. When Roscoe acquired the house some of the timbers were rotten, and he decided to pull this part down and rebuild an east wing on a uniform plan, to correspond with the earlier eighteenth-century centre and wing. Roscoe was delighted with his new estate, praising its advantages and good air. He liked the fact that 'I am a mile and a half from my neighbour, but at that distance I have on every side of me some of my most intimate and valuable friends'. Here he could pursue both his botanical and agricultural interests, and he decided to keep all of the lands surrounding the hall under his own control. In a letter to Henry Fuseli in 1799, he revelled in the fact that:

> I am surrounded with cows, hogs, turkeys, geese, hens and pigeons; which, according to the good old maxim, ("Take, Peter, kill and eat") I plunder and slaughter without mercy; and shall be very angry with you if you tell me (as is not unlikely) that I am keeping up my petty existence at the

expense of the lives of a number of beings, each of which
is ten times happier than myself'.[52]

Given Roscoe's early experience of shooting and his reaction
to the death throes of a bird, one assumes that this letter was
written with his tongue firmly in his cheek. The new wing
containing his library and music room was finally completed
by 1812. Roscoe was very anxious to use the new library but
feared that he had moved into the newly built room too soon
when he was almost immediately struck down with a violent
attack of sciatica.

Roscoe took great pleasure in arranging his books, and
decided to prepare a printed catalogue that he felt might prove
useful to others studying the literary history of the period. This
period saw the rise in England of a passion for books that was
dubbed 'bibliomania'. The famous bibliographer T.F. Dibdin
(1775–1847) was its apostle. Born in Calcutta (now Kolkata),
he took orders in the Church of England where he had several
appointments. United by their love of books, Dibdin and
Roscoe became close friends and associates.[53] Roscoe's library
was particularly strong in examples of early Italian printing
from Venice, Bologna, Naples, Milan, Rome and Florence.
Works by Italian poets, including early editions of the poetical works of Lorenzo de Medici, comprised the largest section
of the library. Of Roscoe's early Italian works, the most
precious was probably the *Canzonieri of Petrarch*, printed in
Venice by Vindelinus de Spira in 1470. Roscoe paid £94 10s
for his copy, a very high price at the time. The book was
described by Dibdin as 'an extremely precious volume; among
the most beautiful, as well as the rarest, of those executed by
Vindelin de Spira'.[54] Roscoe's library was also well stocked
with the varied riches of English literature, including a first
folio of Shakespeare (1623) and editions of Langland (1561),
Chaucer (1561), Donne (1639), Marvell (1681) and Dryden
(1687). He had first editions of Gibbon's *Decline and Fall of*

*the Roman Empire* (1776) and Robertson's *History of Charles V* (1759).[55] There were also classics of botanical literature, and Roscoe's was possibly the finest private botanical library at the time.[56] Ill-health and other business cares delayed the proposed work, but an indication of the contents of the volume can be deduced from the draft title page:

> Catalogue of a Private Collection of Books, Pictures, Drawings, Medals, and Prints, illustrating the Rise, Vicissitudes, and Establishment of Literature and Art in Europe: to which are added, <u>Collectiones Medicianae,</u> or Pieces chiefly relating to the Family of the Medici, from MSS. and rare Books in this Collection, with numerous Portraits, Facsimiles, Engravings, and Vignettes, and occasional Remarks, biographical, historical and critical.

Sadly, within two years Roscoe was engaged on a similar task, but this time he was preparing a catalogue for the sale of his books and pictures, necessitated by his impending bankruptcy (see Chapter 7).[57]

At Allerton Hall, Roscoe entertained distinguished visitors from all parts of the globe,[58] including the botanist and author Sir James Edward Smith, the first president of the Linnean Society of London. The two men became close friends, and Smith later dedicated his book *Exotic Botany* to Roscoe. Roscoe was a keen member of the West Derby Agricultural Society and delivered learned lectures on such matters as farm leases and relationships between landlords and tenants. He also made a point of reminding the society and its members of the need to introduce new and improved modes of cultivation suitable to the district.

Allerton Hall can still be visited today, although the interior was very severely damaged by fires in 1994 and 1995. It has been refurbished and reopened as 'The Pub in the Park'. What still survives is a room at the west end with panelled walls, Kentian overdoors and a stucco ceiling with thin rococo decoration, and parts of Roscoe's grand neoclassical library towards the other end of the house, with a back screen of fluted Ionic columns. The park was opened to the public in 1926 and for many years had a collection of ponies, goats, rabbits and geese, although these have now been dispersed.[59]

Contentedly settled at Allerton Hall, Roscoe happily looked forward to the rest of his life, which he expected to devote to agricultural, cultural and literary pursuits. Following the success of his *Life of Lorenzo*, he decided to embark on a biography of Lorenzo's son, who became Pope Leo X. However, his rural idyll was destined to be short-lived; his strict sense of morality ensured a return to the world of business when the bank of his old friend William Clarke found itself in difficulties. Although reluctant, he felt morally bound to help the close friend who had been so instrumental in the success of his literary work. Under the guidance of Roscoe, confidence was restored in the bank before its final collapse in 1816. His humanitarianism ensured that he played an active role in both the campaign to abolish slavery and the cause of reform, encouraging him to enter the political arena (see Chapter 6). His belief in the compatibility of commerce and culture, fuelled by his interpretation of Medici Florence, ensured that he worked tirelessly to create a cultural infrastructure for his native town. To the end of his life he remained convinced that the preoccupation of Liverpool's merchants with the accumulation of wealth could be redeemed by the conjunction of commerce with culture, and that education would ensure that Liverpool led the way in creating a new generation of scholar-businessmen who would serve as examples in the national and international arenas.

# CHAPTER 3

# Roscoe the Littérateur

Under the auspices of the House of Medici, and particularly through the ardour and example of Lorenzo, the empire of science and true taste was again restored.[1]

William Roscoe's claim to literary immortality rests squarely on his historical writings, but at first poetry was his preferred method of self-expression. George Chandler suggests that Roscoe's poems fall into four natural groups: the early published poems on Liverpool (1774–1777); the unpublished early love poems (mainly 1773–1784); the early (1787–1792) and late (1807–1812) political poetry; and miscellaneous, mainly personal poems (1796–1831).[2]

Roscoe's first published poem was his *Ode on the Institution of a Society in Liverpool for the Encouragement of Designing, Drawing, Painting etc.* (1774), in which he considers the influence of painting in relation to other branches of the arts. The poem was described as 'pretty' and 'ingenious' by the *Monthly Review*, but a more recent assessment dismissed it as 'an example of the imitative arts ... unenlivened by any trace of originality' and 'full of vague abstractions, classical references and Latinized diction'.[3] His next published poem, *Mount Pleasant* (1777), although associated with his native town, imitated Dyer's *Grongar Hill* (1727). Much of Roscoe's poetry was derivative; the influences of Shenstone, Gray, Dyer and Pope were clearly discernible. After *Mount Pleasant* and his early love poems, firstly to Maria Done (who remained unmoved) and then to his future wife Jane Griffies (referred to as Julia), Roscoe moved on to didactic political poetry that attacked the slave trade and supported the French Revolution.

Among his contemporary poets, Roscoe particularly admired Byron and Robert Burns. Roscoe and Burns both sympathized with the ideals of the French Revolution (which earned them unpopularity), although later they became disillusioned with its excesses. Burns did not manage to fulfil his intention of visiting Liverpool before his early death, in 1796, at the age of 37. Roscoe was angry at what he considered to be the unfair treatment Burns received from his fellow countrymen, and he encouraged James Currie to edit a volume of Burns's work with a biography and criticism. Currie hoped to create an edition that would provide some financial security for Burns's family, which had been left in straitened circumstances.

Initially Roscoe's poetry was well received and gained literary recognition for Liverpool. Sir Joshua Reynolds was effusive in his praise, while his old mentor Reverend William Enfield claimed that Roscoe's poems 'cannot fail of being highly acceptable to every reader of classical taste'.[4] However, Roscoe was writing at the dawn of the Romantic era and his work, belonging as it did to the 'classical tradition', held little appeal for members of the new generation such as Thomas De Quincey, who found Wordsworth and Coleridge more to their taste. Coleridge's *Lyrical Ballads* (1798) were greeted with some reserve by Roscoe. Although he had viewed Coleridge's first volume of poems favourably, praising the poet's genius, he had ended his analysis with the warning 'he ought not for a moment to forget that he writes for immortality'.[5]

The reaction of the new generation of poets against the classical tradition is encapsulated by Thomas De Quincey's later bitter tirade against Roscoe and his circle. In his

*Autobiographical Sketches* (published in 1837), he portrayed
Roscoe's circle as a group of pseudo-intellectuals suffering
from delusions of grandeur. De Quincey's impressions were
based on a holiday he had spent at a cottage in Everton oppo-
site the home of William Clarke, Roscoe's close friend, in
1801. Clarke made the precocious De Quincey welcome in his
house and invited him to join in the literary and political
discussions that took place there. Clarke's kindness was
repaid with a harsh diatribe in which De Quincey reduced
Roscoe and his friends to a group of transient caricatures.
Roscoe he dismissed as a 'mere *belle-lettrist*', and he scorned
the Liverpudlian's poetry, amusing himself with the observation that although these men lauded Roscoe as a poet of some
significance, not one of them had heard of Wordsworth. De
Quincey's article caused great offence in Liverpool and a spirited defence was launched by William Shepherd (the only
member of the coterie still alive in 1837), who ascribed De
Quincey's vitriol to his opium addiction.[6] However, a more
recent assessment suggests that De Quincey's condemnation
of Roscoe's poetry was the natural reaction of a new generation against the taste of its predecessor.[7]

One of Roscoe's poems did, in fact, earn him lasting recognition. Originally written for the entertainment of his young
son Robert and composed in a simple style, *The Butterfly's
Ball and The Grasshopper's Feast* was first published in the
*Gentleman's Magazine* of November 1806, and is recognized
as one of the nursery classics. Its air of artless fantasy and
simplicity of line suggest that Roscoe might have achieved
lasting fame as a children's poet had he been content to limit
himself to this genre. Roscoe hoped that his personification
of animals large and small would encourage children to appreciate the world of nature. Lacking the didacticism and moral
content of many of his poems, it has been aptly described as
having 'not the least touch of archness, patronage, grown-up-
ness, be-good-ness in the description'.[8]

Come take up your Hats, and away let us haste
To the Butterfly's Ball, and the Grasshopper's Feast.
The Trumpeter, Gad-fly, has summon'd the Crew,
And the Revels are now only waiting for you.

So said little Robert, and pacing along,
His merry Companions came forth in a Throng.
And on the smooth Grass, by the side of a Wood,
Beneath a broad Oak that for Ages had stood,

Saw the Children of Earth, and the Tenants of Air,
For an Evening's Amusement together repair.
And there came the Beetle, so blind and so black,
Who carried the Emmet, his Friend, on his Back.

And there was the Gnat and the Dragon-fly too,
With all their Relations, Green, Orange, and Blue.
And there came the Moth, with his Plumage of Down,
And the Hornet in Jacket of Yellow and Brown;

Who with him the Wasp, his Companion, did bring,
But they promis'd, that Evening, to lay by their Sting.
And the sly little Dormouse crept out of his Hole,
And brought to the Feast his blind Brother, the Mole.

And the Snail, with his Horns peeping out of his Shell,
Came from a great Distance, the Length of an Ell.
A Mushroom their Table, and on it was laid
Water-dock Leaf, which a Table-cloth made.

The Viands were various, to each of their Taste,
And the Bee brought her Honey to crown the Repast.
Then close on his Haunches, so solemn and wise,
The Frog from a Corner, look'd up to the Skies.

And the Squirrel well pleas'd such Diversions to see,
Mounted high over Head, and look'd down from a Tree.

Then out came the Spider, with Finger so fine,
To shew his Dexterity on the tight Line.

From one Branch to another, his Cobwebs he slung,
Then quick as an Arrow he darted along,
But just in the Middle, — Oh! shocking to tell,
From his Rope, in an Instant, poor Harlequin fell.

Yet he touch'd not the Ground, but with Talons
                                         outspread,
Hung suspended in Air, at the End of a Thread,
Then the Grasshopper came with a Jerk and a Spring,
Very long was his Leg, though but short was his Wing;

He took but three Leaps, and was soon out of Sight,
Then chirp'd his own Praises the rest of the Night.
With Step so majestic the Snail did advance,
And promis'd the Gazers a Minuet to dance.

But they all laugh'd so loud that he pull'd in his Head,
And went in his own little Chamber to Bed.
Then, as Evening gave Way to the Shadows of Night,
Their Watchman, the Glow-worm, came out with a
Light.

Then Home let us hasten, while yet we can see,
For no Watchman is waiting for you and for me.
So said little Robert, and pacing along,
His merry Companions returned in a Throng.

The poem found favour with George III (who was not
Roscoe's favourite person) and Queen Charlotte, who asked
Sir George Smart to set it to music for their daughters, the
Princesses Elizabeth, Augusta and Mary. Roscoe published a
further poem, *The Butterfly's Birthday*, in 1809, and *Poems*

*for Youth* in 1820. Roscoe's children's poems were among the first of the animal books, and he can be considered a pioneer of the genre. He may well have influenced later writers such as Beatrix Potter, Lewis Carroll and Kenneth Grahame, to name just a few.

In 1798, Roscoe – inspired by his Italian studies and grasp of the language – translated Tansillo's *La Balia* into English under the title *The Nurse*. The didactic and moral intent of the poem, an earnest promotion of the merits of breastfeeding, appealed to Roscoe. Some lines near the end of Tansillo's poem alluded to certain aristocratic ladies of the time. Roscoe decided to introduce an aristocratic reference from his own country, and asked a friend to enquire whether this would be acceptable to the Duchess of Devonshire, who against the fashion of the upper classes of the time insisted on breast-feeding her children. In a letter to Roscoe she stated how pleased she had been that her name was mentioned and the satisfaction she felt 'in seeing the practice of nursing, of which she had ever been an enthusiastic advocate, so honoured and recommended as it was by the poem Mr Roscoe had beauti-fully translated'. The manner in which his wife chose to feed her children was announced to the world at large in a dedi-catory sonnet; one assumes Jane agreed to its publication.

> And whilst delighted, to thy willing breast
> With rosy lip thy smiling infant clings,
> Pleased I reflect, that from those healthful springs
> Ah not by thee with niggard love represt –
> Six sons successive, and thy later care,
> Two daughters fair have drunk;[9]

Reviews of the translation were favourable, with reference to the elegance of its translation and the 'correctness' of Roscoe's taste.[10]

Some of Roscoe's later poems were in the form of hymns,

and in 1818 Roscoe and some of his Unitarian friends compiled a new edition of a hymnbook for the congregation of Renshaw Street Chapel, of which he was a life-long member. Roscoe wrote seven hymns for the book.

The first collection of Roscoe's poems, entitled the *Poetical Works of William Roscoe*, was published in 1853 to celebrate the centenary of his birth. In 1953, George Chandler, the city librarian, compiled a further selection to form the second part of his biography of William Roscoe. In his introduction to the biography, Sir Alfred Shennan admits that the poems were not 'offered as the work of a poet, even moderately great, though they are the product of a great man'. Rather, they exemplified 'the muse, domestic and celebratory, of a cultured eighteenth-century English gentleman of a Whiggish way of thought. And they help to illustrate the century's poetic combination of classical tradition and the awakening interest in human rights and emancipation.'[11]

It was Roscoe's Italian writings, particularly his biography of Lorenzo de Medici, that earned him an international reputation as an historian and littérateur. Although he had long been interested in fifteenth-century and sixteenth-century Italian history and was convinced of the need for 'a complete history of these times', his family and business commitments meant that his writing was confined to his leisure hours. Roscoe acknowledged that to write a complete history of the period was too great an undertaking for him – 'a mind of greater compass, and the possession of uninterrupted leisure, would be requisite'[12] – and decided to narrow his focus to the Medici family, and in particular Lorenzo. Roscoe's long interest in Italian writings and poetry had drawn him to conclude that 'every thing great and excellent in science and in art, revolved round Lorenzo de Medici, during the short but splendid era of his life'.[13] Spurred on by 'the real admiration I have of the character of my hero', Roscoe believed it was his mission to make such an extraordinary man more generally known.[14] According to Roscoe, 'certain it is that no man was ever more admired and venerated by his contemporaries, or has been more defrauded of his just fame by posterity, than Lorenzo de Medici'.[15] Roscoe saw in Florence and its ruler the apotheosis of the union between culture and commerce. 'Earnest in the acquisition of wealth, indefatigable in improving their manufactures and extending their commerce, the Florentines seem not, however, to have lost sight of the true dignity of man, or of the proper objects of his regard.'[16] His interest (he declared) was literary and cultural rather than political: 'It appeared to me that the mere historical events of the fifteenth century, so far as they regarded Italy, could not deeply interest my countrymen in the eighteenth; but I conceived that the progress of letters and of arts would be attended to with pleasure in every country where they were cultivated and protected.'[17]

While Roscoe's biography of Lorenzo was a pioneering study of its subject in English, highlighting the Anglo–Florentine entente between commerce and culture, it was also clearly hagiographic: not so much an analysis of Lorenzo as politician, diplomat or statesman, but more a celebration of Lorenzo as merchant prince and self-made man, the patron who was single-handedly responsible for raising the culture of Italy. 'The protection afforded by him to all the polite arts, gave them a permanent foundation in Italy. In the establishment of public libraries, schools and seminaries of learning, he was equally munificent, indefatigable and successful.'[18] Lorenzo emerged as a paragon with few human weaknesses and no inconsistencies.[19] Roscoe wrote that the book had no relevance for contemporary problems: 'the truth is, it is a tale of other times, bearing but little on the momentous occurrences of the present day'.[20] This denial could have been Roscoe's way of reconciling Lorenzo's cultural achievements with the autocratic means by which Lorenzo controlled and maintained power. The significance of politics was played down, and Roscoe largely ignored the economic base of Lorenzo's patronage. Roscoe much preferred to picture his hero at his desk, in his library or immersed in discussions with learned Platonists as he strolled in his gardens. Roscoe admitted that he had 'on all occasions, avoided violent and extreme opinions and perhaps may be accused by some of having taken some pains to display the glossy side of aristocracy'.[21]

The work did, however, showcase Roscoe's industriousness and his skilful use of sources. The influence of historians such as Robertson, Hume and Gibbon, who insisted on verifiable documentary references to the main body of text, is evident. Roscoe spent a lot of time and money building a substantial private library; when bankruptcy forced its sale, the catalogue listed some 2,000 separate items. The sale of the Crevenna and Pinelli libraries proved particularly useful, yielding Italian material that ranged from the early Florentine history of Machiavelli and Ammirato, to Valori's near-contemporary life of Lorenzo, the annals of Muratori, and later critical work by Bandini, Crescimbeni, Baldinucci and Tiraboschi (the latter being deeply admired by Roscoe).[22] The only recently-published books Roscoe found to be of real value were a Latin life by Fabroni printed in 1784 (sent to him by William Clarke), and Tenhove's *Memoires Genealogiques de la Maison de Medici*, which appeared when the first few sheets of Lorenzo were already at the printers. On receiving it, Roscoe deliberated over whether he should give up his own work and concentrate on translating Fabroni's. However, he decided that the main focus of Fabroni's work was political matters, whereas he intended to make the state and progress of letters and the arts the central themes of his book. He did, however, acknowledge the helpfulness of Fabroni's work, particularly in directing him to relevant primary sources. Access to these primary (not printed) sources posed him some problems. With his business commitments and large family,

Roscoe was reluctant to travel abroad. He did not appear to feel any regret at not visiting Italy. As John Hale points out, Roscoe was not alone in feeling there was no need to physically visit the home of his subject; it was a habit of English historians at least as late as Grote.[23] Although his unwillingness to travel abroad caused some difficulties for Roscoe, it can also be argued that it allowed him the freedom to fictionalize his subject to some extent, and to draw imaginative parallels between late fifteenth-century Florence and eighteenth-century Liverpool.

Fortunately for Roscoe, in 1789 his close friend William Clarke travelled to Fiesole for health reasons and readily agreed to Roscoe's request for help with his research. Access to archives in Florence was granted freely and Clarke was able to consult material in the Riccardi and Laurentian libraries and in the Palazzo Vecchio. We do not know what Clarke's exact instructions were, but anything he considered might prove helpful was copied or extracted and sent back to Liverpool; he signed his letters 'G. Le Clerc'. Roscoe acknowledged that the help he received from his friend 'went far beyond even the hopes I had formed'.[24] Given that it was Clarke rather than Roscoe who selected the material, it seems fair to assume that he may have had some influence on the work. Among the material that Clarke sent home was a collection of previously unpublished poems by Lorenzo (which Roscoe published separately with a dedication to his friend);[25] Roscoe's biography pays considerable attention to Lorenzo as a poet. According to Roscoe, Lorenzo (like himself) began to write poetry in his youth, and he called Lorenzo ' the restorer of the lyric poetry of Italy, the promoter of the dramatic, the founder of the satire, rustic, and other modes of composition'. He claimed that Lorenzo was 'not merely entitled to the rank of poet, but may justly be placed among the distinguished few, who, by their native strength, have made their way through paths before untrodden'.[26]

The book was very readable and was an immediate success. The French Revolution and the Napoleonic Wars created a cultural space in the English imagination; Italian literature and history replaced the now-suspect French corpus.[27] Although the two volumes were dated and printed in 1795, the book was published in February 1796 by Edwards of Pall Mall at Roscoe's expense. Roscoe then sold the copyright for £1,200 to Cadell and Davies, a London publisher, and a second edition, carefully corrected by Roscoe, appeared in the autumn of 1796. Seven editions in English were published during Roscoe's lifetime, and after his death his son Thomas edited four more. The book attracted much attention abroad. By 1799 it had been translated into French by Francois Thurot and into German by Kurt Sprengel of Halle. An edition appeared in the USA in 1803. Lord Lansdowne praised it in the House of Lords, while Fabroni, until now the greatest living authority on the Medici, cancelled the translation of his own work into Italian and personally arranged instead for the translation of Roscoe's by Cavaliero Gaetano Mecherini.[28] This translation was published at Pisa in 1799.

The reception given to Roscoe's biography was partly explained by the fact that there was not much competition in this field of historical study. The sparse existing Italian literature on Lorenzo was based on Valori's brief early life. Roscoe felt that Valori, a friend and contemporary of Lorenzo, had failed to explore in sufficient depth the 'strength, extent, and versatility' of the mind and extraordinary talents of his subject.[29] This lack of precedent was in Roscoe's favour as his critics had little with which to compare his work, and their reviews were overwhelmingly approving. The book did meet with some later criticism, particularly from specialist historians; the most prominent was the Swiss historian J.C.L. Simonde de Sismondi, who had begun work on his sixteen-volume *Histoire des républiques italiennes du moyen âge* in

1796, the year Roscoe's work was published. Although Roscoe and Sismondi had used the same sources, their interpretations were very different. While Roscoe romanticized Lorenzo, presenting him as an ideal man who created a cultured and civilized state, Sismondi portrayed him as tyrannical in his pursuit of political and economic ends. Sismondi's criticisms stirred Roscoe to publish in 1820 a whole volume of primary data, the *Illustrations of the Life of Lorenzo*, to vindicate his portrayal. Roscoe claimed he relied on 'the unperverted pages of history' to authenticate his account. Not to be outdone, in the next edition of his book Sismondi included a long list of bloody executions for which he believed Lorenzo to be responsible, adding: 'As for M. Roscoe, I do not know whether there is enough blood here to satisfy him... I have carefully cited my authorities at the foot of the page, and have noted with scrupulous attention the edition, the book and the page of the writer in whom I have placed my trust.'[30] That both men insisted on the incontrovertibility of their sources but produced such contrasting accounts emphasizes the importance of the individual historian in selecting, organizing and interpreting facts. However, despite their differences on the subject of Lorenzo, the two men became friends, with Sismondi visiting Roscoe in 1826.[31]

The book stimulated English interest in the Italian Renaissance and earned Roscoe a national reputation as a writer and historian. He now stood as living proof that humble origins, a remote northern birth-place[32] and the pursuit of a business career were not incompatible with the highest intellectual achievement:

> I can scarcely conceive a greater miracle than Roscoe's history – that a man whose dialect was that of a barbarian and from whom in years of familiar conversation I have never heard an above average observation, whose parents were servants ... that such a man should undertake and

write the history of the fourteenth and fifteenth centuries,
and the revival of Greek and Roman learning, that such a
history should be to the full, as polished in style as that of
Gibbon and much more simple and perspicuous ... is really
*too*.[33]

Roscoe's historical writings also earned him recognition internationally, notably in the USA. His ability to combine the
literary world with business proved perplexing to the author
Washington Irving, who declared: 'To find therefore the
elegant historian of the Medici mingling among the busy sons
of traffic, at first shocked my poetic ideals'.[34] However, it was
this very ability that appealed so strongly to many of the USA's
aspiring businessmen. The fact that Roscoe was a self-made
man who now owned the very estate where his father was
reputed to have been a gardener and his mother a housekeeper
made him an attractive role model for American merchants
and professionals seeking to establish their civic and social
positions. For many Bostonians he symbolized 'the intellectual breadth and elegance which might lift a Boston
businessman to a loftier social and cultural level'. Numerous
Americans visited or corresponded with Roscoe, and at least
two Bostonians named their sons after him.[35]

The book also brought some reappraisal of Liverpool's
image. One critic marvelled that this 'model of literary
endeavour' had been written and printed 'in the remote
commercial town of Liverpool, where nothing is heard of but
Guinea ships, slaves, blacks and merchandise'.[36] On Roscoe's
insistence the book had been printed under his control in
Liverpool by John McCreery, who had established a press
there.[37] The two men became friends (and eventually died in
the same year). Roscoe believed that 'the town which cannot
produce books finely must remain a mere intellectual suburb
of the town that can', and the printing of the book did much
to prove 'to the world that London itself could not surpass

this town in some kinds of elegant typography'.[38]

The acclaim accorded to William Roscoe can scarcely have failed to impress Liverpool's elite. The equating of Liverpool with Renaissance Florence must also have been gratifying. Despite Roscoe's assertions that the book had no contemporary relevance, it was surely to Renaissance Florence that he looked for a role model for his native town. The success (in Roscoe's view) of Lorenzo's academies, schools, libraries and associations provided him with the blueprint for the future construction of a similar infrastructure in Liverpool. Looking to Renaissance Florence rather than to the metropolis for a role model would have been particularly appealing to Liverpool's merchants, who sought to rival rather than emulate London.[39] The wide impression made by Roscoe's Italian vision is shown by the way it continued to be evoked, after his death, by men of all shades of political and religious opinions in public speeches, lectures, and in papers read at Liverpool's scientific and literary societies. Although contemporary observers in other parts of the country traced analogies between their towns and Italy, only Liverpool was in the fortunate position of claiming the country's acknowledged leading authority on the Medici as one of its own. The significance of the book cannot be over-emphasized. It was undoubtedly a turning point, if not the starting point of Liverpool's cultural life. If, as Jon Stobart argues,[40] the turn of the century saw Liverpool experience a second 'urban renaissance', here was its inspiration.

Among the many congratulations Roscoe received for *Life of Lorenzo* was a letter from Lord Bristol professing his admiration of the work. In a second letter, the peer offered Roscoe the use of apartments in Rome and Naples in order to further his researches, but the home-loving Roscoe did not take up this opportunity. Lord Bristol suggested that Roscoe should embark on a sequel, taking Lorenzo's son Giovanni, who became Pope Leo X, as his subject. He stated, 'Tis the sequel of Lorenzo that I propose to you, in the life of his son, Leo X. You see at once, Sir, what a glorious, animating era it embraces; and who is so fit to paint the manhood of arts, of science and religious information, as the happy and elegant writer who has so satisfactorily sketched and delineated their infancy?'[41]

The suggestion attracted Roscoe, who may have been influenced by the fact that Fabroni had embarked on a biography of Leo shortly after the publication of his *Life of Lorenzo*. Roscoe explained the reasoning behind his choice of subject in the Preface to his *Life of Leo*. He wrote that his *Life of Lorenzo* had stimulated his interest in the ensuing period, and he felt compelled to continue, not least because of the many original documents that his friends had discovered both at home and abroad. In addition, Roscoe explained that there was no historical work in English covering Pope Leo X and his period of office, although 'the elegant and pathetic poet, William Collins, was said to have planned in the mid-eighteenth century to write a biography of Leo X, which was to include a history of the revival of literature, learning and the arts during his time.'[42] This work had never come to fruition.

Roscoe began his new project in the autumn of 1798 and his intense effort was remarked upon by his son Henry. Roscoe was already familiar with the earliest history of his subject, that of Paola Giovio in Latin, translated into Italian and published in Florence in 1549.[43] He stated that the work 'contained much authentic information and was less satirical in spirit than Giovio's other writings'. He also had some knowledge of the histories of Guicciardini and the writings of Muratori. He was fortunate that Fabroni's *Leonis Pontificis Maxima Vita* was published in Pisa in 1797, just a year before he began his own biography. In a letter to Lord Bristol, Roscoe said that he did not think it was sufficient to merely synthesize the works of Giovio, Muratori and Guicciardini, as he thought that they did not provide enough information about the political, artistic and literary history of the period. As with his previous work, Roscoe benefited from the help of friends and acquaintances in collecting relevant manuscripts and contemporary documents from Florence, Rome, Paris and Venice. Henry Roscoe wrote that in an unpublished tract written after the publication of his biography of Leo, his father claimed that his new work could be viewed as a continuation of his earlier *Life of Lorenzo*.[44]

As Roscoe became immersed in his new project, the range of the work increased and he experienced some difficulty with its planning. Substantial help with his researches came from Lord Holland, who obtained permission from the Grand Duke of Tuscany for a Mr Penrose, 'the British resident' in Florence, to supervise the copying of a large number of letters and papers illustrating the early life of Leo X. These formed two folio volumes, each of which contained over 300 pages. In addition, Roscoe was keen to acquire as much information as possible from the Vatican archives in Rome. Here he encountered another difficulty; they were designated 'Secret Archives', not open to the public. Just as Roscoe began to accept that he was pursuing a lost cause, he received an offer of help from a Mr John Johnson, who had been travelling in Italy. 'Having learned' wrote Johnson 'from Signor Bandini, that you are employed in writing the "Life of Leone X", I take the liberty of informing you that I propose passing the ensuing winter in Rome, where it is probable that, from my acquaintance with the Cardinal Borgia, the Abbé Marini, Prefetto dell Archivio Vaticano, &c. &c., I may be able to procure you some materials for your work.' Johnson asked Roscoe to give him details of any documents he wished to have analysed.

In his reply, Roscoe explained that he had almost finished the first volume of his book, and said that what he needed most was information from the archives in Rome about Leo's immediate predecessors, Alexander VI and Julius II, and about Leo himself. Roscoe seemed remarkably vague about what he was seeking. He gave Johnson little direction and appeared content to leave the selection of documents to the traveller. He wrote 'with respect to the pontificate of Leo X, everything that refers to it will be of importance to me, whether it concerns his political transactions and negotiations, his encouragement of literature and art, his conduct, both in public and in private life; in short whatever has any connection with his history, or with that of any branch of his family', a spectacularly wide brief.[45] Luckily for Roscoe, Johnson managed to obtain numerous printed books in addition to valuable primary documents available only in Rome. He then paid a visit to Venice, where the librarian of St Marco, the Abbate Morelli, gave him a bibliography of books and documents that were relevant to a biography of Leo X. This contact opened up an important channel of communication between Morelli and Roscoe.

William Shepherd was another friend who made a valuable contribution to Roscoe's researches. Roscoe wanted to study the diary of Paris de Grassis, a native of Bologna who was master of ceremonies at the Pope's chapel during the tenure of Leo X. In 1802 Shepherd visited France and examined the diary; on returning home he gave Roscoe his findings, including information on the history of Leo X and the manner of his death.

The sheer volume of information threatened to overwhelm Roscoe, and the stress of trying to organize it into a lucid form had an impact on his health. Under doctor's orders he was forced to rest for a few months. His literary studies were also hampered by his return to the business world, when he became a partner in William Clarke's bank. Clarke had been an invaluable friend to Roscoe in his researches for the *Life of Lorenzo* and Roscoe felt that he had no alternative but to assist him in his hour of need. After five years, *The Life and Pontificate of Leo the Tenth* was published in the summer of 1805 in four volumes by Cadell and Davies, and Roscoe's reputation ensured that the first impression of a thousand copies sold out immediately. It was translated into German (1806), French (1808) and Italian (1816).

Roscoe sent a number of copies to friends and distinguished acquaintances (including Thomas Jefferson, then President of the USA), and was pleased with the reception his work received. However, he knew that the subject matter of the book and his analysis might not meet with universal acclaim. Anticipating criticism, he wrote to Lord St Vincent shortly before publication: ' a publication on this subject must comprise topics of considerable delicacy, as well in religion as in politics, as in morals and literature; and in other words, must involve questions which have given rise to dissension and persecution in all subsequent times. In the account of the Reformation I am aware that my book will give satisfaction neither to the Catholics nor to the Protestants; yet of the two, I apprehend most the displeasure of the latter.'[46]

Although his established reputation ensured the book's success, reviews were less favourable and Roscoe's prediction that he would please neither side of the religious divide proved correct. He was accused of inaccuracies and misrepresentation, and of using the work as a vehicle to express his own beliefs and opinions on a wide variety of topics. Above all, Roscoe's portrayal of Luther was controversial. Although Roscoe approved of Luther as 'an opponent of the Roman See', he argued that he freed his followers from papal domination only to 'establish another despotism, in many respects more intolerable'. As a Unitarian, Roscoe was opposed to strict dogma, but he should have considered that he was writing of an era in which its importance was unquestioned and viewed as something worth fighting for if necessary. While praising Roscoe's industry and extensive research, the *Edinburgh Review* criticized his use and organization of material: 'the nice discrimination and selection of incidents, form no part of Mr. Roscoe's ideas of historical excellence ... the author, who is unable to give coherence to the different parts, and to preserve the connection of successive events, has no pretensions to the title of an historian'. The reviewer accused Roscoe of favouring Leo at the expense of Luther, and also took him to task for attempting to whitewash the character of Lucrezia Borgia (the daughter of Pope Alexander VI) by questioning the veracity of her alleged incestuous relationship with her father and brothers. Roscoe implied that many of the accusations against her had been made by Protestant authors to denigrate the Pope. This discussion concluded the first volume, and it remains something of a mystery why Roscoe should attack the previously unchallenged view of Lucrezia, thereby laying himself open to the charge of favouring the Papacy.[47] The reviewer conceded that despite his harsh criticisms, Roscoe's writings 'impress us with one uniform conviction, that he is a truly amiable and benevolent man', although by implication this was scarcely an adequate substitute for rigorous historical scholarship or likely to gain Roscoe literary immortality.[48] The *Christian Observer* declared that Roscoe was 'uniformly hostile to Christianity' and charged him with having 'received a retaining fee from the Pope'. On the other side of the religious divide, the Pope's opinion was demonstrated when he placed the Italian translation on his list of banned literature.[49]

The hypersensitive Roscoe was urged by his friend William Smyth not to mind his critics and certainly never to answer them. But Roscoe, although he denied being perturbed by his critics – 'To malicious interpretations, ignorant cavills, and illiberal abuse, I entertain the most perfect indifference' – responded to his critics in a preface to the second edition. Despite his denials, it is perhaps telling that Roscoe now turned his attention away from any further historical writings on Italy, apart from his volume of primary data, *The Illustrations of the Life of Lorenzo de Medici*. According to his son Henry, subjects were suggested to him but he refused to undertake them. In a letter to Lord Buchan, who had proposed that Roscoe should consider writing the history and progress of literature and the fine arts in Italy, he declared that this 'is, indeed a noble subject, but to execute it would require a fortunate union of talents, acquirements, and circumstances which it has not fallen to my lot to enjoy'.[50] However, Roscoe had devoted fifteen years to his writings on the Medici, and they informed his thinking on the conjunction of commerce and culture throughout his entire adult life.

For Roscoe, the Medici were heroes and it was his duty to recount their history in a way that would both instruct and reform later generations. However, historians such as Hale and Bullen have tended to echo the objections made by Roscoe's contemporary Sismondi; in contrast to Roscoe, they considered Cosimo de' Medici and particularly Lorenzo to be tyrannical in their intentions towards the city.[51] Recent scholarship has also seen a reappraisal of the exact nature of Lorenzo's academies and patronage, and Roscoe's interpretation has been dismissed as myth rather than reality. There is little doubt that Roscoe's personal circumstances coloured his view of the fifteenth century. *The Life of Lorenzo* has been described as utopian history, with Roscoe projecting the ideals and aspirations he cherished onto fifteenth-century Florence. However, despite its flaws Roscoe's historical writing played a formative role in developing a new appreciation of the architectural and aesthetic importance of the Italian Renaissance across urban culture, and it was also important in changing external perceptions of Liverpool. For Washington Irving, the parallels between Roscoe and his hero were clear for all to see: 'like his own Lorenzo de Medici ... he has interwoven the history of his life with the history of his native town, and has made the foundations of its fame the monuments of his virtues.'[52]

# CHAPTER 4

# Liverpool's Cultural Icon

> The town of Liverpool, rich in the fruits of its commercial
> enterprise, has not neglected to furnish its citizens with that
> useful mental training which endures when worldly
> comforts fail, or when the luxuries of life fail to give enjoy-
> ment.[1]

In March 1853 a celebration was held in Liverpool to
commemorate the centenary of William Roscoe's birth. The
organizing committee was comprised of delegates from the
Liverpool Literary and Philosophical Society, the Liverpool
Polytechnic Society, the Historic Society of Lancashire and
Cheshire, the Architectural and Archaeological Society, the
Chemists' Association and the Royal Institution. The day
began with a public breakfast in the Philharmonic Hall,
presided over by the Lord Lieutenant of the county who,
together with 560 guests, listened to numerous eulogies on
William Roscoe's contribution to the cultural infrastructure
of his native town. Throughout the day, cultural institutions
opened their doors to the town's inhabitants; the day ended
with a 'brilliant soirée' at the Town Hall attended by over a
thousand of Liverpool's leading citizens.[2]

  The level of the town's cultural provision, as demonstrated
at this celebratory function, was in stark contrast to that of
1753. Although the earlier forays into cultural provision
attempted by the youthful Roscoe had resulted in a conspicuous lack of success, the publication of his *Life of Lorenzo*

and the subsequent national and international acclaim saw a remarkable change of attitude by Liverpool's merchant elite, illustrating their keenness to redefine their own and the town's cultural identity.

The first evidence that Roscoe's new-found cultural eminence had impressed his fellow townsmen came in 1797 with the founding of Liverpool's most enduring cultural institution, the Liverpool Athenaeum in Church Street (now in Church Alley). Although a circulating library had existed in the town since 1758, it was considered to be 'not sufficiently select in its choice of books' and to have too many subscribers.[3] When engaged on the research for his biography of Lorenzo, Roscoe had felt himself 'deprived of the many advantages peculiar to seats of learning', and was determined to rectify this omission. The Athenaeum was to consist of a newsroom and a library. Roscoe attended a meeting at the Theatre Tavern where a prospectus outlining the proposals was drawn up; this was later circulated to the leading 500 citizens of the town to gauge public support. Although, as with the earlier failed initiatives, the founders consisted largely of men associated with dissent and reform, the reception given to the plan was very different. The Athenaeum was welcomed by the common council, which saw it as an ornament to the town and granted it a reversionary interest in its premises. George Case, the first president, was a member of the council, and the mayor was elected as an honorary member. Initially, 350 shares were issued at 10 guineas each. In 1799, 75 more shares were offered, but now at 20 guineas; these were taken up in just 48 hours. The following year, another 75 shares were offered at 30 guineas, and this time it took just 24 hours to sell them. The subscription list was then closed, and the value of the shares jumped immediately to as much as 40 guineas. Within two years, membership of the Athenaeum had become an emblem of status for Liverpool's commercial aristocracy. Its importance is illustrated by the fact that when the business of Thomas Fletcher, one of the original members, collapsed and he was forced to relinquish his share, his fellow Unitarian Charles Booth regarded it as a particularly cruel blow, and he promptly presented Fletcher with a share as a gift.[4]

The Athenaeum also seems to have acted as a unifying factor in an otherwise divided merchant elite. Although its founding came at a time of strong political feeling in the town, the subscription list confirmed the claim of the Athenaeum's catalogue of 1864 that 'men of all shades of opinion, political and religious, concurred with equal zeal in promoting the success of an institution, designed to facilitate the acquisition of knowledge'.[5]

The newsroom opened on 1 January 1799, and the library on 1 July of the same year. James Touzeau, a historian of Liverpool at the beginning of the twentieth century, claimed: 'It was then and still remains a favourite and exclusive resort of Merchants and other gentlemen of position in Liverpool, and is therefore looked upon as one of the finest institutions of its kind in the town'.[6] William Roscoe was vice-president of the Athenaeum from 1799 to 1801, and president from 1803 to 1804. Thereafter he remained an active committee member, devoting much time and attention to the library. In 1802 the first catalogue was published, detailing over 6,000 volumes. The second, published in 1820, contained about 10,000 volumes; the third, issued in 1864, contained about 20,000 volumes.[7] In 1817, as a consequence of Roscoe's financial troubles, a number of his personal books were purchased by his friends and donated to the Athenaeum to form a Roscoe Collection.[8]

The founding of the Athenaeum and its Roscoe connection also helped to establish Liverpool as a cultural role model. The Boston Athenaeum, founded in 1807, based its laws on the Liverpool institution, with one of its founders claiming the intention to 'make ours as much like that as the different

circumstances of the countries will admit'.[9] The Bostonian
Joseph Buckminster reported to his Anthology Society in
1806:

> The City of Liverpool has now reached that point of
> wealth, at which societies, which have been hitherto
> merely mercenary and commercial, begin to turn their
> attention to learning and the fine arts, that is they perceive
> that something more than great riches is necessary to make
> a place worthy of being visited, and interesting enough to
> be admired.[10]

At the annual general meeting of the Athenaeum in 1831
shortly after Roscoe's death, tribute was paid to the vital role
he had played in its foundation. Great regret was expressed
that the Athenaeum could 'no longer be benefited by the
advice and assistance of a man whose literary, scientific and
benevolent exertions so justly entitled him to their esteem and
admiration.'[11] The Athenaeum is still thriving today, having
moved in 1928 to a new home in Church Alley, near Bluecoat
Chambers. In 1803 the Athenaeum was emulated by the
Lyceum, which was opened in Bold Street and housed the
Liverpool Library. The Athenaeum was, however, regarded
as more exclusive than the Lyceum.[12]

In 1802 came the successful launch of a botanic garden in
Liverpool, a long-held ambition of Roscoe's. He was again
following the Italian example; the first botanic garden for the
cultivation and scientific study of plants had been established
in Pisa in 1543, closely followed by Padua and Florence.
Gardens were also founded in Switzerland, France and
Germany in the sixteenth century. Britain established gardens
in Oxford (1621), Edinburgh (1667), Chelsea (1673) and Kew
(1759).[13] Roscoe first considered the viability of a botanic
garden for Liverpool in 1799. It was to be funded by subscription and the allotting of shares. In conjunction with his friends

Dr Rutter and Dr Bostock, Roscoe drew up a prospectus in which he made clear the importance he placed on the study of nature in man's artistic and cultural development:

> Even the cultivation of the fine arts, however alluring in its progress, and dignified in its object, must yield the superiority to the study of nature; for who will venture to compare the most finished productions of the painter and the sculptor with the originals whence they derived their ideas of beauty and proportion?[14]

However, Roscoe the businessman did not lose sight of the economics of the situation, and took care to appeal to the commercial instincts of the town's wealthy merchants as well as their cultural aspirations. The garden would be a place of beauty and a source of 'elegant amusement', but it could also, through botanical experiments, contribute to advances in medicine, agriculture and manufacturing. Even the subscription might be recouped by the distribution of rare seeds and surplus plants among the subscribers. This two-pronged appeal (beauty allied to utility) proved successful and the shares in the garden, priced at twelve guineas with an annual subscription of two guineas, were quickly appropriated. As with the founding of the Athenaeum, civic pride allied with self-interest overcame any antipathy towards the founders and the subscription list was representative of wealthy men of all shades of political and religious opinions.[15] A triangular plot of five acres of land, bounded by Myrtle Street, Melville Street and Olive Street, was granted by the corporation for the use of the institution, and the garden was opened in the summer of 1802. Roscoe, now president, gave the opening address in which he outlined plans for a library of works of natural history and a first-class herbarium (a reference collection of preserved plant specimens). Liverpool's Botanic Garden had already, claimed Roscoe, 'excited a spirit of emulation in some of the principal towns of the Kingdom, where proposals have been published for institutions on a similar plan'.[16] This did not only apply to Britain. The Botanic Garden at Philadelphia, for example, was based on the plan of the Liverpool institution.[17]

Promoting and extending the collection of plants became a prime concern of Roscoe's. Together with the curator John Shepherd, Roscoe enlisted the help of ship's captains and travelling merchants to bring back rare plants from overseas, and entered into correspondence with anyone whom he felt might further the garden's cause. One of the first of his correspondents was Sir James Edward Smith, then President of the Linnean Society of London and the foremost botanist of his time. Smith visited Liverpool on a number of occasions, delivering lectures to the proprietors. He claimed 'my lectures are numerously and brilliantly attended and seem to stir up a great ardour and taste for botany'.[18] Other correspondents included Sir Joseph Banks (1743–1820), President of the Royal Society; Dr Nathaniel Wallich (1786–1854), Superintendent of the Calcutta Botanic Garden; and Dr William Carey (1761–1834), who established a garden at Serampore that became famous. There are over 200 letters in the Liverpool Record Office between William Roscoe and his botanical associates.

The foundation of a herbarium at the botanic garden was of particular interest to Roscoe. In 1799 he had purchased for himself the herbarium of Dr Johann Reinhold Forster of Halle. Forster and his son had sailed with Captain Cook on his second voyage around the world (1772–1775), and the collection included many rare plants from the southern oceans. It also contained specimens from the collections of Peter Simon Pallas in Siberia, Carl Thunberg in South Africa and Japan, Pehr Forsskål in Egypt and Yemen, and Olov Swartz in the West Indies. Roscoe donated the herbarium to the botanic garden. It was also boosted by the gift of up to 5,000 specimens from Sir James Edward Smith. The first consignment of 2,000, containing many specimens of newly described species, arrived in 1806 and helped to raise the profile of the garden. The committee proceeded to elect Sir James Smith to honorary membership 'as a testimony of their respect and gratitude for your many valuable presents of plants and seeds'. Roscoe continued to search for additions to the herbarium, and in 1809 purchased a set of eight bound volumes of seaweeds (most from the south coast of England) mounted by Thomas Velley (1748–1806). When the herbarium was transferred to the City Museum in 1909, it contained more than 11,000 species.[19]

Roscoe was elected a Fellow of the Linnean Society of London in 1804,[20] and in 1806 travelled to London to present the first of three papers, 'A new Arrangement of Plants of the Monandrian Class usually called Scitamineae'. The publication of this paper served to establish Roscoe's name in botanical circles in London.[21] While staying in London Roscoe dined with Sir Joseph Banks, who later gave him several important books that initiated the botanic garden's library. Roscoe's second botanical paper, 'On Artificial and Natural Arrangements of Plants', was read before the Linnean Society in November 1810; his third and last paper, 'Remarks on Dr Roxburgh's Descriptions of the Monandrian Plants of India', was delivered in February 1814.[22] By 1808, the catalogue of the garden's living collections listed 4,823 different varieties and species of plants, many of which had only rarely been seen before in cultivation.[23]

In 1808, at Roscoe's instigation, the committee of the botanic garden agreed to fund an innovative expedition to the mid-western USA, led by John Bradbury, to collect rare American plants. Bradbury sailed to the USA in 1809 and spent three years embarking on perilous expeditions before returning with a unique collection of plants for the garden.[24] By 1820, the botanic garden was becoming renowned for the cultivation of many species of orchids, and Roscoe played a pioneering role in establishing natural species and introducing them into the conservatories of Britain. Liverpool became widely regarded as the main centre for orchids in the first half of the nineteenth century. Although the popularity of orchids waned from around 1890, an orchid collection remained a feature of the garden until the glasshouse collection of plants was destroyed by bombing in the Second World War. The work of rebuilding the collection was started at Harthill and Calderstones once peace was restored. Liverpool now has one of the largest collections in municipal hands.

Until the end of his life Roscoe remained interested in acquiring new specimens for the garden. An exhibition held in Liverpool's Central Library from August to October 2007 displayed previously unpublished documents from the Raffles Family Collection (acquired by the British Library in January 2007), which reveal a connection between Roscoe and Sir Thomas Stamford Raffles. Raffles had close family connections with Liverpool through his cousin, the Reverend Dr Thomas Raffles, Minister of Great George Street Chapel for fifty years. Although best known as the founder of Singapore, Raffles also threw himself into the study of the Malay language, literature, history, law and especially natural history. A letter dated 4 July 1826 from Raffles to his cousin reveals that he was planning to send a specimen of Rafflesia – the largest flower in the world, which had been discovered by him – to Roscoe. The sudden death of Raffles on 5 July 1826 complicated matters, but the specimen was forwarded on 11 July. Whether because of its 'somewhat decayed state' on receipt, the mode of transport or possibly bomb damage during the Second World War, the specimen can, unfortunately, no longer be traced in Liverpool today.[25]

The garden also fulfilled a social role; special functions were organized, attended by the proprietors (shareholders) and their families, who would wander round the grounds or through the conservatories to the strains of music provided by a band hired for the occasion. According to Maria Edgeworth, it was this social aspect 'as a public parade walk to shew themselves' that held the most appeal for the proprietors and their families.[26] The garden attracted distinguished visitors, including the Prince of Wales and the Duke of Clarence,[27] and was seen by a contemporary historian as affording 'an additional proof of the advances made by the inhabitants of Liverpool in the cultivation of taste and the liberal arts'.[28] Although access to the garden was initially restricted, in 1840 (when it had moved to a larger plot in Edge Lane) the corporation purchased the right of free access for the whole of the town's population on a Sunday and one weekday. The garden was important not only in providing a role model for other towns, but also as an encouragement to succeeding generations of Liverpool citizens to endow open spaces and parks in their native town.[29]

In 1812 the founding of the Liverpool Literary and Philosophical Society provided another outlet for Roscoe's cultural ambitions. Such societies (and the dates of their establishment) were of considerable cultural and civic importance in nineteenth-century cities. This society is generally seen as the first of the enduring middle-class societies in Liverpool. Although the Liverpool Literary and Philosophical Society (or Lit. and Phil.) was founded in 1812, local chroniclers (doubtless hoping to claim a Liverpool 'first') invariably point to its connecting links with the short-lived Liverpool Philosophical and Literary Society, which existed from 1779 to 1783. Nevertheless, the Manchester Literary and Philosophical Society (which developed from private informal meetings at the house of Dr Thomas Percival in 1781) is generally acknowledged as the prototype for many later societies of a similar type. This has led to the conclusion that their development was closely associated with the new interest in applied science arising from the Industrial Revolution.[30] Although Arnold Thackray questions this assumption, and suggests that the main impetus for the Manchester society stemmed from the demands of the new industrial middle classes for a cultural forum in which they could forge their own distinct identity, nonetheless it was science that they chose as their mode of self-expression. In 1822 John James Taylor, a member of the Manchester society, observed, 'Mechanics and chemistry are all the vogue in this district ... literature is quite beaten off the field by science – even though we have a Literary and Philosophical Society'.[31] John Dalton (1766–1844), the eminent chemist, read a total of 116 papers before the Manchester society, raising it 'in the esteem of scientists at home and abroad, from a provincial meeting of more or less reputable scholars interested in a curious variety of subjects, to one from whose proceedings they had much to learn'.[32] Science was also the dominant ethic in the Newcastle Literary and Philosophical Society (1793); its progenitor, the Unitarian minister William Turner, unequivocally saw its prime purpose as bringing science to bear on the primary economic needs of the district. He placed papers on coal and lead firmly at the head of his agenda.[33]

The pattern of the Liverpool Lit. and Phil. was markedly different, with Liverpool's gentlemen seeking to define themselves through a general intellectual and literary culture in which science and the arts were allotted equal attention. Although it never achieved the eminence of the Manchester and Newcastle societies, the Lit. and Phil. nonetheless fulfilled an important role in Liverpool's intellectual life, attracting an elite membership and orchestrating a number of public cultural activities that earned Liverpool recognition in a wider intellectual arena.

The society met on the first Friday of each month from October until May, with meetings being held at the Freemason's Hall in Bold Street until the opening of the Royal Institution in 1817. Membership was open to all who lived within five miles of Liverpool. The entrance fee was one guinea, and an annual subscription was half a guinea, which in comparison to other such societies was relatively cheap: Newcastle's annual subscription, for example, was one guinea. Ability to pay, however, was not the sole criterion for membership; all prospective members were balloted for, and three-quarters of the votes had to be in a man's favour before he could join. In 1814 this was increased to four-fifths, and the minutes record that at least one prospective member fell foul of this regulation in the early years of the society.[34] Women were excluded throughout most of the nineteenth century. It was not until October 1883 that the first women were elected to full membership, and even they customarily attended only the less academic lectures No woman was appointed to the society's council until about 1927.[35]

Surprisingly, Roscoe's name is absent from the initial membership roll although he was part of the original founding group, most of whom had been associated with him in the embryonic literary societies of the eighteenth century. A poem written by one of the founder members in 1812 indicates that the society thought of him as a mentor and the formative influence on its intellectual development:

> Long may attention's raptured ear
> Our Roscoe's tuneful numbers hear;
> The beauties of his native stream
> At once his pleasure and his theme.[36]

The most likely explanation for his omission was the bout of ill-health he suffered during the year of the society's inauguration, which kept him confined to his home.[37] Roscoe's entry into the society appears to have been further delayed by his involvement with the founding of the Royal Institution, and by his impending bankruptcy. His formal application was finally received in 1817 when the society moved to its new accommodation in the Royal Institution.[38] The society immediately offered Roscoe the presidency, a position which he accepted and retained until his death in 1831. He offered his resignation as president in 1825 (although he wished to remain a member) as he felt that his ill-health and old age prevented him from carrying out his duties efficiently, but the society persuaded him to remain on the understanding that he need attend only when his personal circumstances permitted.[39] Despite his health and business worries, Roscoe chaired a number of meetings and presented six papers before the society on themes particularly close to his heart, notably 'On the Effects and Impolicy of War' (1819) and 'The Principles of Morality applied to the Intercourse of States' (1829), in which he attacked the concept of political expediency, insisting that moral principles were equally applicable in both personal and public life.[40]

Although the early membership of the Lit. and Phil. included many reformers and dissenters (eighteen known Unitarians, three Quakers), it also included men of conservative political opinion and men of conformist religious beliefs; and it continued to elect to membership West Indian merchants, Anglican priests and a wide variety of other men from established sections of the middle class. This has led to the suggestion that an important aim of the society was to provide a forum for a broad section of Liverpool's wealthier classes to join together to discuss literary and scientific topics in a relatively informal, congenial and non-controversial atmosphere.[41] Law 23 of the society ruled that 'Papers, or subjects for conversation may be selected from any branch of philosophy, or general literature: but all discussions on the particular party politics of the day, and the peculiar creed of any sect of Christians, shall not be admitted by the Society'. Although this rule was applied in other societies throughout the country, this was a time when divisions between Liverpool's American and West Indian merchants had been exacerbated by the serious effect that the American embargo was having on Liverpool's trade. Liverpool's American merchants feared for their livelihoods and were critical of what they felt was a lack of support from the town's West India merchants, who were not affected. The Lit. and Phil. was thus important in helping to create a sense of common consciousness among Liverpool's merchant elite.[42] Members' reminiscences of the early meetings confirm that they were pleasant, friendly occasions. Many years later, the Reverend H. Higgins recollected that William Rathbone 'had often spoken to him of the delightful associations of those early times, when members of the Society frequently met in each other's houses, and, after spending the evening in literary and scientific discourse, concluded with oysters and porter'.[43]

However, the society did not attract the immediate support that had greeted the Athenaeum (and later the Royal Institution), probably because a rule of 1812 insisted that 'no gentleman can be balloted for membership, who has not previously submitted a paper'. The commitment of many of Liverpool's middle-class seekers of polite culture was apparently more rhetorical than real; membership of the Athenaeum, an appearance at a musical or theatrical concert, or even attendance at a lecture were all less demanding ways of making a cultural statement than active participation in a learned society. Significantly, this law was omitted from the revised code of 1814 and membership then began to increase, although, as in the majority of societies, the main work of the Lit. and Phil. seems to have fallen on a small group of activists. In 1817 the secretary felt impelled to 'make some remarks on the attendance ... and on the small number who have taken a part in its public business'.[44] By 1821, however, the names of 146 members had been entered on the roll and numbers then stabilized at between 120 and 145 members (including corresponding members). From the outset the Lit. and Phil. sought to dignify its status by electing as honorary members distinguished men from home and abroad, particularly the

USA. The first honorary member, a resident of Boston, was elected in April 1812. Other honorary members in the early years included Peter Mark Roget (1812), Benjamin Rush, a doctor and politician of Philadelphia (1813) and William Buckland, clergyman and geologist, and later Dean of Westminster (1814).

Links with the wider intellectual community were fostered by activities such as the collection of unusual artefacts, and in particular minerals, which was begun by the society at its inception.[45] Interest in geology was common to many of the provincial societies that were scattered about the country in areas of widely varying geological character. The comparison of their different geological situations by means of correspondence provided an excellent way of establishing contact with each other and with more traditional centres. In 1813, for example, the Reverend Warner of Bath presented the society with a collection of minerals from his locality.[46] When the Lit. and Phil. moved to the Royal Institution in 1817, the collection was deposited in the Institution's Museum of Natural History, with Lit. and Phil. members granted free access on the day of their meeting.

Eliciting the support of other societies on matters of national scientific concern performed a similar function. In 1824 William Rathbone mobilized the society to lobby Parliament and the King for a change in the law regarding the procurement of dead bodies for medical research, and circulated the petition round the other provincial societies. It asked for unclaimed bodies in workhouses, hospitals and prisons to be used for anatomical research 'under proper restrictions and with a decent burial to follow'. Dr Traill, a fellow member, stated that there was a precedent for the government being influenced by groups such as the literary and philosophical societies, and claimed that a paper on customs duties on minerals read by him before the Liverpool Lit. and Phil. had been instrumental in obtaining a reduction in that duty.[47]

Collective action of this kind by the society not only promoted common feeling with the outside intellectual world but also helped to create a sense of common identity within the Lit. and Phil. itself.

During the society's first ten years, a total of 117 papers were presented by 40 individuals, and 95 written communications were received. The occupational status of the presenters reflected the bias of the membership roll, with merchants and brokers forming the largest group, followed by medicine and the church. The number of papers on architecture, which was a feature of the society's programme in its first years, was indicative of both the concern of the members with the physical fabric of their rapidly-expanding town, and the presence in the society of the architect Thomas Rickman, who delivered thirteen papers during the society's first ten years. Rickman (like many others at that time) was at work on the actual facts and principles of the Gothic style. Considerable time and energy went into the problems of terminology and there was also a debate on the origins of the pointed arch. Rickman examined both of these questions and presented his findings. In 1817 Rickman published a book, *An Attempt to Discriminate the Styles of English Architecture, from the Conquest to the Reformation*, based on the information he had transmitted to the gentlemen of Liverpool; it became the cornerstone of the Gothic revival, providing a framework for the development of an authentic Gothic vocabulary with a system of classification by periods. Terminology such as 'early English', 'decorated' and 'perpendicular' quickly passed into common usage.[48] It has been claimed that it was through the work of Thomas Rickman that 'a play style of the eighteenth century became a demonstration of serious intent'.[49]

Among the audience at the Lit. and Phil. were members of building committees for new public buildings and churches, and although they did not repudiate the neo-classic form, it has been argued that Rickman's influence ensured that Liverpool witnessed 'the birth … of the Gothic revival'. It has been claimed that Liverpool also saw the last gasp of the Gothic revival in the form of the town's Anglican cathedral, 'a final blaze of Gothic, in scale unprecedented – a fitting consummation of a great period'. [50] Rickman taught by example as well as by words, forging a friendship with the Liverpool iron founder John Cragg and designing a number of Liverpool churches using cast iron inside and out. These included St George's, Everton (1814), St Michael-in-the-Hamlet (1814) and St Philip's, Hardman Street (1816). These three buildings led to the development of pre-fabricated cast-iron churches, which were shipped in large numbers from Liverpool and Bristol to be erected in the USA and Australia. [51] After Rickman moved to Birmingham at the beginning of the 1820s papers on architecture became markedly less frequent. However, the Lit. and Phil. continued to be a sounding board for the discussion of architectural projects for the town; it was, for example, before the society that Sir James Picton first formulated the scheme for a Liverpool cathedral. [52]

The major contributors to science papers in the early years were the Edinburgh-trained physicians Dr Traill and Dr John Bostock. However, motivated by the town's shipping and mercantile interests, papers were read on subjects such as 'The Destruction of Copper Sheathing in Iron-Fastened Ships' (1816), with discussions being held on the current state of research in that field. The society also acted as a sounding-board for various improvements designed to increase the efficiency and prosperity of the port. Papers such 'The Proposal for a Floating Pier' (1825), 'Suggested Improvements in Warehouses to Facilitate Loading and Unloading' (1827) and 'Plans for Docks and a Ship Canal at Wallasey Pool' (1828) were presented to an audience that not only had a vested interest in such matters, but that was in a position to exert its influence to effect relevant improvements.

Many of the papers offered under more general headings were used to stress the importance of literary and scientific pursuits in enhancing personal worth, and to reiterate the Roscoe motif of the compatibility of culture with commerce. William Dixon used his paper, entitled 'The Advantages of the Interchange of Ideas in Literary Societies', to emphasize this theme and 'refute an assertion ... that the pursuits of literature, the investigations of sciences, or the gratifying researches of natural philosophy, are repugnant to those habits of plodding industry, which are deemed most essential to commercial prosperity'. He also seized the opportunity to defend Liverpool merchants against the 'illiberal and unjust aspersion which has not infrequently been advanced, that, they are as conspicuous for ignorance as for wealth'.[53] That Dixon felt it necessary to do so underlines the extent of the merchants' resentment of this charge and their recognition of a need for a redefinition of their image.

After Roscoe's death the society continued to fulfil a useful role in promoting the town's image, hosting a very successful visit by the British Association for the Advancement of Science in 1837. It beat off intense competition from Manchester, which sought to become the first industrial city to be visited by the association. The society also continued to be regarded as a fitting venue for the presentation of detailed, statistical and revealing reports on local problems, and discussions of contemporary urban problems. Dr William Henry Duncan, the country's first medical officer of health, chose the platform of the Lit. and Phil. from which to present his influential three-part paper 'On the Physical Causes of the High Rate of Mortality in Liverpool' in 1843. This paper was subsequently published by the society, with an abridged version being printed in the *First Report of the Health of Towns Commission* in 1844, and was recognized locally as having helped to promote sanitary reform in Liverpool.

In common with literary and philosophical societies in

other towns, the second half of the nineteenth century saw the influence of the society decline. However, it survived until 1979 and was an important prototype for many of the societies that proliferated in Liverpool throughout the nineteenth century. When delivering his inaugural address before the Liverpool Philomathic Society (founded 1825), Robert McAdam, its first president, concluded his address with a tribute to William Roscoe (who had never been a member), underlining how important the Roscoe connection was seen to be in Liverpool by organizations seeking to establish their intellectual credentials. In 1847, a new institution aimed at nurturing the social and cultural aspirations of the growing numbers of young clerks and tradesmen in the town called itself the Roscoe Club. According to its committee, the widespread support it received owed much to its namesake: 'Whenever the name of Roscoe has been mentioned, an immediate and lively interest has been excited, a hallowing influence seems to be associated with the name of Roscoe'.[54]

In 1814, Roscoe was a founder member of the Liverpool Royal Institution, the culmination of a generation of cultural endeavour and a realization of his dream of establishing a prestigious cultural centre that would exemplify the Liverpool conjunction of commerce and culture. It was, claimed Professor Ramsay Muir:

> An attempt to institute in the midst of a great trading city a place which should be a perpetual focus for every intellectual interest, a perpetual radiator of sane and lofty views of life, a perpetual reminder of the higher needs and aspirations of men in the midst of the fierce roar of commercial competition and the clangorous appeal of those surroundings to the vulgar lust of money.[55]

Although, as the choice of name suggests, it was partly inspired by its London namesake, it was never planned as a purely scientific establishment. From the outset its stated aims were 'uncompromisingly cultural in character', a reflection of Roscoe's generalist approach to the arts. It played a significant part, particularly in its early years, in enhancing Liverpool's status by gaining recognition as one of the major provincial organizations devoted to the diffusion of learning.[56]

The original idea of the scheme has been attributed variously to: Dr Thomas Traill; William Corrie, a Liverpool broker; John Theodore Koster, an English gold merchant from Lisbon who had taken refuge in Liverpool; and Major-General Alexander Dirom, a former Indian Officer who was at this time commander of the Liverpool garrison. All accounts, however, acknowledge the seminal role played by Roscoe.[57] He was the chairman of the general committee (formed in 1814) and the first president in 1822, despite his acute personal financial problems. At a series of meetings in 1814, plans were made for the erection of a building that would house a museum and scientific apparatus, and the compilation of a lecture programme on varied subjects was begun. Close cooperation with local cultural societies was a particular aim, in order to coordinate and encourage cultural provision within the town. There were hopes of designing a school on a new model, incorporating commercial subjects into the curriculum.[58] A sum of £20,000 was required to adequately fund the enterprise; the founders set about raising the money by selling shares of £100 and £50. A proprietor holding a £100 share was entitled to a silver ticket that granted him and members of his family free admission to the institution; holders of £50 shares were entitled to a discount of 50 per cent. The term 'family', it was stipulated, was to include wives, children, brothers and sisters of the proprietors, but definitely not housekeepers; this was an indication that the institution had no intention of drawing its patrons from the town's lower classes.

As with the Athenaeum and the botanic garden, the venture unified the town's elite and gained wide support; £13,500 was raised in just four weeks. Encouraged by this success, Roscoe together with seven other members of the committee prepared an address to the public, citing the rapid growth of the town as a major factor in the foundation of the institution. The committee hoped that the institution's role would prove multi-functional, not only providing increased educational facilities but also helping to upgrade Liverpool's cultural profile and possibly even bringing commercial benefits to the town. The proposed school, for example, would not only relieve local parents of 'the expence [sic] and anxiety of sending their Children to a distance', but might also attract trade to Liverpool from outlying areas by encouraging 'Strangers to bring their families here for that purpose ... especially such as may intend any of their sons for trade, as they could then unite here, in some measure, Scientific with Commercial education.'

By 20 June 1814 the target had been surpassed, and was raised to £30,000. A new 21-man committee chaired by Roscoe was appointed to direct and oversee the future development of the project. This committee included West India and American merchants, Anglican clergymen, Unitarian ministers and members of the town council, emphasizing from the outset the scheme's success in uniting divergent groups among Liverpool's middle classes. A promise of financial help from the town council indicated that the civic authorities, too, recognized the benefits that such an institution might bring, not only to the subscribers but to the civic and cultural image of Liverpool, nationally and internationally.[59] Confident now of the viability of the project, the committee compiled a comprehensive plan that was a reflection of Roscoe's intellectual interests in literature, art, science and education. Roscoe was asked to become Professor of History, a position he accepted although he declined to lecture.

However, it was three years before any further progress reports were issued. One reason for the delay was the failure of the institution's bankers, Roscoe, Clarke and Roscoe, which not only resulted in the loss of about £5,000 of funds but also enforced the retirement of William Roscoe from public life for twelve months. His financial plight and the repercussions for the institution do not appear to have diminished the respect and high esteem that the committee members felt for their chairman, and it has been seen as 'a tribute to his [Roscoe's] hold upon his associates that during those twelve months the committee did little more than mark time'.[60] It was July 1817 before the committee was able to report that preparations for the new institution were near to completion. Much time had been spent on the search for premises, and as no land was available for a new building, a decision was made to purchase a house in Colquitt Street for £9,000 and to undertake major reconstruction work to the designs of the architect Edmund Aikin (the youngest son of Roscoe's old friend John Aikin). The redesigned mansion included: 'a handsome apartment' for the use of the subscribers, 'supplied with such periodical works, on literary and scientific subjects as the Committee ... may think proper'; a large lecture theatre capable of holding 500 people; committee rooms; a library; a museum; an observatory; a laboratory; and a meeting room for the Liverpool Literary and Philosophical Society. The entire second floor of the institution was to be reserved for the establishment of academic schools. The committee planned to 'carry [this] into effect with the least possible delay [to] so important a measure'.[61] Provision was also made for the Liverpool Academy of Artists. Cooperation between the new institution and the Liverpool Academy had always been an ambition of the founders (see Chapter 5). The committee planned to launch the institution's activities with a series of public lectures delivered by eminent men. The first lecture was to be delivered by William Roscoe.

On 4 August 1817 the insitution was granted permission to adopt the title the Liverpool Royal Institution, and the formal opening ceremony took place on 25 November 1817. His severe financial problems and the threat of bankruptcy made Roscoe initially reluctant to preside at such a public and auspicious occasion. However, persuaded that it was his duty and assured by his friends of their unswerving support, he delivered the opening discourse. In front of a very large audience, which included the eight-year old future Prime Minister William Gladstone, he was 'received with the most flattering applause, which was repeated at the conclusion of the lecture'.[62] In his address, he questioned the idea of 'art for art's sake', and attempted to justify his thesis that literature and art could not and should not be disassociated from commerce:

> If you will protect the arts, the arts will, and ought to remunerate you. To suppose that they are to be encouraged upon some abstract and disinterested plan, from which all idea of utility shall be excluded, is to suppose that a building can be erected without a foundation. There is not a greater error, than to think that the arts can subsist upon the generosity of the public... Utility and pleasure are thus bound together in an indissoluble chain, and what the author of nature has joined let no man put asunder.[63]

He traced an historical link between intellectual improvement and commerce, concluding that 'in every place where commerce has been cultivated upon great and enlightened principles, a considerable proficiency has always been made in liberal studies and pursuits'.[64] He reiterated his belief in the significance of cultural associations, using Liverpool's Athenaeum and Lyceum as contemporary examples of the efficacy of such organizations. The Royal Institution would now confirm Liverpool as a cultural as well as a commercial centre of excellence:

It is to the union of the pursuits of literature with the affairs of the world, that we are to look forwards towards the improvement of both; towards the stability and foundation of the one, and the grace and ornament of the other; and this union is most likely to be effected by establishments in the nature of the present Institution.[65]

If Roscoe's celebration of commerce was pleasing to his merchant audience, his contention that manufacturing was less suited to intellectual development would have also ensured him a warm reception:

The effect of manufactures is different and on the whole not so conducive ... to the formation of intellectual character ... it is much to be feared that the unavoidable tendency of these employments is to contract or deaden the exertions of the intellect, and to reduce the powers both of body and mind to a machine, in which the individual almost loses his identity and becomes only a part of a more complicated apparatus.[66]

This was reassurance indeed for Liverpool's gentlemen and a heart-warming contrast with the neighbouring Manchester men! However, this may well have been rhetoric on Roscoe's part, aimed at pleasing his audience. In the printed version of the address, Roscoe avoids giving offence to a wider readership by adding a footnote in which he claims that recent improvements in manufacturing rendered his comments no longer applicable.

A version of the address was published and received many reviews. Roscoe was recognized as 'a living witness that in no situation is elegant literature irreconcilable with attention to the more active duties of life'. The Liverpool merchants received equal praise as a reward for their investment:

Of all examples of prompt and enlightened liberality among English merchants, we do not hesitate to say, that we consider this as by far the most remarkable. If things go on as they have begun, we expect that ere long the effects of their exertions will be such as not only to create a mighty improvement in their own neighbourhood, but to excite in many other quarters a spirit of honourable emulation.[67]

From the USA came praise from Thomas Jefferson, who recognized the Royal Institution as a prototype for the university he was establishing.[68] Dr Aikin, writing to congratulate Roscoe on the *Discourse*, was equally certain of the importance of the new institution, seeing its potential to 'one day convert Liverpool into an Athens or a Florence'.[69] When the Royal Institution finally received its charter of incorporation in 1822, William Roscoe's position as Liverpool's cultural leader was reaffirmed with his appointment as the institution's first president. It is worth noting, however, that this appointment did not meet with universal approval. John Gladstone expressed the view that the time had now arrived for a change in Liverpool's cultural hierarchy, allowing new and younger men to take over the leadership of Liverpool's intellectual life. Despite his professed admiration for Roscoe's abilities, he believed that his nomination as president was 'tantamount to the chair being placed in perpetuity':

Do not suppose that I do not feel all the respect for Mr R. that you or any of your warmest friends can entertain, but I have a conviction we are injuring the interests of the Institution, by this, as it were monopolising those situations.[70]

However, although Gladstone proclaimed his own readiness to resign from the committee in favour of new blood, he allowed himself to be nominated vice-president. While his view may have been entirely altruistic, it is possible (despite his rhetoric) that his increasing personal animosity towards Roscoe influenced his opinion. In his early years Gladstone had responded, at least in part, to the ideas of Roscoe and Currie. However, he later became hostile to them. As the owner of large West Indian plantations, Gladstone found Roscoe's chairmanship of the Liverpool Anti-Slavery Society a particular grievance. By the latter years of the 1820s, Gladstone considered Roscoe to be 'a senile and detested meddler'.[71] However, the men shared similar aspirations for Liverpool's intellectual development, enabling them to work in tandem to ensure the wellbeing of the Royal Institution. In the event, Roscoe held the presidency for one year only, succeeded in 1823 by Benjamin A. Heywood, although he remained concerned to promote its aims until his death in 1831.

By 1820 the major part of the institution's programme had been achieved. Lecture courses were well received and the founders intended to appoint a permanent staff of lecturers. The 'establishment of academical schools' had been the first objective listed in the detailed plan of 1814, aiming to give the proprietors and their social peers the opportunity of educating their sons 'in the highest departments of science and literature, without the necessity of sending them to distant and expensive establishments'. The original plan indicated that the members favoured a school that would be innovative in its curriculum, moulding young Liverpool gentlemen who would exemplify Roscoe's tenet that the union of commerce and culture was both possible and desirable. This theme was reiterated in Heywood's addresses of the early 1820s: 'The successful union of commercial and mechanical knowledge with literature is of all others the most congenial object of our contemplation.'[72] Although Roscoe, in particular, remained convinced of the importance of a classical education, the pupils were also to be given the opportunity to study scientific and commercial subjects. This broad field of studies suggested that the model adopted by the committee of 1814 owed as much to the dissenting academies of the eighteenth century as to established public schools. However, when the school opened in 1819 it was organized in only two departments, classical and mathematical,[73] and within a short time these had been combined into a single school that throughout the 1820s became increasingly wedded to the classical tradition. Although these changes did not go unchallenged, the proprietors in general did not appear perturbed by this departure from the original plan, apparently not convinced of the value of science in an effective education. Within a year of its foundation, the classical school was reported as 'already enabled to support itself',[74] and among the first pupils were the sons of a number of leading Liverpool merchants, including Charles Horsfall, William Laird and Robert Gladstone. John Gladstone, however, remained convinced that social and political power was still best achieved via the traditional route of Eton and Oxford. By 1840 the curriculum was broadened again, and the idea of combining commercial and classical education led to the Liverpool Royal Institution School becoming a model for proprietary day-schools in other large provincial cities; by 1864 there were about one hundred of them.[75] The school closed its doors in 1892, mainly because of the refusal of the institution's committee to accede to the headmaster's demands to move to more salubrious surroundings. In 1883 the upper school of the Liverpool Collegiate had moved to new buildings near Sefton Park and gradually assumed the position previously held by the Liverpool Royal Institution School.

A Museum of Natural History was established and proved one of the most popular of the institution's activities. At its inception, the committee was fortunate in acquiring the services of William Swainson, the well-known naturalist and bird illustrator, who undertook the task of arranging the collections that had already been obtained. Swainson planned to utilize Liverpool's overseas connections to develop the museum's collections, drawing up a short manual on the best ways of collecting and preserving zoological specimens. Two hundred copies were distributed to local sea-captains and others who might be likely to bring specimens home. The first printed catalogue (1829) listed 2,467 specimens of rocks and minerals (over a quarter of which were deposited by the Literary and Philosophical Society), 99 mammals and 826 birds. A large number of the specimens were of foreign origin, an indication that Swainson's efforts to involve the seafaring and commercial community in the museum's welfare had proved successful.[76]

The institution also provided a home for the Literary and Philosophical Society, uniting 'under this roof in promoting and extending the knowledge of the Arts and Sciences'. The Royal Institution offered encouragement and accommodation (at a moderate rent) to other societies 'whose objects are in perfect harmony with the design of the institution', with the usual proviso that controversial theology and party politics were to form no part of the societies' agendas. In 1847 four societies were reported to be meeting in the Royal Institution; by 1868 this had risen to nine, with a total membership of 2,000; by 1880, this number had doubled.

Particular attention was paid to the exhibition room for the Academy of Art. The role of the institution in promoting art and architecture was seen as being particularly significant at a time when the town was in a period of rapid expansion. Many of the institution's proprietors were on building committees for new civic and business buildings, and it was considered vital for the future architectural heritage of Liverpool that they had the knowledge to make informed choices: 'it is highly important in this growing town, to adhere to what is correct in architecture and cultivate the taste to appreciate and adopt what is excellent'.[77]

By 1822 Heywood (then president) felt able to assure his audience that the institution was already proving influential, both in stimulating intellectual development among the citizens of Liverpool and in helping to redefine Liverpool's cultural identity. 'At this moment it has a higher literary character than most provincial towns, and there is undoubtedly more general desire of mental improvement.' Although the institution was still in its infancy, Heywood believed that the signs were positive for its permanent success. He ascribed the problems that had beset the short-lived eighteenth-century cultural organizations to the fact that Liverpool, at that time, had still been primarily preoccupied with establishing its commercial position. He reassured his listeners that the town had now reached 'a more mature era' of prosperity, and that the lessons of the past would serve to ensure that cultural provision in Liverpool would 'extend and flourish, delayed for a time, only to be achieved with the more perfect success'. Heywood also recognized the value of communal cultural projects in helping to forge a strong sense of civic identity in a town whose ranks were constantly swelled by fortune-seeking newcomers:

> This earnest seeking after something more and better, makes Liverpool what it is; and its readiness to respect and adopt valuable suggestions, gives to intelligent settlers their best welcome and imbues the perfect stranger with as lively an interest in the prosperity of his adopted town, as though it had been the scene of his earliest associations.[78]

The institution attracted visitors not only from Britain, but also from the USA, Belgium, Portugal, Denmark, Jamaica, Russia, Italy, Peru, France, Germany and Canada.[79] In 1824 Heywood took particular pleasure in asserting the institution's status (and by association the proprietors' and the town's) as a model for 'the numerous institutions ... which have been founded upon similar plans in various parts of the kingdom'.[80] The Plymouth Institution, for example, based its rules and regulations on those of the Liverpool Royal Institution. The Reverend Robert Lampen of Plymouth declared: 'The Liverpool Institution excites both astonishment and admiration.'[81] Furthermore, he contended, this 'had not been confined within the limits of this country', quoting in justification of his claim a committee in New York that was planning to establish a similar institution in its city:

> The example of Liverpool has been frequently held out to our citizens as worthy of imitation, and none can be adduced more apposite. The two cities have risen into importance almost pari passu, have been mutually conducive to each other's progress, and are most intimately connected in the bonds of a constant and ever active intercourse.[82]

However, despite the optimism of the early annual reports and addresses, it was apparent even in the 1820s that the original aims of the founders would be modified. Great efforts were made to provide systematic lecture courses on literature and science. The arts lecture programme covered a wide range of subjects, including English poetry, Italian, French and German literature, ancient and modern history, philosophy, political economy and music. Lectures on scientific subjects were also given fairly frequently during the institution's early years. Among notable visiting lecturers was Dr P.M. Roget (later famous for his thesaurus), who lectured on physiology in 1829.[83] However, it was only in medical subjects that the institution provided anything resembling systematic coverage, a development that contributed greatly to the establishment (within the institution) of the Liverpool Medical School in 1834, the forerunner of Liverpool University's Faculty of Medicine. This aspect of the institution's work was undoubtedly impressive, and in his detailed analysis of the lecture programme Professor Ormerod concludes that the Royal Institution had quickly 'developed within itself at least the nucleus of a modern University College ... which if circumstances had been more favourable, might well have come into existence much earlier than was actually the case'.[84] Unfortunately, the financial resources of the institution proved inadequate to carry out this function, and by 1840 the lecture courses had been abandoned, although occasional courses were organized independently.

In many ways, the Royal Institution did not fulfil the hopes that Roscoe had entertained. By the middle of the nineteenth century it was fighting a losing battle against the rising tide of public enterprise. Its waning fortunes can also be seen as a reflection of J.W. Hudson's analysis that 'institutions, like all great works, flourish or decay in proportion to their value and utility to the age in which they exist'.[85] Liverpool's merchant elite was now legitimate and secure, and consequently less concerned with asserting its group identity through joint cultural enterprise. During the institution's early years, the possession of a silver ticket – like membership of the Athenaeum – was regarded as an impressive badge of status. With the passing of the Museums Act (1845) the era of municipal provision was dawning. In 1850, shortly before the Public Libraries Act, there were negotiations between the Royal Institution and the town council regarding making the institution 'an admirable nucleus for a public institution worthy of the town of Liverpool'. The chairman of the new library committee, Sir James Picton, although not himself a proprietor of the Royal Institution, linked this new venture to William Roscoe, seeing it as a way of ensuring that 'the great object proposed by Mr Roscoe in the establishment of the institution – the encouragement of art and science in a commercial community' would be a continued by future generations.[86] These negotiations failed, mainly due to financial considerations, and the town lost a number of the institution's important collections, although it retained a large part of the art collection. However, Roscoe's dream of a cultural infrastructure for Liverpool lived on in the imposing classical buildings built in the second half of the century, including the William Brown Library and Museum (1860), the Walker Art Gallery (1877), the Picton Reference Library (1879) and the Hornby Art Library (1906). Surrounding the Walker Art Gallery's porch are three statues: Raphael on one side, Michelangelo on the other and Commerce on the top.

# CHAPTER 5

## *Art in the City*

If gentlemen were lovers of painting, and connoisseurs, this would help to reform themselves, as their example and influence would have the like effect on the common people.[1]

William Roscoe is inextricably linked with the rise of art in Liverpool, and for the first thirty years of the nineteenth century he played a major role in the establishment of art societies in the town and in guiding art patronage. Roscoe believed that art had a relevance to a community's hopes and ideals and that exposure to the fine arts would somehow help to civilize or reform society at large. He was far from alone in this belief; it was a proposition widely held and propagated throughout eighteenth-century England, as well as on the continent. As Trevor Fawcett points out, how this was actually to work was never really explained; presumably it was to be by example. Once the upper classes were correctly motivated and inspired by art exhibitions and so on, they would, through the reformation and raising of their own sentiments, inspire those around them; 'thus a spirit of enlightenment would spread in ever-widening circles.'[2] In commercial Liverpool the dissemination of such lofty ideals was to prove far from easy for Roscoe. Although some of Liverpool's wealthier residents shared Roscoe's views, it seems reasonable to suppose that for others, art patronage was regarded as a mark of social arrival, with their pictures being 'hung as

trophies rather than for decoration'. A friend once wrote cyni-
cally to the artist John Constable that the chief reason men
bought pictures was that others coveted them.[3]

Throughout his life Roscoe always maintained that coop-
erative enterprises devoted to the cause of art were valuable
and necessary to a town's cultural development, in the
provinces as well as in London, and to this end he had played
a leading role in the short-lived art societies and exhibitions
of late eighteenth-century Liverpool. An art society was
founded in the town in 1769 but the scheme lasted only a few
months. However, in 1773 the twenty-year-old Roscoe was
instrumental in the foundation of a Society for the
Encouragement of Designing, Drawing, Painting Etc. He
composed an inaugural ode, read before the society on 13
December 1773, in which he emphasized his belief in the civilizing and moral influence of art on society at large:

> Tis true – the BARD'S harmonious tongue
> May draw the landscape bright and strong:
> Describe the dreadful scenes of war,
> The crested helm, the rattling car;
> The generous thirst of praise inspire,
> And kindle virtue's sacred fire:
> Yet still may PAINTING'S glowing hand
> An equal share of praise command:
> In every province claim her mingled part,
> The wondering sense to charm, or moralize the heart.[4]

Roscoe stressed that the study of great works of art would
enrich the personalities and the lives of businessmen and he
characterized the artists themselves as 'potential agents of
morality and bulwarks of the honest state'.[5]

The society held an exhibition in 1774 (the first of its kind
outside London) at which Roscoe exhibited an Indian ink
drawing entitled *The Mother*. Its aim was to improve the

quality of the designs of local artists and craftsmen, and thus to improve the taste of the local patrons. Although there were only 85 exhibits, these included not only paintings but samples of applied art; Matthew Gregson, an upholsterer (and later a leading citizen and antiquary) contributed furniture designs. Gregson and Roscoe were united in their belief that design should not be divorced from utility; in exhibiting his designs Gregson was intent on fulfilling the aims of the founders.[6] However, in 1775 the society collapsed and its effects were sold off. Roscoe attributed this failure to 'the loss of a very ingenious and spirited member now resident in Germany' (probably the engraver P.P. Burdett), and hoped that some day it would be re-established.[7] However, these were years of economic adversity for Liverpool with trade severely affected by war with the USA and France. It seems likely that in times of straitened circumstances, even those merchants who were prepared to invest in the arts would probably have seen it as one of the first areas in which to prac-tise economy.

Although the society floundered, Roscoe was subsequently associated with every attempt in Liverpool to establish an academy and annual exhibitions. In 1783 the Society for Promoting Painting and Design in Liverpool was founded, and set out to make a deliberate appeal to the commercial men of the town, promising to provide 'a rational and liberal amusement for those few hours of leisure which an active and mercantile place affords its inhabitants'.[8] Henry Blundell of Ince, the collector of classical marbles and primitive Flemish and Italian masters, was president; William Roscoe was vice-president and treasurer. Roscoe and Blundell, although they differed in their political beliefs (the latter fearing that the abolition of slavery would ruin Liverpool), were united in their belief in the civilizing effect of art on society at large. In 1784 the society held an exhibition in Rodney Street, then being developed as a fashionable residential street. This was a shrewd blending of London and provincial talent which pleased patrons and public. Following the example of the 1774 exhibition, the catalogue reiterated the theme that 'It is the aim of the present times to unite beauty with utility; and even the mechanic who would wish to arrive at eminence ought not only to cultivate his taste, but to acquire the practical knowledge in the art of design, without which abilities may frequently be misapplied and industry fail of its reward'.[9] However, this exhibition was, in fact, traditional. Painting and in particular romantic painting dominated. There were 206 exhibits; two were by Sir Joshua Reynolds, the President of the Royal Academy, including a portrait of General Banastre Tarleton. Roscoe was especially grateful to Reynolds, who assured Roscoe of his support: 'I am very glad to hear of the success of your exhibition. I shall always wish to contribute to it to the best of my power.' The exhibition, wrote Roscoe's brother-in-law Daniel Daulby, had 'increased the taste of the town for the arts', and many pictures that had been exhibited 'without any particular interested view, (but merely to promote a general taste for the arts) have been purchased and remain in the town'.[10] Significantly, there were no examples of industrial design and no exhibits from Matthew Gregson.

The society now seemed on the road to permanency, inaugurating lecture courses to which Roscoe was a willing contributor. In 1785 he spoke 'On the History of Art', outlining the achievements of the great masters of the past and on occasion lauding a modern artist such as Fuseli. Other papers included 'On the Knowledge of the Use of Prints', and 'On the History and Progress of the Art of Engraving'. Roscoe presented his lectures in a style calculated to appeal to the amateur, and carefully emphasized the moral and historical lessons to be learned from a study of these works. A second exhibition was held in 1787; contributors included Fuseli, Thomas Gainsborough, Reynolds and Joseph Wright.[11] This time the catalogue paid no lip-service to applied art, stating that the exhibition was 'prompted by the desire of contributing to public amusement'.[12]

Despite its auspicious beginnings, in a few years the society was no more. Daniel Daulby's explanation was that in a mercantile town like Liverpool, it was extremely difficult to meet with gentlemen who had the leisure to conduct such a society. Henry Smithers attributed its demise to outside events; 'from the year 1792 all was convulsion, anarchy and tumult' and 'no fragments of time or of attention remained to cultivate steadily the civilising arts of peace'.[13] However, the ethos that was to dominate the nineteenth-century institutions had been established, and when the Liverpool Academy re-emerged it was firmly wedded to the classical tradition. The failure of Gregson's efforts to further the cause of applied art through the medium of art societies is illustrated by the comments of the silversmith and collector of antiquities Joseph Mayer (1803–1886), who in 1876 reprinted a catalogue of the 1774 exhibition in which he included biographical details of the contributors. When he came to Matthew Gregson, he disdainfully remarked: 'Matthew Gregson was an upholsterer, dwelling on the west side of Castle Street. He might have chosen works very much more creditable to his taste and spirit than Palmyrean bedsteads.'[14] However, that Roscoe empathized with Gregson's views is evidenced in a letter he wrote to Gregson in 1817, stating: 'If others had been as zealous in promoting the arts connected with design as you and I have been for the last 40 years and upwards, they would have stood upon a different footing than they do at present in this part of the kingdom'.[15]

Despite the failure of these early efforts to establish art societies, Roscoe's belief in the efficacy of such institutions remained unshaken and in 1810 he was instrumental in the founding of the Liverpool Academy. Although William Carey (a tireless advocate of British art), in his survey on the state of the fine arts in Liverpool, claimed that the re-emergence of the Liverpool Academy owed much to the successful institution of the Northern Society at Leeds, he nevertheless acknowledged the seminal role of Roscoe in its foundation. Carey ascribed the failure of Roscoe's earlier efforts to their prematurity, but asserted that since that era, Liverpool had 'undergone extraordinary changes' and that the present times were far more propitious to success.[16] He reiterated Roscoe's belief in the importance of such institutions not only in furthering the cause of art, but in helping to foster a sense of local civic pride: 'The institution of three or four Provincial Academies must prove a means of introducing British Art to a more general and intimate acquaintance with the public. A strong local interest would group round and feel a pride in supporting them.'[17] If London could have its academy and exhibitions, it was argued, so too could the provinces. Why should the arts be 'confined to a *glutted* metropolis?... They should be planted in *every* apt soil.'[18]

Probably spurred on, as Carey suggested, by inter-town rivalry, the Liverpool Academy was established at a meeting at the Crown and Anchor Tavern in April 1810, and immediately announced that it would hold an annual exhibition to encourage art and to raise the funds necessary for the establishment of an academy of painting, sculpture and architecture. It was also decided that 'the laws of the Royal Academy of London be considered the ground-work for the regulation of this institution'.[19] There were seventeen original members, four associates and two honorary members. Among these were Charles Towne, the animal painter; and Thomas Hargreaves and John Turmeau, both miniature painters. Henry Blundell was the first patron, the sculptor George Bullock was president, and Roscoe was the treasurer. Dr Traill was appointed lecturer on anatomy, W. Strachan was lecturer on chemistry, and later, in 1813, Thomas Rickman was lecturer on architecture.

The first exhibition was held in August 1810 at Thomas Winstanley's Gothic Rooms, Marble Street, and was surprisingly big and impressive, with 348 exhibits from 116 contributors. Eminent London artists were invited to submit works, including Benjamin West, William Etty and J.M.W. Turner; local artists also made important contributions. This exhibition appears to have been well supported, as the takings were sufficient to cover all the expenses and leave a surplus of £200. Some Liverpool exhibits found purchasers, but no London ones.[20]

The following year, the academy emulated the metropolis in holding a banquet before the opening of its second exhibition. This attracted many of the town's elite: 'the company was numerous and of the highest respectability'.[21] It was an occasion for celebration, as Roscoe had succeeded in securing the patronage of the Prince Regent. Notification had also been received of a bequest of £1,600 (from the estate of the recently deceased Henry Blundell) towards the cost of a permanent home for the academy. In his address to the artists and patrons, Roscoe stressed that increasing wealth, interest in the fine arts and the presence of well-trained artists in the community augured well for the academy. He 'now looked forward with confidence to a period when the Liverpool Academy might produce artists of the highest talent, and perhaps might eventually rival the great Institution in the capital', and he envisioned a future when the name of the Liverpool Academy would be known throughout the world.[22] He then turned to a favourite theme – that art for art's sake was neither viable nor desirable – and he discussed what he saw as the realities of the current mode of patronage. He stressed that while the artists of Liverpool could depend on the schools of the academy for their education, they must then be prepared to stand or fall by their own merit, not by soliciting patronage as a matter of favour. He insisted that no artists 'ought to expect as a bounty that which ought to be the reward of talent alone. No person ought to be expected to purchase a work of art for any other reason than because he approves of it. To act otherwise was in fact an injury to the artist who was thus led to content himself with mediocrity instead of aiming at excellence.'[23]

The academy continued to hold annual exhibitions until 1814, on much the same lines as the first, with 300 to 400 works each time and always with good support from London and from the more artistically-minded members of the town's elite.[24] Despite the fact that the finances of the academy were always precarious, the exhibitions would probably have continued but for a new development: the plan to establish the Liverpool Royal Institution, to which the academy was invited to contribute.[25] Roscoe and Liverpool's merchants were now concentrating their attention on the creation of this prestigious cultural centre to the detriment of the academy. When the Royal Institution was finally inaugurated in 1817, the academy was defunct; this was an indication of the importance of the input of the lay community. A committee was immediately appointed to ensure that this was merely a temporary glitch in the academy's history. The exact date of the reconstitution of the academy is unclear, but it was mentioned in the institution's report of 1820, which stated that an exhibition room had been constructed, helped by the grant of £1,600 from Henry Blundell. The academy had taken possession of the accommodation by 1822 and a sum of money for the instruction of pupils (presumably in the school of design) was awarded to the academy in December 1822. Exhibitions commenced in the same year, with seven exhibitions being held in the Royal Institution. Roscoe's views on the didactic uses of art exhibitions and societies were shared by many of his fellow proprietors of the institution. In 1824 Benjamin Heywood, a leading merchant and banker and then president of the Royal Institution, suggested that education was the main function of an exhibition: 'probably its greatest

use would be to instruct and improve the taste of the specta-
tors'.[26] At the academy dinner in 1824, the wealthy lay
supporters recognized the role of art in their quest to assert
Liverpool's status, and they offered toasts galore to 'the fine
arts and may the town of Liverpool, second only to the
metropolis in commercial enterprise and opulence, hold the
same rank in taste, judgement and liberality'.[27]

The times seemed propitious in 1827 when 'The fourth
exhibition of the works of living artists' was advertised to
open in 'the Rooms of the Academy of the Royal Institution'.
A total of 270 paintings were exhibited (including works by
Copley, Fielding, S. Austen, Barber, Williamson and
Mosses).[28] At a dinner on 24 August to mark the opening of
the exhibition, speaker after speaker emphasized the importance of art to the community and to the reputation of
Liverpool. Following Roscoe's example, the art dealer
Thomas Winstanley appealed to the commercial instincts of
his listeners by stressing the soundness of investment in
English art, citing the large sums paid for English works at the
sale of the late Lord de Tabley's collection. He also noted that
the mayor and common council were seriously considering
ways in which they could support art. Possibly, these municipal leaders realized the influence that successful exhibitions
could have on Liverpool's image and were now determined
that the town's artistic profile should be enhanced. At this
exhibition, leading citizens not only viewed but purchased.
On 27 August, the correspondent of the *Liverpool Mercury*
noted: 'We are glad to learn that the attendance at the exhibition is considerably more numerous than it has been on
former occasions, 150 daily – and the sales of pictures have
been effected to a very considerable amount'.[29]

Roscoe's views on the didactic purpose of art exhibitions
and societies and their importance in promoting the civic
image of Liverpool appear to have born fruit when, in 1828,
municipal support for art in Liverpool was forthcoming. The

common council granted three premiums of twenty guineas
each for the best specimens of painting, drawing and sculpture, with John Gladstone boasting that a town that had
succeeded so triumphantly on the economic front could excel
equally in fostering the cause of art and artists in Liverpool,
thus achieving a cultural identity to rival that of London.[30] In
December of the same year the corporation voted the sum of
one hundred guineas to the academy exhibitions. Its careful
stipulations as to how it was to be apportioned indicated the
desire of some of its members to play a controlling role in
directing art patronage in Liverpool. An increasing interest in
art at this time is also attested to by the fact that six or seven
Liverpool newspapers published critical opinion on the fine
arts more or less regularly.[31] It seemed that more men now
came regularly to the aid of the artists and 'in the succeeding
years not only were the exhibitions popular social events, but
Liverpool's expenditure on art could be compared favourably
with other cities'.[32] Exhibitions were held in 1829 and 1830
in the Royal Institution before the academy moved to new
exhibition rooms in Old Post Office Place for the 1831 exhibition. Although the reasons for this move have been ascribed
to the desire of the academy to free itself from the undue influence of the Royal Institution and dissatisfaction with its
quarters there, relations between the two bodies appear to
have remained friendly. At the close of 1830, a movement was
made to form a 'Society of Amateurs' to assist and encourage
art in the town and by 1831, 'a society of gentlemen of taste
and opulence' for the purpose of the 'encouragement of the
fine arts' was being mentioned. The mayor was the chairman,
and the society included 7 aldermen, 12 members of the
corporation and 54 other leading citizens, many of whom
were serious collectors.[33] A later academy catalogue acidly
commented that its inception 'was no doubt due to a desire
on the part of members of the corporation to have some say
in the expenditure of money provided by the municipality'.[34]

A sum of money was placed at the disposal of this committee by the corporation, and it dispensed some £100 to £150 yearly in prizes.[35] Although it seems inevitable that some of the influential members of the society would be likely to adopt a proprietary attitude and antagonize the artists who preferred to be in charge of their own affairs, relations, at least on the surface, appeared to be cordial. In a preface to its catalogue, the academy duly paid tribute to the contribution of the gentlemen.

Thus, on his deathbed in 1831 William Roscoe might have felt justified in allowing himself a sense of satisfaction. His life-long commitment to promoting the cause of art in Liverpool appeared to have been realized with the creation of a lasting infrastructure that attracted support not only from the artists but also from the town's commercial community. His belief in the compatibility of commerce and culture seemed vindicated, at least in the realm of art. Regrettably, his conclusions were premature. In 1832 the prizes were again awarded by the lay society, but in 1833 no exhibition was held because of renewed financial difficulties and in 1834 the lay society is not cited in the exhibition catalogue, although it stated that the mayor and committee had granted prizes to the amount of £135. In 1835 the mayor and corporation were thanked for their patronage, but from 1837 onwards, prizes came out of academy funds 'in consequence of the Corporation having declined to contribute their annual grant of £100 for prizes at the exhibition, this Academy deems it incumbent to award out of its funds the sum of £50'.[36] However, municipal support was not entirely withdrawn; the corporation granted the academy an annual sum to cover the cost of the rent on its exhibition rooms.[37] No further mention was made of the Society of Amateurs, which appears to have been disbanded. According to C.P. Darcy, this probably reflected (as in other towns such as Birmingham and Edinburgh) the clash between the belief of the patrons that an

informal lay-dominated academy met all the basic needs of
art, and the artists' dislike of any form of lay control. The
hopes cherished by Roscoe and other merchants that the
academy's school would bring honour and glory to the name
of Liverpool were destined to remain unfulfilled. Arguments
over the award of its prizes to Pre-Raphaelite exhibitors
resulted in a split into two separate organizations in 1857.
After a short period of artistic competition, exhibitions by
both societies petered out. However, the Liverpool
Corporation now came forward to sponsor exhibitions, the
first of which was held in 1871 in the newly opened Liverpool
Museum in William Brown Street. Finally, Andrew Walker,
a brewer and distiller, donated the money for a permanent
home for the annual exhibition, and the Walker Art Gallery
opened in 1877.

While Roscoe's efforts to promote organized art societies
did not meet with universal or lasting support from his fellow
businessmen, it is clear that they were impressed by his
knowledge and taste and he became the single most important influence guiding art patronage in the first thirty years of
nineteenth-century Liverpool. Roscoe developed a close
association with the Swiss-born British painter Henry Fuseli,
who once described Roscoe as 'the man nearest my heart'.[38]
As an example of patronage, the Fuseli–Roscoe association
was remarkable. The two men were very different in temperament but shared similar political views, and hated slavery.
They first became acquainted in 1779 when Fuseli visited
Liverpool, meeting again in the spring of 1782 when Roscoe
visited London on business and saw Fuseli's paintings, which
seem to have impressed him deeply. From this time the two
men appear to have met quite frequently, with Roscoe
publicly declaring his enthusiasm for Fuseli's work in 1785.
Roscoe gave Fuseli considerable financial help (about £700
between 1790 and 1800) and a welcoming place to stay in
Liverpool.[39] Without Roscoe's considerable generosity,

support and sound practical advice, Fuseli would not have been able to open his Milton Gallery. Fuseli valued Roscoe's opinion (more on practicalities than on his art) and in a letter to him in 1790 concerning plans for his Milton Gallery, he asked for Roscoe's views on the project: 'tell me your opinion with your usual openness'. The preparations for the gallery and its two public showings covered a span of ten years, during which time Fuseli used Roscoe as an emotional crutch. He once confessed, 'I have got rid of a violent oppression by writing all this querulous stuff to you'. Even when the scheme proved a failure, Roscoe remained calm and encouraging throughout, reassuring Fuseli 'if your works possess real merit the neglect of the present day will only enhance that merit in the eyes of posterity'.[40]

Roscoe promoted Fuseli to his friends, and gave him advice on the best way of framing the pictures and the most cost-effective way of showing them.[41] At least 40 of Fuseli's paintings were imported into Liverpool for sale to Roscoe's friends, and he owned 15 himself. Roscoe's dining room at Allerton Hall was reputed to be hung solely with Fuseli's paintings; Roscoe commissioned *The Death of Lorenzo* for the chimneypiece.[42] The family donated this piece to the Liverpool Athenaeum, but it was hung in an unfavourable position and the picture gradually perished. It was last heard of in 1875 when Sir James Picton mentioned it in his *Memorials of Liverpool*.[43] Roscoe seems to have had a genuine admiration for Fuseli, as much for his personal qualities as his artistic abilities, and his patronage of him was not founded on fashion. In a letter to Fuseli's biographer, Roscoe wrote: 'He was indeed a most extraordinary & accomplished person, & notwithstanding his eminence in his profession it may be doubted whether this was the most interesting, or the most valuable of his acquirements.'[44] Jane Roscoe appears to have been less impressed than her husband, claiming that 'to be on terms of Friendship with Fuseli there is a degree of Servility necessary... I can never think his merit as an artist adequate to the defects of his character in other points.'[45]

Because of Roscoe, Fuseli supported the Liverpool exhibitions, showing three works in 1787 and nine in 1812, all of which were for sale. Fuseli was able to help Roscoe with his *Life of Lorenzo*, advising him on the chapter concerned with painting. In a letter of 28 November 1791, Fuseli wrote that he had read all of the art historian Vasari, and had made a note of anything that might be useful to Roscoe relating to the period before Michelangelo. Fuseli later reviewed Roscoe's book favourably in the *Analytical Review* of 1796. Roscoe also consulted Fuseli (probably, at this time, one of the best informed men concerning the history of art living in England) on the chapter in *Leo the Tenth* devoted to the arts.

Despite Roscoe's financial generosity, in 1816 – when Roscoe found himself in difficulties and facing the dispersal of his most treasured assets – it does not appear to have been reciprocated. There are no letters from Fuseli expressing sympathy and support for his friend, either at this time or when he was declared bankrupt in 1820, although, as Hugh Macandrew charitably points out, these may not have survived.[46] The altruistic Roscoe appears not to have expected any return for his patronage or to have been upset by this lack of support. Roscoe and his son Henry both attended Fuseli's funeral in 1825, and most of Roscoe's friends assumed he would write the life of Fuseli. In the event a biography was written by John Knowles, bad health preventing Roscoe from carrying out his original intention.

Roscoe encouraged the sculptor John Gibson (1790–1866) to visit Allerton Hall to study original drawings and engravings from his collections. In his *Life of Lorenzo* Roscoe described Lorenzo's patronage of the young Michelangelo and stressed the importance of patronage in the furtherance of the arts. Gibson's first encouragement came from the miniature painter John Turmeau who kept a stationer's shop in Liverpool. He then became apprenticed to a firm of cabinet-makers, and quickly persuaded his employers to alter his indentures so that he could decorate furniture rather than make it. However, on being introduced to the marble works of Samuel Franceys he soon lost interest in wood-carving and, after some difficulty, again had his indentures transferred. It was while working with Franceys that he became acquainted with William Roscoe, who came in one day to order a chimney-piece for his library at Allerton Hall. Gibson was subsequently given the job of executing a bas-relief for the centre of the chimney-piece. Roscoe specified the subject, lending Gibson a print from which to copy his composition. Gibson completed the piece, although it is not known whether it was ever installed. At Roscoe's death it was bequeathed to the Liverpool Royal Institution and is now in the Hornby Library in Picton Library.[47] Roscoe was so impressed by Gibson's work that he decided to take the young sculptor under his wing: 'I was invited once a week to Allerton Hall, and there he opened all his portfolios of prints from all the great masters. He had also a considerable collection of original drawings, for which he had paid great sums. He advised me to copy some of those fine drawings, so that I might learn to sketch in the same masterly manner.' Roscoe urged Gibson to study anatomy and arranged for him to attend lectures being given to young surgeons by a certain Dr Vose, who (on Roscoe's recommendation) allowed Gibson into his dissecting room. All of Gibson's drawings were given to Roscoe for his advice, and Roscoe tempered the sculptor's growing enthusiasm for his prints after Michelangelo by reminding him that in the long run the purest models were the Greeks. It was Roscoe, too, who conceived the plan for Gibson to visit Rome for three years and who provided him with vital introductions; for example, Roscoe asked Fuseli to give Gibson an introduction to Canova in Rome.[48]

Fig. 1 Bust of William Roscoe lent to the William Brown Library in 1931 by the Royal Institution to mark the centenary of his death. Wreaths were laid by the Lord Mayor, all the leading institutions and societies and the descendants of Roscoe to remember and honour his contribution to the city.

Fig. 2 Lithograph of Roscoe's birthplace, the Old Bowling Green Inn at the corner of St Mary's Lane and Mount Pleasant.

Fig. 3 Allerton Hall c. 1800, around the time that Roscoe bought the house.

Fig. 4 Allerton Hall in 1824, showing the new east wing that Roscoe built after he acquired the house.

Fig. 5 Allerton Hall as it is now, having been refurbished and converted into a pub. Sadly very little of the original interior remains as a result of extensive fire damage.

Fig. 6 Jane Roscoe with her son William Stanley, from the painting by John Williamson in the Walker Art Gallery, c.1790

Fig. 7 The Athenaeum, founded in 1797 as a subscription library for the gentlemen of the town, showing its original premises in Church Street, 1810. Roscoe was active in the development of the Athenaeum from the outset, and a large part of his personal library is held there today.

Fig. 8 William Roscoe helped found the Royal Institution in 1814. The building was opened in 1817 with Roscoe, who later became its first President, delivering the inaugural address.

Fig. 9 The Botanic Gardens were opened in 1802, fulfilling a long-held ambition of Roscoe's for the improvement of the town. He was active in expanding its collections until the end of his life.

Fig. 10 The Roscoe memorial garden in Mount Pleasant, near the former site of the Renshaw Street chapel, where Roscoe's funeral was held in 1831.

Figs 11 and 12 City centre street names are one of the ways
Roscoe is commemorated in modern Liverpool.

Fig. 13 and 14 The Roscoe Head pub is not far from Roscoe's birthplace, while Roscoe Junior School has adopted the butterfly as its badge in honour of its namesake's best-known poem.

Gibson remained conscious throughout his life of all he owed to Roscoe. In a letter to Roscoe he declared 'whenever my imagination glides to Allerton, it is with a deep feeling of gratitude and respect; for it was there my inexperienced youth was led to the path of *simple art*; it was there it caught the flame of ambition; it was there the suggestion of Rome was given birth to'.[49] In 1827 Gibson presented a bust of William Roscoe to the Liverpool Royal Institution, accompanied by a letter where again he speaks of his gratitude to his patron. 'To that gentleman I am indebted for what little merit I may possess as a sculptor. He first inspired me with ideas worthy of my profession and kindled within me an ardent love of fame in the pursuit of it'. Without the help and patronage of Roscoe, John Gibson would have found it hard to escape from a life spent in making stone tablets and the manufacture of plain marble chimney-pieces for Liverpool's commercial elite.

Although these were the two most notable illustrations of Roscoe's patronage, there were many others: for example, the sculptor William Spence (1793–1849), who was born in Chester but trained in Liverpool and who was for many years Professor of Drawing at Liverpool Academy. Spence's bust of William Roscoe was exhibited at Liverpool Academy in 1813. Roscoe was not only involved in promoting private sculptures but was also on committees concerned with erecting expensive and comparatively large public statues commemorating national figures such as Lord Nelson (1813) and George III (1822), which allowed Liverpool not only to parade its loyalty and patriotism but also to assert its wealth and civic pre-eminence over rival towns.[50]

A glowing tribute to Roscoe's success in encouraging Liverpool's merchant elite to patronize the cause of art (whatever their underlying motives) came from Benjamin Haydon, the great anti-Royal Academician, who lectured at the Liverpool Mechanics' Institution on several occasions between 1830 and 1840. In September 1837, through the agency of Mr Lowndes and with some help from Thomas Winstanley, Haydon was commissioned to paint *Christ Blessing the Little Children* (since lost) for the Asylum for the Blind in Hardman Street, while most of 1839 was spent painting the Wellington portraits now in St George's Hall. He commented in one of his lectures: 'Liverpool is the only distinguished town since the Reformation which has the moral courage to employ native historical painters on the true, thorough-bred principles of patronage, which produced such glorious results in Italy and Greece!' According to Haydon, this was mainly due to Roscoe's views on art and art patronage: 'Such was the opinion of one whose name is synonymous in every city in Europe with elegant accomplishments... His literature and his love of art have cast a halo round the name of Liverpool, which is felt in conjunction with its commercial power in every part of the world; its taste for elegant embellishment and accomplished literature, can never die, while each successive generation pronounces with respect and gratitude the name of Roscoe, the father of its accomplishments and its tastes.'[51]

Roscoe's own collection of art was to prove his greatest legacy to future generations of Liverpool citizens. He was an avid collector of works of art and prints, and like Lorenzo (according to Roscoe's interpretation) he had a specifically didactic purpose. His collection, he claimed, was 'chiefly for the purpose of illustrating, by a reference to original and authentic sources, the rise and progress of the arts in modern times';[52] it was an 'instructive and informative' collection rather than one to 'delight and move'.[53] To this end, his paintings and prints were arranged in historical order at his home at Allerton Hall. Maria Edgeworth, who visited Allerton Hall in 1813, gives us a vivid description of the collection, despite finding Fuseli's work not to her liking:

Allerton Hall is a spacious house, in a beautiful situation
– Fine Library – every room filled with pictures, and a
gallery of pictures... Many of them are presents from
persons in Italy who admired his Leo the 10th ... There is
a picture of Tasso ... it has a sort of mad vigilance in the
eyes – looks as if he saw his genius that haunted him that
instant at the window... I may just mention that Mr
Roscoe has I think arranged his collection admirably so as
to shew in chronological order and edifying gradation the
progress of painting. The picture which he prized the most
was painted by one of Raphael's masters (Francesco
Francia I think),[54] not in the least valuable for its own sake,
but for a frieze below the original picture by Michael
Angelo. The picture a holy family is in distemper highly
varnished. The frieze about a foot deep represents the
destruction of the oracles and Moses breaking the tables.
It is a gray colour something like the colouring of the
figures at the Temple. Mr Roscoe thinks it one of Michael
Angelo's earliest performances, and he says it is conceded
that this is the only Michael Angelo certainly original in
England. Of this I know nothing, but I know that it struck
me as full of genius, and I longed for you and Margaret
when we looked at a portfolio full of Michael Angelo's
sketches, drawings, and studies. It is admirable to see the
pains that a really great man takes to improve a first idea.
Mr Roscoe is free from all the cant of a connoisseur and
speaks of painting as a philosopher. Turning from the
drawings of Michael Angelo to a room full of Fuseli's
horribly distorted figures I could not help feeling astonishment not only at the bad taste, but at the infinite conceit
and presumption of Fuseli! How could this man ever make
himself a name! I believe he gave Mr. Roscoe these
pictures, else I suppose they would not be here sprawling
their fantastic lengths, like misshapen dreams. Instead of
*le beau ideal* they exhibit *le laide ideal*.[55]

Roscoe's first foray into the world of art collecting was his attempt to build up a historical collection of prints. His poem, *The Origin of Engraving*, showed the considerable knowledge he had on the subject. He wrote an introductory essay to Joseph Strutt's *Biographical Dictionary of Engravers, 1785–6*, and contributed two essays ('Remarks on Etching' and 'Idea of a Chronological Collection of Engravings') to a proposed but never-published third volume.[56] In the 1780s he appears to have purchased prints on his regular visits to London, probably under the guidance of his brother-in-law Daniel Daulby, who was a connoisseur of fine prints and for whose catalogue of Rembrandt etchings Roscoe later wrote a preface. Works of art were also sent up from London on approval. For example, in 1795, the London dealer Thomas Philipe notified Roscoe of a shipment and enclosed a list of prices for the prints and drawings. 'The case containing the items has been dispatched by post coach to Birchfield... The above articles are sent to you for your amusement, and if they in any degree answer the purpose, you may have frequent parcels in the same way'. A letter of 1796 notes that Philipe had received the returned items and was sending his account for articles retained. 'I shall be happy to have the Honour of serving you here and if in the meantime you wish for any amusement in any way I am always ready to serve you, and with more pleasure, as there is a congeniality in our Taste.' A letter of the same year reveals that Philipe, on occasion, acted as agent for Roscoe in London, purchasing prints at auctions on commission.[57] The extent of Roscoe's collection can be estimated from the sum of £1,915 1s 0d realized by the 1,352 lots at the eventual sale of his most of his prints. These included Italian, Flemish and German copper engravings, Italian, Flemish, Dutch and French etchings, Italian and German woodcuts, illustrations of classical sculpture and books of prints.[58]

Most of Roscoe's collection of paintings was brought

together in the first fifteen years of the nineteenth century. The two most prominent dealers in Liverpool were Thomas Vernon and Thomas Winstanley, who both handled Old Masters and contemporary works, though the latter was more active in handling the earlier schools of art. Indeed, Winstanley was the principal agent of Roscoe for the procurement of his historical collection. Many of Winstanley's bills survive, and it is clear from them that he took a major part in helping Roscoe to build up his collection. Roscoe bought 50 or 60 pictures from him. It is impossible to tell whether Winstanley had any influence on the taste of his patron, but the date of his establishment in Liverpool coincides loosely with the date at which Roscoe seems to have begun collecting most actively.[59]

Roscoe's collection of early Renaissance art is now regarded as one of the most significant private galleries of Italian and Netherlandish 'Primitives' formed in the early years of the nineteenth century. The catalogue of Roscoe's collection, compiled by him in 1816, contains 43 pictures that he judged to be by Primitive painters, 32 of them attributed to Italians. He is also thought to have had at least three more which are not in the catalogue.[60] It is not known exactly when Roscoe began to form his collection of Primitives; the earliest established date is 12 May 1804. All his purchases took place between 1804 and February 1813, by which time he had written his manuscript catalogue.

Whether Roscoe's art collection owed more to luck than good judgement is a matter of conjecture. Many of the pictures in his catalogue are wrongly attributed, and he seems to have had a problem distinguishing between Italian and their later Flemish imitators. However, to be fair to Roscoe he did not pretend to be an authority on art, either as a connoisseur or as an historian; he always turned down suggestions that he should write histories of art, although he did sometimes buy pictures for friends. His biographies of Lorenzo and Leo X each have only one chapter on the history of art, and these lack in-depth analysis; much of the content is lifted from Vasari and other obvious sources. Roscoe conceived his own collection of paintings as a pedagogical tool, writing in 1816 of his desire to have formed a more extensive one and to have 'rendered (it) subservient to some object of public utility'.[61] He explained that his prime reason for his purchase of fourteenth-century and fifteenth-century works of art was:

> Chiefly for the purpose of illustrating, by a reference to original and authentic sources, the rise and progress of the arts in modern times, as well in Germany and Flanders as in Italy. They are therefore not wholly to be judged by their positive merits, but by a reference to the age in which they were produced. Their value chiefly depends on their authenticity, and the light they throw on the history of the arts.[62]

This was in accordance with Roscoe's belief that experiencing art could have both an ennobling and an educative effect on all viewers, the working class as well as the elite. Yet although the amateur Roscoe may not have fully grasped the significance of the paintings he collected, and they were, in the words of Edward Morris his 'slide library', his determination led him to acquire interesting and important paintings.[63]

In 1816 financial pressures forced Roscoe to dispose of his collection; the sale made £2,823 and 19 shillings. Five of the most desirable paintings were acquired by Coke of Holkham (he spent at least £1,868). They included Raphael's *Leo X with his Cousin and Nephew*, Ghirlandaio's *Madonna and Child*, and the Leonardo *Head of Christ*. Some of Fuseli's paintings were bought anonymously and returned to Roscoe.[64] Although Roscoe stated both publicly and privately that he had no intention of buying in at the sale, it appears likely that he may well have bought in part of his historical collection through local dealers.[65] Certainly, by June 1818 any unsold pictures together with some of those bought by local dealers were back in Roscoe's possession. This collection was valued by Thomas Winstanley at 1,553 guineas and Roscoe then generously offered it to the Royal Institution for 1,200 guineas, stating, 'I shall think myself sufficiently gratified if the liberality of my townsmen shall so far second my wishes as to prevent a collection form'd with a view to public utility from being dispersed.' A group of leading merchants[66] then joined together to raise the necessary funds, and 35 of Roscoe's early Italian paintings were presented to the Royal Institution. Emulating Roscoe's didactic intent, they were displayed with the purpose of improving taste and design in Liverpool. This appears to have been the first time in England that Old Master paintings had been deliberately acquired for public display with the aim of fostering the public appreciation and practice of art.[67]

A few individuals conceiving, that as the following PICTURES form a series from the commencement of Art to the close of the fifteenth century, their value would be enhanced by being preserved together, have united in purchasing and presenting them to the Liverpool Royal Institution in the hope that by preventing the dispersion of a collection interesting to the history, and exemplifying the progress of Design, they may contribute to the advancement of the FINE ARTS in the Town of Liverpool.[68]

A tribute indeed to Roscoe by his friends, and also evidence that he had succeeded in disseminating his ideas on the civilizing effects of art on society to fellow members of Liverpool's merchant elite.

Although as a collector Roscoe has been criticized for lacking connoisseurship, for his didactic and moralistic stance towards art and for his failure to fully appreciate the significance of some of his pictures, he nevertheless managed to amass a collection that arguably would prove his greatest legacy to his native town. Roscoe had lived through the opening of many of the great national public collections of Europe and it was his hope that one day his collection would be available for public viewing. All the pictures that were in the original purchase by the Royal Institution (with others) were deposited on loan at the Walker Art Gallery in 1893, and were finally presented to the gallery in 1948. They are currently enjoyed freely by all sections of Liverpool society, a circumstance that would have brought Roscoe much satisfaction.

# CHAPTER 6

# Roscoe the Radical

His great desire was to witness the removal of those restraints upon the freedom of thought and action which subject one set of men to the caprice, the ignorance, and the malice of another.[1]

Roscoe's reputation as an active and influential participant in the abolition of slavery and as a radical politician has been variously subjected to both hyperbole and censure. In the anti-slavery campaign, Roscoe's promotion of gradualism was to earn him criticism not only from contemporaries but also from later historians of the slave trade. Posterity, it has been observed, has been somewhat unkind to the small band of Liverpool abolitionists, with the major histories of abolition according them an insignificant place in the history of the movement.[2] Although the leading anti-slavery campaigner Thomas Clarkson praised them for the help they gave to the London committee during the opening period of the campaign, the desire of the Liverpool abolitionists to maintain a low profile contributed to this lack of national recognition.

Considerable effort has been employed by some historians of Liverpool to redress this balance and to play down Liverpool's domination of the slave trade. George Chandler described Roscoe as the 'leader of the movement for the abolition of the slave trade', an overstatement that has justly received criticism. Northcote Parkinson excused Liverpool's slave-trading merchants on the grounds that they were 'no worse than their neighbours' and joked: 'As for the poor African, we may fairly conclude that, with the comings of the modern dance band, he has been only too horribly avenged.'[3] A more recent account, however, castigates Liverpool's abolitionists, arguing that even when they did speak up against the slave trade, they were careful do so in the language of political moderation, and that Roscoe in particular warned of the dangers of immediate abolition given the huge sums of money invested in it by Liverpool's merchants.[4] Probably the fairest assessment comes from F.E. Sanderson, who points out that the historical significance of these men's activities lay in demonstrating that Liverpool in this period was not entirely motivated by self-interest.[5]

The publication of Roscoe's poem *The Wrongs of Africa* heralded the start of his well-documented career as an opponent of the slave trade and a politician. Although this was not the earliest of Roscoe's poems on this theme (*Mount Pleasant* had been written when Roscoe was only nineteen although it was not published until 1777), it was a more direct piece of propaganda and the first to receive widespread notice. The first part of the poem was published anonymously in 1787 and depicts the Africans living a simple, idyllic existence, free of materialism, before the arrival of the Europeans. The second part was published the following year and emotively describes the horrors of the middle passage (the ocean crossing between Africa and the Americas). The poem made clear Roscoe's opposition to the slave trade, with humanitarian motives informing his thinking. However, interestingly, even at this early stage he also introduced economic arguments, suggesting that a trade in Africa's natural resources would be more profitable than the trade in slaves:

Cou'd not Afric's wealth,
Her ivory, and her granulated gold,

To her superfluous, well repay the stores,
(Superfluous too) from distant Europe sent;
But liberty and life must be the price,
And man become the merchandize and spoil.[6]

In the same year as the publication of the first part of the
poem, the London Society for the Abolition of the Slave Trade
was founded by Thomas Clarkson, Granville Sharp and a
group of Quakers, including two (Dr Binns and William
Rathbone) from Liverpool. In 1788 eight Liverpudlians are
listed on the roll of subscribers, including William Roscoe,
and one listed as anonymous, almost certainly James Currie.[7]
Through the medium of his friend John Barton, a Quaker
member, Roscoe offered to donate the entire profits from his
poem to the London committee, although it is not clear how
well the poem sold. According to Clarkson, the committee
was particularly impressed that the work had emanated from
Liverpool: 'To find friends to our cause rising up from such a
quarter, where we expected scarcely any thing but opposition,
was particularly encouraging'.[8] In the winter of 1787 one
thousand copies of another pamphlet by Roscoe, A *General
View of the African Slave Trade, Demonstrating its Injustice
and Impolicy; With Hints towards a Bill for its Abolition*,
were distributed. It contained little that was new except for a
statement of Roscoe's gradualist philosophy, but the reaction
in Liverpool is evidenced by John Barton's letter to Roscoe: 'I
rejoice to find that thy pamphlet has occasioned a ferment
amongst the African merchants at Liverpool'.[9]

In a town that considered its prosperity to be dependent
on the slave trade, it is not surprising that Roscoe was considered by many of his fellow-townsmen 'as a busy-body, as a
meddler, as a mischief-monger, whose wish and object were
to injure and destroy the town and trade of Liverpool'.[10] The
town's workmen were bombarded with pamphlets and squibs
warning them that if the abolitionists succeeded, the commer-

cial ruin of the town and the subsequent loss of their livelihoods were inevitable.

> If our slave trade had gone, there's an end to our lives,
> Beggars all we must be, our children and wives:
> No ships in our ports their proud sails e'er would spread,
> And our streets grown with grass, where the cows might
> be fed.[11]

In 1787 at the start of the abolitionist campaign in Parliament,
37 out of the 41 Liverpool councillors were slave-ship owners
or major investors and suppliers to the trade. All of the 20
mayors of the borough between 1787 and 1807 had some
connection with the slave trade.[12] The corporation was thus
solidly anti-abolitionist, and during the course of the
campaign Liverpool sent at least 64 petitions to Parliament
opposing abolition, compared to 14 from the London
merchants and 12 from the Bristol corporation and
merchants. Given that Anglican livings were in the gift of the
corporation, it is hardly surprising that only one Anglican
minister, the Reverend Henry Dannett of St Johns, was associated with the abolitionist movement. Even among the
Unitarians, a sermon against slavery by the Reverend John
Yates in 1788 was reputed to have given great offence to many
influential members of his congregation.[13] Respectable and
prosperous dissenting merchants such as the Heywoods, the
Boltons, the Booths and the Fletchers preferred to concentrate
on the reform of the Test and Corporation Acts and gaining
access to the patronage of the municipality. Roscoe, Rathbone
and (in particular) Currie, Shepherd and Rushton made rather
uncomfortable political allies.[14]

In the abolitionist campaign of 1788–1792, Roscoe
appears to have acted as a propagandist for the London
committee. In this, he was supported by many within the small
literary circle to which he belonged. James Currie wrote that

'in a very little while, almost all these had declared themselves in favour of the Abolition'.[15] Roscoe and Currie tended to maintain a low profile publicly although they were active privately. Following the founding of the abolitionist committee and the visit by Thomas Clarkson to Liverpool in the autumn of 1787, Roscoe and Currie supplied information and propaganda to the campaign organizers in London and were also in touch with the Manchester committee, which was formed in 1787, although Roscoe strongly advised against the formation of a similar committee in Liverpool, given the climate of opinion. In opposing the vested interests of the town, they risked not only social ostracism but also financial loss or even violent retaliation. William Rathbone recounted how, when he summoned a Liverpool doctor, the cautious practitioner asked if he could pay his visits after dark for fear that his carriage would be seen and recognized outside the Rathbone home, which would almost certainly result in his practice suffering.[16] Both Roscoe and Currie, in their communications with Wilberforce, insisted on strict anonymity. On his receipt of *The Wrongs of Africa* in 1787, John Barton wrote 'Depend upon it, I will strictly observe injunctions that have accompanied it, and have also cautioned R.F. against any hints concerning the quarter from whence it comes.'[17]

Clarkson received first-hand knowledge of the depth of hostility towards his campaign on a visit to Liverpool during which, together with Alexander Falconbridge, he endeavoured to collect information on conditions of the trade. John Barton privately asked Roscoe and Rathbone to keep an eye on the pair, adding of Clarkson, 'His zeal and activity are wonderful, but I am really afraid he will at times be deficient in caution and prudence.'[18] This proved to be true, as the less than discreet Clarkson proceeded to give great offence to some of the respected merchants of the town and was soon subjected to threats and abuse, culminating in an attempt on his life on the Pier Head. Clarkson undoubtedly gained material for his work, but the position of the Liverpool-based anti-slavers must have been made more difficult and feelings ran high in the town. Although the views of Roscoe and Rathbone on the visit have not survived, it seems likely that they were in accordance with those of Currie, who complained to William Wilberforce that it was a near-disaster. By April 1792 workmen in Liverpool were openly boasting that some houses in the town (which they had marked) would be pulled down if the abolition campaign was successful.

Although unswerving in their condemnation of the trade, Roscoe and Currie recognized the need to adopt a more conciliatory approach towards the views of Liverpool's African merchants, some of whom they counted as friends. In December 1787 Currie wrote to Wilberforce: 'It is a truth, that those in my acquaintance, who are and have been masters of Guineamen, a great majority are men of general fair character – that some of them are men of considerable improvement of mind – and that I could point out amongst them more than one instance of uncommon integrity and kindness of heart. The same may be said of the body of merchants concerned in the slave trade.'[19] Matthew Gregson, an ardent anti-abolitionist who had collaborated with Roscoe in the foundation of the Society for Promoting the Arts in Liverpool in 1783, was still referring to Roscoe as 'my friend' in 1791.[20] Roscoe preached that gradual restriction of the trade was the fairest course of action, and in January 1788 he sent a communication to the London Committee entitled 'An account of the opinions that prevail in Liverpool respecting the African reform'. Roscoe advised the committee that an all-out attack on the slave trade was unwise and might be counterproductive. He tried to impress on them the severe economic dislocation that Liverpool would suffer with total and immediate abolition. Liverpool's merchants had large amounts of capital tied up in the trade, which had until recently been seen as a legitimate commercial venture.

However, the London committee appeared to feel that any concessions were unacceptable and opposed Sir William Dolben's bill of 1789, which was aimed at relieving some of the worst of the abuses of the trade. Nothing but total abolition was acceptable.

Despite Roscoe advising against the formation of a Liverpool abolitionist society, he continued with his writings. In the summer of 1788, his 'Scriptural Refutation of a Pamphlet lately published by the Rev. Raymond Harris entitled "Scriptural Researches on the Licitness of the Slave Trade"' was an answer to a tract written by a Jesuit priest who endeavoured to justify the slave trade on moral grounds, claiming to show that slavery was countenanced by the Bible and was a divinely approved institution. Harris had skilfully extracted verses from the Old Testament suitable to his purpose, commenting on them at length. He claimed that 'every transaction of Abraham's life' demonstrated 'positive approbation' and 'sanction of Divine Authority' in favour of the slave trade. Not surprisingly, this gained Harris the gratitude of Liverpool's merchants and also a pecuniary reward of £100 from the common council.[21] Harris's pamphlet was extensively advertised in Liverpool and London and promoted by Lord Hawkesbury, the President of the Board of Trade, who claimed that it contained unanswerable arguments in favour of the slave trade. Liverpool's abolitionists were incensed and the usually cautious James Currie declared that 'a little scoundrel, a Spanish Jesuit priest, has advanced to the assistance of the slave-merchants, and has published a vindication of this traffic from the Old Testament. His work is extolled as a prodigy by these judges of composition, and is, in truth, no bad specimen of his talents, though egregiously false and sophistical, as all justifications of slavery must be. I have prompted a clergyman, a friend of mine, to answer him, by telling him that if such be religion, I would none on't.'[22] The clergyman Currie refers to was the Anglican Reverend

Dannett, who bravely published a pamphlet under his own name, despite the fact that as a minister of the established Church his living was in the gift of the corporation, and he might well be putting his future prospects in jeopardy. He claimed that 'His object was to defend his calling and to show that the Church of England possessed a true friend to humanity in the heart of Liverpool.'[23]Although it was Dannett's work that appeared to annoy Harris the most, it was William Roscoe's answer that received the most attention. He carefully refuted all of Harris's points, demanding a more rational interpretation of the Bible, and a wider interpretation of the Christian doctrine of equality. He argued that it was ridiculous to claim that actions authorized in the distant past validated them in the present. If Harris's premise was accepted then one would be bound to approve of incest, fraud, lying, theft, murder and polygamy, since all these acts were unpunished, even rewarded by the God of Israel. Many crimes are not explicitly forbidden in the New Testament but, stated Roscoe, omission can never safely be construed as permission.[24] His work impressed the London committee, and a demand was made for copies for special circulation. John Barton claimed, 'we are all unanimously of the opinion that it is the <u>work of a master</u> and by much the best answer that Harris has received'.[25]

After 1788 the activity of the Liverpool abolitionists became muted, not only because of the hostile atmosphere in Liverpool but also because between 1789 and the latter part of 1791 the main emphasis of the campaign was on parliamentary debates (in which only two MPs, both representatives of Liverpool, spoke out in justification of the trade),[26] and on the evidence submitted to select committees. Roscoe and Currie still maintained their interest and Roscoe might well have attended debates on his visit to London in 1791.[27] In 1789 and 1791 two motions for abolition were brought before the House of Commons, both of which were defeated.

The slave rebellion in Santo Domingo increased resistance to abolition as reports of slave atrocities against the planters were exploited. In 1792 Roscoe's third pamphlet, 'An Enquiry into the Causes of the Insurrection of the Negroes in the Island of Santo Domingo', was published, 1,500 copies of which were printed and circulated by the London committee. He urged that the evils of slavery were responsible for such occurrences, not the abolition movement. Post-1792, the issue of abolition faded from the political scene. As Currie wrote, 'it was swallowed up in the volcano of the French Revolution',[28] but to some extent the battle was already won. In the Commons, Pitt stated that 'The point now in dispute between us, is, a difference merely as to the time at which abolition ought to take place.'[29]

Between 1789 and 1792 Roscoe was an active and enthusiastic participant in the movement for political reform stimulated by the French Revolution. His interest in the subject was not new. On 16 November 1788 a service was held at Benn's Garden Chapel for which Roscoe wrote his first political poem, *A Secular Song for the Revolution of 1688*, in which he gave his wholehearted support to the national constitution and the peaceful means by which it was accomplished. In some ways this reflected his later political thinking. While he supported parliamentary reform, it must not be at the expense of the constitution; rather, he favoured increasing Parliament's representational base and correcting its more obvious corruptions. Inspired by the reforming activity demonstrated in France, Roscoe's poem *Ode to the People of France* (imitating a canzone of Petrarch) was published in Liverpool in 1789. In it he celebrated the French people's efforts to free themselves from tyranny. It ends with a plea that Europe would be similarly inspired:

Thus rise the notes from BRITAIN'S neighbouring strand,
That hail the welfare of a sister land;

To distant nations emulous to trace
This noblest effort of the human race:
Till wond'ring EUROPE hear th' inspiring strains,
And dash to earth her Tyrants and her chains.[30]

Further poems were written by Roscoe to be read at celebratory dinners held on the first and second anniversaries of the fall of the Bastille. *Unfold Father Time* (also known as *Millions be Free*) appeared in 1790, and *The Song for the Anniversary of the French Revolution* in 1791. The latter proved very popular, although it did not bear Roscoe's name and as late as 1812 it was not widely known that he was the author. [31]

Initially, such sentiments were echoed throughout the country and the revolutionary events in France during the summer of 1789 met with widespread approval. Newspapers of the summer of 1789 confirm this, but the consensus was destined to be short-lived. As events in France took a violent turn, the mood in Britain changed. Edmund Burke, initially a supporter of reform, deserted the Whigs and wrote his *Reflections on the Revolution in France* (1790), which exposed the excesses of the Revolution and warned that Britain could find itself in the midst of a bloody revolution if it was not careful. This work found fertile ground in the popular and violent loyalist associations of the early 1790s. Nearly 20,000 copies of Burke's *Reflections* were sold in its first six months. In response to Burke, the Anglo-American political writer Tom Paine produced the first part of *The Rights of Man* in 1791–1792, in which he supported the French Revolution and called for an overthrow of the British monarchy and universal male suffrage. Paine's work quickly became the radical bible. Roscoe played a minor role in the national debate inspired by Burke's *Reflections* when he published in 1791 his highly critical account of *The Life, Death, and Wonderful Achievements of Edmund Burke*. In it he expressed his admiration for Mary Wollstonecraft,[32] one of the leading protagonists of the revolutionary cause, who in 1790 had replied to Burke's *Reflections* with *A Vindication of the Rights of Man*, in which she portrayed Burke as an apologist for oppression and a toady to power. Roscoe also referred admiringly to Tom Paine:

An lo! An Amazon stept out,
One WOLSTONECRAFT her name,
Resolve'd to stop his mad career,
Whatever chance became.

An oaken sapling in her hand,
Full on the foe she fell,
Nor could his coat of rusty steel
Her vig'rous strokes repel.

But heavier ills on EDMUND wait,
He seeks to 'scape in vain,
For out there rush'd a fiercer foe,
Whose dreaded name was PAINE.[33]

When Roscoe visited London in 1791 he became personally acquainted with Wollstonecraft, and correspondence between them continued throughout 1791and 1792. Roscoe was very impressed by her and even commissioned a portrait of her.[34] The feeling appears to have been mutual, with Wollstonecraft consulting Roscoe on legal matters and asking him to secure a situation for her brother in Liverpool.[35] The *Wonderful Achievements* was reprinted in 1792 (Edinburgh), 1793 (London) and again in 1800 (Edinburgh), evidence of its popularity in democratic circles.[36]

However, as news of the events in France filtered through, support for the revolution waned in Liverpool as elsewhere. An intimation that attitudes in Liverpool were hardening came when Joseph Priestley (whose outspoken support of the French Revolution had aroused public and governmental suspicion) decided against coming to Liverpool to open the new Paradise Street Chapel, possibly on the advice of the Liverpool Dissenters. Significantly, there are no reports of an anniversary dinner for the Revolution in 1792. This might have been abandoned because of the violence of the Church and King riots in Birmingham the previous July, or simply because local newspaper editors refused to allow the Liverpool radicals any publicity.[37]

Roscoe's sympathies (like those of Paine) were with the Girondin party. He particularly admired the deputy Pierre Vergiaud, a lawyer and brilliant orator. Roscoe felt that 'if ever the love of his country was apparent in any man, it was so in him',[38] and celebrated 'the spectacle of a great nation rising up, as one man, to regain the station and the happiness from which it had been disbarred by centuries of misgovernment.'[39]

His continuing support for the Revolution led to Roscoe and his circle being dubbed the 'Liverpool Jacobins' by their opponents. Jacobinism in Liverpool, it should be noted, was entirely a middle-class protest movement; no branch of the London Corresponding Society was ever formed among the town's loyalist working people.[40] For Roscoe, the excesses of the Revolution resulted in a degree of disillusionment. He claimed that the events in France had brought him to a 'dislike not only to the French but to my species. Sorry I am to say that this dislike is not much removed by anything I can see in my own country, where the same selfish and slavish spirit that has contributed to bring on the enormities of France is apparent in the prosecution of all those who aim, by a cool, rational, and deliberate reform, to prevent a similar catastrophe here.'[41] However, he was still convinced of its original justification, claiming that the escalation of violence resulted from the 'degraded and servile state in which the people had long been plunged'; they now had no conception of how to behave in a just society.[42] He was, however, no ardent republican: 'I think that a monarchy is capable of being as well constituted for the happiness of a people as a republic.'[43] It seems likely that his sympathies lay with a limited constitutional monarchy; he rejected many elements of Burke's *Reflections* but he did value the fact that the British political system provided stability and opportunity.

For those holding such anti-establishment views, the early 1790s were a dangerous time, particularly as the Liverpool Jacobins were also identified with the campaign for religious toleration and repeal of the Test and Corporation Acts. A warning note was sounded when, at the end of November 1792, the recorder and mayor of Liverpool ordered 10,000 copies of an anti-Jacobin declaration to be printed and distributed in the town. This document (subsequently called the *Resolutions*) was threatening in tone and implied that violence against the local reformers was justified. Roscoe and Rathbone immediately replied with a pamphlet entitled *Equality*, which they tried to get published in the *Weekly Herald*, the only paper in Liverpool favourable to their cause. The article was essentially mild in tone and did not preach against personal wealth or property owning: 'The inequality derived from labour and successful enterprise, the result of superior industry and good fortune, is an inequality essential to the very existence of society, and it naturally follows that the property so acquired should pass from father to son.' However, in 1792 the very word 'equality' was enough to set alarm bells ringing, and Hodgson, the newspaper's proprietor, was prevailed upon to refuse to insert it, to discharge the editor and to change the name and politics of the paper. Rathbone then printed the article as a handbill and had it distributed throughout the town. One of his reasons for doing this was that the newspapers were full of reactionary advertisements addressed to the 'loyal population of Liverpool'.

Rathbone declared that if any of the Liverpool mob acted on the advice offered to them in the advertisements, then those who had printed them would be responsible for any ensuing violence. After being threatened with a libel action, a quid pro quo was agreed: the handbills were withdrawn and the advertisements ceased to appear.[44]

Pressure from the moderate Whigs finally forced the mayor to summon a general meeting of the inhabitants to the Town Hall on 8 December so that a true sense of Liverpool opinion could be sent in an address to the crown. An address, prepared by Roscoe, voicing the reformers' desire for moderate reform and their disapproval of war was delivered to the meeting in the hope that it would have 'conciliated all parties and put an end to our political dissensions in Liverpool'. After a noisy debate, the address was surprisingly agreed to by a large majority. However, any hopes that Liverpool might possibly give a lead to the nation in the campaign to avoid war overseas and reaction at home were soon shattered. Before the address could be signed, inflammatory handbills were circulated denouncing the sentiments of the address. At the appointed time for signing, a riotous mob threatened and abused anyone trying to sign his name, and eventually seized and tore up the address. The mayor was summoned, and after telling the reform leaders that unless they were prepared to withdraw their address he could no longer answer for the peace of the town, one of the ultra-loyal Tory drafts previously rejected by the meeting was later sent up with more than 11,000 signatures.[45]

The Liverpool Jacobins were now marked men, and in January 1793 the execution of Louis XVI saw public opinion harden further against them. The mayor of Liverpool wrote to a correspondent that 'the horror and consternation here are not to be described. Everybody means to put on mourning.'[46] Revulsion was also evident among the radicals, with Dr Currie viewing the act as 'a deliberate and dreadful murder, calculated to awaken the horror of men in an extraordinary degree.'[47] For Roscoe, the final blow came with the execution of the Girondin deputies in the autumn of 1793 and the triumph of the Jacobins. To Roscoe, who hated all warfare, the war with France was doubly odious. In 1793 he published *Thoughts on the Causes of the Present Failures* in which he blamed the war for the nation's economic ills. James Currie, under the pseudonym Jasper Wilson, issued a *Letter to Mr Pitt Commercial and Political* on the same theme, and urged that negotiations should be immediately instituted to end the war. The increasingly repressive measures of William Pitt, the suspension of habeas corpus in 1794 and the Treasonable Practices and Seditious Meetings Acts of 1795 (which made any kind of political organization, public meeting or political writing dangerous) caused Roscoe to despair of reform in England. He wrote to Lord Lansdowne, 'The leaders have apostatised and the disciples perish.'[48]

The Liverpool Jacobins, having regard to 'the lunacy of the town' as Rathbone put it, opted for discretion and retreated from the political arena, calling a halt even to their literary society meetings; 'suspicion has for some time gone abroad about us ... and, in the present state of things, we have thought it expedient to suspend our future meetings'.[49] Their radicalism appears to have incited more anger than their anti-slavery campaigning. James Currie immersed himself in his medical work among the poor, although as a precautionary measure he borrowed £1,200 and made inquiries about a property in Virginia. The Reverend William Shepherd also secured a property in Kentucky, while Rathbone – so shocked by the events of late 1792 that his hair was reputed to have turned white overnight (hence his nickname 'the hoary traitor') – decided he would devote the rest of his life to religious enquiry. Roscoe was advised by Shepherd to retire from the 'intestine broils and foreign rage' to the enjoyment of his 'domestic comforts', advice that Roscoe prudently accepted.[50]

The following few years saw the Liverpool Jacobins on the defensive. They were not alone in pursuing a policy of caution; radicals in other towns were also forced to adopt a policy of 'quiet resignation'.[51] However, Roscoe, Rathbone and Currie conducted a vigorous campaign to try to improve the conditions of the French prisoners of war held in Liverpool, and Roscoe earned himself a considerable reputation at Westminster as an anti-war pamphleteer, corresponding regularly with Lord Lansdowne, Lord Holland and the Duke of Gloucester. In 1796 Roscoe was in print again with his *Strictures on Mr. Burke's Two Letters*, in which he argued for the re-opening of peace negotiations with France. In 1797 Lansdowne introduced him to Whig society, and he had an hour's 'familiar conversation' with Charles Fox, whose anti-war stance he greatly admired.[52] In the same year Roscoe sent an article on the same theme as his *Strictures* to the *Morning Chronicle*, but it was not allowed to appear, leaving Roscoe and Rathbone in despair.

1806 heralded Roscoe's return to the political spotlight with his election as MP for Liverpool. He had not been the the Whigs' first choice; they had tried to persuade Lord Sefton to stand, and after his refusal had moved on to Sir Thomas Hesketh, Admiral Sir Isaac Coffin and Thomas Earle before turning to Roscoe.[53] Although he had already rejected informal approaches, the proprietor of the *Liverpool Chronicle* circulated handbills throughout the town suggesting Roscoe as a candidate. The proposal elicited considerable support, and there were many discussions about the viability of his candidature and the availability of the necessary funds. Support among Roscoe's friends was not unanimous; William Rathbone, in particular had reservations although he was not prepared to advise him not to stand.[54]

Roscoe's election cannot be seen as indicative of a sea change in attitudes among his fellow townsmen; references to the slave trade were minimal throughout the electoral campaign. There was the odd warning that Roscoe was 'a distinct enemy to the Africa Trade' and the prediction of dire consequences to Liverpool's economy, but these apparently went unheeded.[55] The stature gained in the public arena from the publication of the *Life of Lorenzo* and the *Life of Leo* meant that Roscoe was now at the peak of his career, and his standing convinced his supporters that any political prejudices of the voters would be outweighed by their respect for Roscoe, the cultural and philanthropic icon.[56] The Liverpool freemen were urged to:

> View him as a HUSBAND, a FATHER, a FRIEND, a COUNSELLOR; the Votary of Science, the Promoter of the Arts!... Look at the School for the Blind, the ATHENAEUM, the LYCEUM, the BOTANIC GARDEN... Such is MR.ROSCOE; such FREEMEN OF LIVERPOOL! is the Man now offered to your choice. His Virtues and his Deeds have already immortalized his Name. It will be recorded and revered by your latest Posterity.[57]

Roscoe was nominated on the hustings by his banking partner, Alderman Thomas Leyland, and seconded by Alderman Thomas Earle; ironically both were prominent slave traders. Lord Sefton and Lord Stanley (heir to the Earl of Derby) both exerted themselves on Roscoe's behalf. Roscoe's success, however, probably owed most to the unpopularity of the other candidates (particularly the incumbent Tarleton, who was felt to have neglected his duties and to have been inconsistent in his political allegiance) and to extensive bribery. Of the three candidates, General Isaac Gascoyne's bill was reputed to be £3,000, General Banastre Tarleton's £4,000 and William Roscoe's £12,000. Despite the fact that these figures come from the Tory camp, Roscoe himself admitted spending that amount.[58] The conclusion that the victory was largely due to 'the combined ideas of ale and independence ... our exertions and the weight of our purse'[59] appears to have credibility. It was later explained that the high expenditure was the result of the relative inexperience of Roscoe's supporters; 'much money was squandered away ... and the chief expenditure arose from the injudicious zeal of persons, who, though unknown to, and unauthorised by, committee, gave orders to a large amount, which the committee thought it incumbent on them to discharge'.[60] Whatever the reasons behind his election success, the end result was that Roscoe was at the head of the poll and General Tarleton lost the seat he had held for sixteen years.

The Liverpool reformers were overjoyed at Roscoe's success, and a few days after the result of the poll he sat down to a sumptuous celebratory dinner at the Golden Lion in Dale Street, attended by 260 of his supporters. At the end of the room was a 'beautiful transparency' exhibiting a bust of Roscoe with the inscription 'An honest man is the noblest work of God'. The food ordered for the dinner was reported to have included 13 pots of turtle soup, 12 dishes of fish, 12 pieces of beef, 12 legs of pork, 6 legs of mutton, 12 saddles of mutton, 12 roast pigs, 12 tongues, 12 hams, 2 turkeys, 12 geese, 12 hares, 24 fowls, 13 pigeon pies, 6 ornamental raised pies, 100 snipes, 36 partridges, 50 woodcocks, 12 wild ducks, 6 pheasants, 12 moor game, 48 lobsters, 20 salads, 18 plum puddings, 50 tarts, 50 jellies, 20 blancmanges and 50 mince pies.[61] It is a tribute to the gastronomic stamina of the diners of that era that anyone felt able to get to their feet to deliver a speech after such a repast.

Despite Roscoe's lack of input on political questions during the campaign, his speech at the banquet revealed that his reforming zeal remained undiminished. He made his views clear on two major issues. In respect of the slave trade, he confirmed that 'my sentiments have long been known and they are now what they ever were ... the trade should be brought to a termination', although he advocated compensation for Liverpool's merchants. He believed that Liverpool would not be financially ruined by abolition, for 'there are other sources to which it can and ought to look to as an equivalent', and he hinted that the ending of the monopoly of the East India Company might be a contributory factor here. He also stressed his support for 'that which is usually called a reform in Parliament'. He outlined the need for 'gradual and temperate measures of improvement in the House of Commons' by way of legislation to curb bribery and corruption, extend the franchise and redistribute the seats of rotten boroughs among the large towns.[62] Roscoe embarked for London and his new political career, pinning his faith on the so-called 'Ministry of all the Talents', a coalition formed after the death of William Pitt the Younger. It was led by Lord Grenville and included Charles James Fox (until his death in September 1806) as Foreign Secretary despite the King's opposition.

Roscoe's radical friends eagerly awaited his performance in the Commons, sure that he would promote the principles for which they had so long fought. They hoped that he would denounce corruption and provide a rallying point for enlightened and dedicated men. William Rathbone in particular urged Roscoe to make his voice heard in the Commons. 'How is it', he wrote, 'we hear so little sound of your voice. Oh Roscoe, if you can see unmoved, if you raise not your voice against a system of fraud ... you are no longer the character for which nature formed you.'[63] However, Rathbone recognized the difficulties that Roscoe faced, particularly on the question of compensation. In a letter to a friend he acknowledged that 'between friends to the slave trade on the one hand and his own friends on the other, Roscoe will have a very narrow path to walk in'.[64] Other radicals also found Roscoe's performance disappointing. Roscoe himself was very apprehensive about his ability to fulfil the expectations of his

Liverpool supporters. His self-doubt was evident in a letter written to William Rathbone soon after taking his seat. He admitted, 'If my friends have formed such high notions of the extraordinary effects which I am to produce in my public character, I fear they will only meet with disappointment, and that I must reconcile myself to that failure with which I am so strongly threatened.'[65] Always the family man, he found the separation from his loved ones, particularly his wife, very hard to bear, and this contributed to a recurrence of a depressive nervous disorder. He stated in verse how much he longed for Jane's arrival:

> O Come! Thy presence shall the clouds dispel,
> Thy voice shall soothe me, and thy counsels guide;
> For thou alone canst soothe the tempest's swell,
> And snatch me, struggling, from the whelming tide.[66]

Jane Roscoe's arrival in London in February 1807 did indeed do much to restore his equilibrium. In a letter to her son, Jane reported that her husband was now feeling happier and had been asked to dine by the Speaker of the House of Commons. Jane appears to have found living in London more to her liking than her husband, and was busy looking for a footman, whom she proposed to dress in the Allerton livery, to ride behind the carriage and walk behind her in the park. She finally engaged 'a Scotch man with yellow hair and long visage'.[67] Just as Roscoe was gaining confidence, however, his worries were revived by Thomas Leyland's unexpected dissolution of their commercial partnership (see Chapter 7).

Although initially Roscoe hesitated to speak, claiming 'I find great caution necessary on my first outset: and my present resolution is not to engage in any hasty or precipitant measures, nor to commit myself in any way where I cannot maintain my ground',[68] he later claims, in a letter to William Rathbone, to have spoken three or four times 'which is, I

believe, as often as any new member, but still find a reluctance
to offer myself to the House'.[69] In his speech to the Commons
on the slavery debate (the ever-forceful William Rathbone had
written one for him, but Roscoe opted to deliver his own)[70]
Roscoe assured the House that despite the opprobrium
heaped on Liverpool for its anti-abolition stance, opinion in
the town was not unanimous. 'On the contrary, a great and
respectable body of the inhabitants are as adverse to the slave
trade as any other persons in these realms.'[71] He argued that
abolition should be gradual and that the question of compensation should be carefully considered. By merchants being
encouraged to spread their areas of trade, the result of abolition would be increased revenue for both the traders and the
country at large. To this end, Roscoe argued that the
monopoly of the East India Company should be ended: 'Let
there be no monopoly but the monopoly of the country at
large.'[72] He concluded,

> It is now upwards of thirty years since I first raised my
> voice in public against the traffic which is the object of the
> present bill to abolish ... I shall always think it the greatest
> happiness of my life, that I have had the honour to be
> present on this occasion, and to concur with those true
> friends of justice, of humanity, and, as I most firmly believe
> of sound policy, who have brought forward this present
> measure.[73]

Roscoe went on to cast his vote in favour of abolition and was
particularly pleased to be assured that his vote, as the Member
of Parliament for Liverpool, was worth twenty.

The 'ministry of all the talents' succeeded in abolishing the
slave trade but had little success in its other reforming measures. Roscoe spoke again in support of Samuel Whitbread's
bill aimed at free education for the poor, and on the issue of
Catholic emancipation, a subject which was to earn him the

anger of his constituents. When the government fell in April 1807 over Catholic emancipation and its conduct of the war, Roscoe returned to Liverpool, which was now facing the effects of abolition. Despite warnings from William Rathbone that his homecoming might not be trouble-free, rather naively Roscoe was not concerned that his vote for abolition would affect his support, claiming, 'I do not augur much opposition for my conduct on the slave trade as my opinions on it were well known'.[74] Accompanied by his main supporters he returned to town on the day after abolition came into force. The procession was peaceful until it arrived at the south end of Castle Street, where it was greeted by a hostile crowd consisting of seamen, mainly from the slaving ships, armed with sticks. Others were dressed in green, the colour of General Tarleton. A vicious riot ensued, and the horses of Roscoe's supporters were attacked with the sticks. The procession managed to reach the corner of Castle Street and Dale Street near the premises of Roscoe's bank, where he got out of his carriage. A stone was promptly hurled at him; a voice cried 'Now is your time!' and shouts of 'No popery' rang out. Lieutenant Colonel George Williams, a commander of a Liverpool volunteer regiment, was pulled from his horse, which was stabbed. Roscoe's legal agent Fletcher Raincock was twice hit in the face, while Wallace Currie, son of the late Dr James Currie, was knocked to the ground.[75] Roscoe tried to subdue the mob but he was not given the chance to speak. The assembly eventually broke up in disorder. Later the same evening, a fight broke out in Highfield Street, in which Edward Spencer, a young man who was one of Roscoe's supporters, was killed.

Roscoe's enthusiasm for active political participation was extinguished, and retreat to Allerton Hall seemed a welcoming prospect. In an address to the people of Liverpool published on 5 May, he declared: 'if the representation of Liverpool can only be obtained by violence and bloodshed I leave the honour of it to those who choose to contend it'.[76] His immediate supporters accepted his decision and his election committee was dissolved. However, the auctioneer Thomas Green was determined that despite Roscoe's protestations, his name should be submitted as a candidate against Gascoyne and Tarleton in the ensuing election. Although support was forthcoming from a few of Roscoe's more ardent supporters and Raincock was engaged as an agent, it was not until the poll had actually opened that a committee was formed.

During the week of Roscoe's unwilling candidature, the opposing Tories inaugurated a campaign that was slanderous even by Liverpool standards. One pamphlet, allegedly signed by the Pope, called on 'all apprentices, Ragamuffins, Presbyterians, Rogues, Methodists, Jail-birds, Whores, etc' (a remarkably eclectic grouping) 'to assist our cause' and vote for Roscoe.[77] Despite the passing of the Abolition Act, Tarleton campaigned under the banner, 'The Church and the slave trade for ever!' and even had two black boys parading through the streets carrying a placard declaring 'The African trade restored'. The Whig response was ineffectual. Ploys aimed at countering Tarleton's tactics, such as hiring black men to march with a banner declaring 'We thank God for our freedom', made no impression on the voters. Roscoe was sick of politics and withdrew his name, but the poll went ahead. The outcome of the election, unsurprisingly, was a heavy defeat for Roscoe; he polled only 377 votes to Gascoyne's 1,227 and Tarleton's 1,461.[78] This time, the image of Roscoe the townsman was superseded by that of Roscoe the politician; one workman was said to have exclaimed, 'He is an ornament to the town, but what have we poor folk to do with ornaments?' Although there was talk of raising a petition against the conduct of the election, nothing came of it. Lord Holland described the result as 'a disgrace to the country', while another correspondent, Dr J.E. Smith, comforted

Roscoe with the reflection that 'the world is not worthy of you'. Roscoe, weakly attributing his defeat to the 'temporary delusion of the public mind'[79] retreated from active politics and refused on religious grounds the offer of a deputy-lieutenancy from the Earl of Derby. He was debarred from office under the Test Act, and felt that it was only by people such as himself adhering strictly to the letter of the law was there any hope of repeal.[80]

Roscoe's brief parliamentary career and its aftermath left him disillusioned with political activism, while the electorate was similarly disenchanted with the performance of the intellectual in politics. It turned to more practical men who would more faithfully represent its views in Westminster. However, although Roscoe eschewed an active parliamentary career, he still espoused the cause of peace and also of reform. He was horrified by the British bombardment of neutral Copenhagen in 1807, and once more turned to writing political poetry:

> Murderers! Whom my soul disowns,
> Authors of your country's shame,
> Recreants to a Briton's name;
> What could prompt your furious rage
> Thus the war with Heaven to Wage.[81]

In July 1807 Roscoe presided over a banquet attended by 300 'friends of genuine principles of the British constitution'. The leanings of the meeting towards the late Whig government were clearly demonstrated in the numerous toasts. William Rathbone defended Roscoe's political performance in the Commons, and Roscoe discussed in detail his activities in Parliament, urging his listeners to continue to press for reform and elect a candidate for Liverpool sympathetic to their aims, although 'I shall not ... ever more present myself as the object of your choice'.[82] A great anniversary dinner was held to celebrate Roscoe's election of 1806, and the resolutions passed on this occasion reminded the local reformers that the battles for parliamentary reform, Catholic emancipation and purity of government had not been won. In April 1811 Roscoe composed a letter to Henry Brougham arguing for a measure of parliamentary reform, voting rights for all householders, the disenfranchisement of rotten boroughs and the exclusion of placemen from the House of Commons. He also corresponded with the reformer Major Cartwright on the question of parliamentary reform but, perhaps regretting the Jacobin enthusiasm of his younger days, did not join the Major's Society of Friends of Parliamentary Reform on the grounds of prudence. A tract of 1812 by Roscoe, 'An answer to Mr John Merritt on the subject of Parliamentary Reform', is almost entirely historical in content and whiggish in tone.[83]

In the event, Liverpool's radicals (especially the merchants among them) found that economic pressures rather than political ideals proved to be their major concerns during these years. Trade was being severely affected by the Orders in Council (economic sanctions on neutrals trading with the French) which particularly affected trade with the USA. William Rathbone IV was afraid that the Orders in Council would not only ruin his family business but would also result in the Americans confiscating the Rathbones' considerable property in America. Roscoe immediately began writing two pamphlets against the orders and a third giving the government his proposals for peace.

With the early months of 1812 seeing increasing distress in Liverpool and war with the USA now a distinct possibility, Roscoe pinned his hopes on Henry Brougham, with whom he began a prolific correspondence. In March 1812 Roscoe chaired a large meeting to demand the opening up of the East India trade, and in April he chaired another to petition for the repeal of the Orders in Council, following which two of Liverpool's leading American merchants presented a petition to the House of Lords (where they found a supporter in Lord

Derby). In August 1812 the orders were finally repealed, although this came too late to avert war with the USA. At a great reform dinner on 5 September, Henry Brougham was feted for the part he had played in the repeal and also for securing the acquittal of 38 reformers recently imprisoned in Manchester. When in October 1812 an election appeared imminent, Roscoe and his friends felt that they should invite Brougham to contest the Liverpool seat on their behalf.

Roscoe was determined to press ahead with Brougham's candidacy, despite the fact that the aristocratic Whigs withdrew their patronage from a candidate they considered to be a newcomer and an upstart. They were even more at odds with the choice of Thomas Creevey as Brougham's running-mate, his lower middle-class background being even less to their taste. The Tories opted for George Canning and General Gascoyne. Brougham's policies were for peace with the USA and France, the opening up of the East India trade and moderate parliamentary reform. Canning, on the contrary, was for pursuing the war with vigour and was strongly against Catholic emancipation. Both sides used the name of Roscoe during the campaign. Brougham, not surprisingly, portrayed him as a far-sighted patriot whose policies, if they had been implemented in 1807, would have saved Liverpool from her present economic distress. Canning and Gascoyne presented Roscoe as a cowardly recluse who hadn't the courage to stand at the election and had even refused an invitation from the radicals at Westminster to uphold their interests.[84]

The campaign soon degenerated into the customary scurrilous squibs and insults. An approach was made to the leading reformers to drop Creevey, agree to a compromise and return Canning and Brougham. However, Roscoe still stubbornly maintained that Canning could be defeated and both reformer candidates could be elected. His judgement was wrong; worse still, the Tories rallied and at considerable expense got enough votes to elect Gascoyne. Brougham was forced to accept defeat. This proved to be a mortal blow to Roscoe's political reputation and he was severely criticized (not least by Brougham) for his misjudgement. Creevey wrote bitterly, 'We had to do with artists who do not know their trade. Poor Roscoe made much too sanguine an estimate of our strength.'[85] This was the end of Roscoe's political career as an active radical reformer, although his support for the cause was to continue until his death in 1831, when he was eagerly anticipating the Reform Act.

Roscoe's interest in the subject of slavery continued until the end of his life even though abolition had been achieved and his parliamentary career had concluded. He attended the inaugural meeting of the African Institution (1807) and was on its committee. From 1807 until 1811 he played a role in ensuring that the merchants did not try to get around the 1807 Act, providing information for Zachary Macaulay, the African Institution's secretary, on illegal slave trading. In 1809 he received the thanks of the African Institution for his efforts in rescuing nine men who had arrived in Liverpool as part of the crew of a Brazilian vessel. The men were slaves and on the request of the ship's captain were immediately arrested, handcuffed and placed in the borough gaol. Although this was supposedly because the men owed the captain money, it was more likely to have been to stop them absconding. When the ship was ready to sail, the men – anticipating their return to slavery – refused to leave the prison. Their gaoler, showing considerable humanity, refused to release them. Roscoe used his legal expertise to have the men bailed, and instituted proceedings that succeeded in having the men released and freed. The Committee of the African Institution congratulated him 'on his having been the instrument of delivering nine human beings from the dreadful state of Negro slavery, and vindicating at the same time the justice of the British laws, which were fraudulently abused for purposes of aggression'.[86]

Now that the Liverpool merchants had turned from

trading in slaves to 'legitimate' trade with Africa, such as palm oil, the Liverpool abolitionists met with little opposition. Poachers had now turned gamekeepers, and as early as 1814 former African slave traders such as Thomas Leyland signed a petition against the slave trade. As Roscoe grew older, the Quaker James Cropper became the leading abolitionist in Liverpool. Cropper persuaded Roscoe to join a society the former had formed with the aim of alleviating the conditions of existing slaves and promoting the gradual and final end of slavery itself. On 14 January 1823 Cropper wrote to Roscoe (now in his seventieth year) informing him that 'for sometime past we have had a small society here for the mitigation and gradual abolition of slavery', and inviting the veteran campaigner to accept the position of president. Initially Roscoe declined, regretting that other engagements prevented him from accepting. However, Cropper persisted and by the end of the month Roscoe had agreed to attend a meeting. This seems to have changed Roscoe's mind, as in March a 'Declaration of Objects' appeared bearing the signature of William Roscoe as president.[87] Cropper's anxiety to associate Roscoe's name with his society illustrates how important he felt this was to its success. Roscoe took a keen interest in the work of the society, but ill-health appears to have prevented him from playing an active role and he did not live to see the society achieve its aims.

In these years Roscoe also took an interest in the improvement of the conditions of the poor and the ways they were affected by the criminal justice system. His interest in the subject was aroused in 1817 when researching a short paper outlining the arguments against the death penalty (he had been asked to prepare this for the Society for the Diffusion of Knowledge on the Subject of Capital Punishment). His 'Observations on Penal Jurisprudence, and the Reformation of Criminals' (1819) was a plea for the amelioration of the criminal code, particularly in the ways in which it affected the poor. He followed this up with two further tracts in 1823 and 1825, and his views stimulated considerable discussion, not least because they were considerably ahead of his time. He believed that reformation rather than the exacting of vengeance was the best way to prevent crime; that harsh punishment was not the answer; and that it was far better to improve the morals of prisoners through education. Roscoe was against corporal punishment and the death penalty. He declared that 'in order to demonstrate to a people that they ought not to be cruel, he [the state] sets them an example of cruelty; and in order to deter them from putting each other to death, he puts them to death himself'. He urged that offenders should be imprisoned and 'set to hard labour till they acquired a habit of industry and had been compelled to repay to those they had robbed the amount of their losses'. Roscoe felt strongly that the time had arrived for a thorough review of the criminal code.[88] Although his writings on penal discipline led him into a frequent and lively correspondence with numerous distinguished people, particularly in the USA, and his work was mentioned in Parliament, he was discouraged by the lack of any real progress in his homeland. He wrote to his old friend John McCreery, 'I have scarce heard a word from the great world about my late publication, from which I conjecture that it does not exactly hit the public taste, and that the old system of hanging, transporting, and flogging will be continued'.[89] Roscoe's summation was right; his views were far ahead of his time.

Roscoe has been both applauded and derided for his political contributions to the abolition of the slave trade and the reform movement. It has been claimed that he was too domesticated and simply 'too nice a man' ever to make a successful politician.[90] He certainly was not a natural orator and lacked confidence in his own abilities. Although the Tory accusation of cowardice is unfair, he did have a natural caution and sensitivity to criticism that prevented him from playing a major role on the national political stage. In many ways, Rathbone's talents made him more suited to the role Roscoe was called upon to play, although business commitments precluded him taking an active role. The pressure that Rathbone put on his friend did little for Roscoe's confidence or his desire to stand for re-election. It has also been argued that Roscoe's disintegration after his election defeat exposed the vulnerability of the idealist intellectual in the harsh, practical world of politics. However, Roscoe's preparedness – against his natural instincts – to offer himself to the electorate and vote in Parliament on issues that were bound to upset his constituents is surely a matter for commendation. His support for gradualism on the subject of abolition was less a matter of caution than of pragmatism. Ideally, he supported the immediate and total abolition of the slave trade. Pragmatically, he realized that it would be easier to gain support for the movement, particularly in his beloved native town, if gradualism and compensation were under consideration. Roscoe was not a major player in the abolition movement and the cause of reform, but his contributions with the pen and in Parliament should not be undervalued.

# CHAPTER 7

## *Roscoe the Businessman*

Attorneys, their fingers in every pie, fixing mortgages and
acting as bankers and political agents as well as handling
litigation, oiled the wheel of business ... and many got
rich.[1]

Although one of William Roscoe's most profoundly held
beliefs was the compatibility of culture and commerce, his
abilities as a man of business have invariably been down-
played by his biographers. His son's biography, in particular,
does little to explain how Roscoe accumulated his wealth,
partly because the biography is based on the subject's
extensive correspondence, which inevitably leads to the depre-
ciation of Roscoe, the Liverpudlian in favour of Roscoe, the
cosmopolitan man. The biography ignores the important
business and social relationship with Thomas Leyland, and
minimizes the close association with those, like Thomas and
William Earle, who were leading slave traders.[2] His everyday
activities must have involved dealing to some extent with the
affairs and finances of fellow citizens whose wealth was based
on the slave trade, privateering and even smuggling simply
because in Liverpool in the late eighteenth century it would
have been impossible to avoid this.

The precise source of Roscoe's wealth has proved difficult
to establish, although the legal profession could prove
extremely lucrative in the eighteenth century, with high fees
being charged.[3] In a rising commercial town like Liverpool

one must assume there was considerable scope for an aspiring attorney such as Roscoe. In Roscoe's correspondence there are letters attesting to his skill. John Barton declared Roscoe 'one of the honestest lawyers' and he one of the most fortunate clients in the world, since, being employed to procure him £49 and two shillings, Roscoe had sent him £49 and four shillings.[4] Although he would have gained a considerable amount of work from his fellow worshippers at Benn's Garden Chapel, he could not have afforded to turn away lucrative work from outside this close-knit group. His frequent absences from home on business testify that his legal abilities were highly valued by the community at large.

The fact that Roscoe, despite his large family, was able to retire from the practice of law at the age of 43 is the best illustration of his success. While he often claimed to dislike the profession, writing to his wife of the law as 'that sometimes wilful and sometimes blindness, which prevents the appearance of truth',[5] it had undoubtedly made him a wealthy man. Despite his criticism of his fellow citizens' excessive preoccupation with profit, he was not averse to surrounding himself with the comforts of life that wealth could provide. It has been claimed that the best proof of a man's success in business is his ability to leave it, and we may assume that this was true of Roscoe.

Although Roscoe withdrew from practising law, his commercial instincts remained active and he was prepared to consider schemes that seemed likely to offer a good return on his investment. One factor that might have influenced his decision to retire from the practice of law was his involvement in 1792 with Thomas Wakefield, a sugar refiner of Liverpool, in a plan to reclaim Chat Moss and Trafford Moss, large marshy tracts of land between Liverpool and Manchester. Early experiments appeared to augur well, with Roscoe convinced that the reclaimed land would prove favourable for both pasture and cultivation. He envisaged that the growth of

Liverpool and Manchester would ensure an ever-expanding market for agricultural produce. He thus hoped to turn his natural affinity to the land into a profitable agricultural and horticultural concern.

Roscoe supervised the work from the outset, the object being to make the mosslands capable of producing a rotation of the best crops. In a letter to his wife in February 1793, Roscoe regrets how much time he is spending away from home but trusts that 'the Moss Scheme will be a capital undertaking', which would 'not only repay the trouble bestowed on it' but would provide for their old age and their descendants.[6] In his book *The Taming of the Flood*, in a section on eighteenth-century 'improvement', Jeremy Purseglove outlines the work undertaken by Roscoe:

> In 1793 Roscoe began work on Trafford Moss, part of the mighty Chat Moss, 2,500 acres of sphagnum, sundew and bog asphodel. Roscoe's ambition was to drain the whole wetland, and to this end he organized ditching, marling and importation from nearby Manchester of boatload upon boatload of human ordure, which was forked by hand on the moss. One of Roscoe's ideas was a windmill plough, whose sails would actually churn up the bog.[7]

In 1796 Roscoe wrote 'The land is now laid dry and upwards of one-third of it is in a state of cultivation with oats, barley and potatoes'. Roscoe corresponded with anyone who could offer him advice, including Sir John Sinclair (the President of the Board of Agriculture) and Sir Joseph Banks, who was less convinced than Roscoe of the suitability of the land for grazing sheep. His experiments in scientific agriculture brought Roscoe some useful and significant contacts, in particular with the progressive landowner Thomas Coke of Holkham in Norfolk (1752–1842). Coke invited him to his home where Roscoe was enthralled by the magnificent library.

The reclamation project proved to be a heavy drain on his capital reserves, which may have contributed to his later financial woes. Interestingly, the reclamation work did prove beneficial for non-agricultural reasons. According to Robert Gladstone, when the Liverpool to Manchester railway was cut across Chat Moss Roscoe's drains were found to be of great service.[8]

Notwithstanding his supposed dislike of the business world, Roscoe had his fingers in a number of other pies. With his partners John Clarke, William German and Charles Porter, he acquired and opened out the colliery at Orrell in 1789. In 1791 a correspondent of Roscoe's declared himself happy to learn that Roscoe's coal business was succeeding.[9] The Roscoe family were importers of Bagillt coal and were also involved in a white lead manufactory. In 1805 at Garstang they began a building for smelting lead, which Roscoe's second son Edward was to manage.[10] It is unclear whether this ever came to fruition, but Edward was obviously interested in this sphere as he became an iron merchant.

Despite much research and speculation, there is no evidence to suggest that Roscoe invested in any ventures associated with the slave trade. In a letter to the Duke of Gloucester in 1809 Roscoe categorically states that 'he himself had never had any share in a shipping adventure'.[11] A letter in the same year from the abolitionist Zachary Macaulay states that he has heard that Roscoe is sending two vessels to enter into a mercantile speculation in the natural produce of Africa, and asks that his vessels should report any suspected cases of illegal slave trading by English or Portuguese ships to the naval authorities. In his reply, Roscoe explains that his second son (Edward) was a partner in a mercantile house under the name of Hamnet, Roscoe and Wilson, dealing with native produce from Africa, which had led to the rumour that Roscoe himself was engaged in sending vessels to Africa. He assures Macaulay that his son would be very willing to help him in his inquiries. He also refers to the prejudice which prevailed against traders who were engaged in a quite legitimate form of trade with Africa.[12] As with most of the town's citizens, Roscoe would have benefited indirectly from the wealth generated by the slave trade but there is no evidence of any direct involvement.

Roscoe also (reluctantly according to his son) entered the world of banking. From the mid-1770s onwards a number of Liverpool merchants involved themselves in banking in addition to their other business affairs. At first they conducted their trading business in tandem with their banking business, but as they grew more successful the tendency was for them to rely entirely on banking. William Clarke, the father of Roscoe's close friend and leading researcher of the *Life of Lorenzo* (William Clarke Jr), fits this pattern. In the first Liverpool Directory of 1766 he is listed as 'merchant and linen draper'; by 1774 he appears as 'banker and linen draper'. In the 1777 directory the firm of 'William Clarke & Sons, Bankers' appears, while the linen business is still in the name of William Clarke alone. In 1781 the linen business was sold and from then on the Clarkes were solely bankers, moving to premises at the corner of Castle Street and Dale Street facing the Town Hall.

On 5 February 1797 William Clarke died at the age of 73 and the running of the bank passed into the hands of the son. The bank had only just managed to survive the crisis of 1793 (initiated by the war with France), and now it came close to insolvency. In an examination of the affairs of the bank, the business of the house was found to be very complicated. The London correspondents were Esdaile and Co., who held in the region of £200,000 of Clarke and Son's paper; they promptly sent Sir Benjamin Hammett, one of the partners of the firm, to investigate matters. William Roscoe was summoned in his professional capacity as an attorney to help sort matters out. Hammett was so impressed by Roscoe's acumen in arranging the affairs of the bank that he suggested that Roscoe should consider becoming a partner with the Clarkes. Repeated refusals from Roscoe resulted in Hammett threatening to put the matter into bankruptcy. Roscoe, conscious of the debt he owed his friend for his contribution to *The Life of Lorenzo,* and satisfied that the bank had sufficient assets to cover its liabilities, reluctantly agreed. 'The step I took was not a matter of choice and inclination, but of imperious necessity ... it was the irresistible claim of friendship.'[13]

The title of the firm now became 'Clarkes and Roscoe'. Clarkes' bank had been far from alone in struggling with the liquidity crises of the 1790s, and by the end of the eighteenth century it had done well to survive as one of the two banks of stature in Liverpool. It became the preferred bank of the new American interest; these clients were free traders and Whigs and it was they who formed the American Chamber of Commerce in 1801. Merchants and traders of the West India connection, who established the Liverpool West India Association in 1799, tended to patronize Gregson, Sons, Parke, and Morland. After it was dissolved in 1805 they took their business to Leyland and Bullin.[14]

In 1802 the firm was strengthened when Thomas Leyland, a wealthy merchant and keen businessman, became a partner. The bank now became known as Leyland, Clarkes and Roscoe. Given Roscoe's views on the slave trade, this appears an unlikely alliance, as Leyland was one of the most active of Liverpool's slave merchants. Leyland was originally engaged with Gerald Dillon in the Irish trade. In 1776 the partners had a stroke of luck when, having invested £7 in a ticket for the state lottery, they drew a prize of £20,000. In 1780 Leyland was elected to the chamber of commerce and the two men went their separate ways. He entered the slave trade and became increasingly prosperous. Between 1782 and 1807 he was responsible for transporting nearly 3,500 Africans to Jamaica alone, and by 1826 his reputed fortune was £73,653.

Both materially and intellectually Leyland was a decided asset to the firm, illustrating perhaps that Roscoe's business instincts could, at times, take precedence over his principles.

In 1805 William Clarke, who had never been robust, died and Roscoe lost not only a business partner but a close friend. John Clarke, William's brother, remained involved in the bank's affairs. In 1806 Roscoe was elected to Parliament, which must have necessitated him having less to do with the day-to-day affairs of the bank. The news that Thomas Leyland had withdrawn from the partnership (made public on 31 December 1806) must also have had an impact on the conduct of the bank's affairs. Following the withdrawal of Leyland, John Clarke and William Roscoe brought the latter's eldest son, William Stanley Roscoe, into the business. From 1807 the firm became known as Roscoe, Clarke and Roscoe.

The reasons for Leyland's departure are the subject of some debate. Henry Roscoe gives no reason in his biography, while James Picton, in his *Memorials of Liverpool*, attributes it to Leyland's acumen in foreseeing impending financial disaster. However, though undoubtedly acute and far-seeing, it seems unlikely that even Leyland could forecast the severity of the monetary crises of 1808–1809, 1810–1812, 1815 and 1816. John Hughes, in his analysis of Liverpool banking, suggests that Roscoe's anti-slavery stance might have been the causative element. Leyland had been making a fortune from the trade and he might have wished to separate himself from a major player in a campaign that could end it. Hughes also argues that Leyland, having mastered the mysteries of banking in the three years with Clarke and Roscoe, might have thought the time was ripe for him to commence a banking business on his own account. This was confirmed on 10 January 1807 when Leyland commenced business as a banker on his own account in partnership with his nephew, Richard Bullin. In about 1809 Christopher Bullin, Leyland's other nephew, was admitted to the partnership. The bank of Leyland and Bullins survived Leyland's death in 1827 and was amalgamated with the North and South Wales Bank in 1901.[15]

At the end of the Napoleonic Wars in 1816 (ironically, something Roscoe had desired for so long) there was a commercial panic. With its assets tied up, the bank of Roscoe, Clarke and Roscoe found itself unable to meet demands, and notice to this effect appeared in the local press on 1 February 1816. A meeting of the bank's creditors was held at the Great Room of Lillyman's Hotel. According to an account in Gore's *Liverpool Advertiser*, Roscoe produced a statement of the bank's affairs from which it appeared that the bank's debts of £315,000 were covered by its assets to the extent not only of satisfying the creditors but allowing the partners a share in a 'handsome surplus'. Mr Roscoe, it was effusively reported, 'submitted the statement with great feeling, but in a clear, energetic and manly tone. He was received, he was heard, and he retired, accompanied with the strongest testimony of attachment and respect ... a single question was not put to him.'[16] A committee of seven was appointed to investigate the bank's affairs and they confirmed Roscoe's estimation that the debts could all be paid and that there would be an eventual surplus of £61,144. Roscoe drew up a proposal that the bank should be allowed six years, at the end of which all the debts should be discharged. This was accepted by most of the creditors.

The partners immediately set about realizing the assets, but property prices were low and the mines in which the bank had invested heavily turned out to be less valuable than they had estimated. Roscoe realized that in order to meet commitments he would need to sell his private property, and the most easily realizable assets were at once put on the market. These consisted of books, pictures and prints belonging to Roscoe, as well as some valuable pictures belonging to John Clarke. Roscoe set about compiling catalogues of his treasured possessions. In a postscript to her friend Mrs William Rathbone,

Jane Roscoe wrote: 'In the course of the ensuing week, I expect the whole of his books and pictures to be gone and I shall not have the misery of viewing Mr Roscoe's silent submission to the painful duty of dismissing his constant companions of nearly 40 years'.[17] Typically, Roscoe wrote a sonnet on his feelings at parting with his books:

As one who, destined from his Friends to part
Regrets his loss, but hopes again erewhile
To share their converse and enjoy their smile,
And tempers, as he may, affliction's dart –,
Thus, lov'd associates! chiefs of elder art!
Teachers of wisdom! who could once beguile
My tedious hours, and lighten every toil,
I now resign you; not with fainting heart –
For, pass a few short years, or days, or hours,
And happier seasons may their dawn unfold,
And all your sacred fellowship restore;
When, freed from earth, unlimited its powers,
Mind shall with mind direct communion hold,
And kindred spirits meet to part no more.[18]

The printed catalogue of his library listed around 2,000 separate items, although only about 1,800 were actually sold at auctions held over 13 days between 19 August and 3 September. The library realized £5,150. The bulk of Roscoe's pictures remained in his home town (today in the Walker Art Gallery), but many of his books were dispersed and only a few were retained in Liverpool in the Athenaeum. Thomas Coke purchased items from Roscoe's library; many others went to Althorp in Northamptonshire, the home of Lord Spencer.[19] The estates belonging to the partners were also put up for sale, including Allerton Hall.

In the same year it was decided to bring a new partner, William Wardell, into the bank. According to Roscoe, 'for the purpose of separating this from our former concern, and of obtaining additional assistance in our bank, we are negotiating to take into partnership a very respectable young man, who was brought up with us'.[20] The new firm was known as Roscoe, Clarke, Wardell, & Co. but it only lasted until January 1820, when the Roscoes and John Clarke were declared bankrupt.

With the landed estates and mining assets proving slow to sell, in 1820 a commission in bankruptcy was issued against William Roscoe, John Clarke and William Stanley Roscoe. Although the majority of creditors had agreed to accept payment over a period of time and were prepared to wait, a minority of others demanded payment and they resorted to legal proceedings against Roscoe. It was only by the allowance of a certificate of conformity that Roscoe could be protected from his creditors. The required signatures were quickly acquired, but a petition against its allowance was presented to the Chancellor by two individuals who wanted to continue their legal case against him. One of the creditors who refused to agree to a settlement was Charles Blundell of Ince, and Roscoe's friends felt that this was reprehensible behaviour. At the sale of Roscoe's assets, Blundell had commissioned a Roman Catholic priest to bid for over 160 drawings from Roscoe's collection. He obviously coveted the drawings for his personal collection as he kept them bound in albums rather than selling them to recoup his losses. Charles had been estranged from his father Henry who, before his death in 1810, had been on friendly terms with Roscoe; this might have coloured his attitude towards Roscoe. However, much of Blundell's behaviour in other spheres of life showed him to be an eccentric.[21]

Roscoe was forced to leave Liverpool and remain at his farm on Chat Moss between February and April 1820. He was separated from his wife and family, and fear of intimidation forced him to remain indoors. It is likely that this time provided a breathing space to recover from the feelings of personal failure resulting from his bankruptcy. This must have been a worrying time for Jane, particularly as Roscoe appears to have been tempted to spend the remainder of his life at Chat Moss. In a letter to her husband, however, her only concern was for him; 'of my own feelings, in the hope of your returning, I say nothing. You know well, that there is one object in this world, in which all my hopes, fears enjoyments – all my earthly enjoyments, centre.'[22] Roscoe's depression lifted and he decided to return to his old life in Liverpool, his inner turmoil now seemingly overcome. He wrote to Lord Lansdowne: 'The struggle is now over ... in the circle of my own family, the society of my friends and the contracted limits of my literary pursuits, I shall look forward to the enjoyment of as much happiness as it is usual for human life to attain.'[23]

Once his certificate was allowed, Roscoe considered going back into business, but his son Thomas wrote that his age and the state of his health meant that this was not a viable option, and he decided to devote himself to literary work, hoping that he could supplement his income with his writings. Although Roscoe's career as a banker ended in failure, this does not negate his abilities as a businessman. Roscoe's bank was not alone in succumbing to the strains of the post-war economy and it has to be remembered that it was only through the efforts of Roscoe that the bank had survived the death of William Clarke Sr. This was remembered by a later generation of the Clarke family who, having built up their assets again, paid a substantial dividend on the liabilities of the old banking firm of Roscoe, Clarke and Roscoe, in response to which the creditors unanimously agreed to an annulment of the bankruptcy in 1843.[24]

Roscoe is generally portrayed as an idealist, but his lack of private means ensured that he also had to be a realist. Despite having no inherited income he took on the financial support of his father and sister and then his wife and large family. Notwithstanding his expressed dislike of the legal world, Roscoe appears to have made a considerable fortune from the practice of law and was a very successful banker until, together with many others, he suffered in the economic strains imposed by over twenty years of war. He was prepared to invest in projects such as mining and land reclamation, and interestingly his commercial instincts did not apply only to business but also to the arts. Roscoe's bankruptcy was not a sign of his inadequacies as a businessman but more a sign of the economic instability of the times. His ability to combine his business career with his literary, artistic and political interests is surely something to be lauded rather than denigrated or ignored. He became a living symbol to his fellow townsmen (and the world at large) that culture was not the preserve of the independently wealthy who could afford to eschew any connection with the grubby world of money-making; rather, it was open to all. That in the year 2008 Liverpool is again seeking to combine its economic and cultural profiles for the benefit of all its citizens is a testament of the successful diffusion of his ideas down to later generations.

# CHAPTER 8

## *Towards Immortality*

Somebody has said, that a king may make a nobleman but he cannot make a gentleman.[1]

Although Roscoe's later years were to an extent clouded by his bankruptcy, he worked hard at building a new life albeit in somewhat straitened circumstances and minus his most treasured possessions. His religious beliefs were a comfort to him and shortly after his return from Chat Moss, he and some of his friends published a new edition of the hymnal used by the worshippers at Renshaw Street Chapel. After the sale of Allerton Hall he lived at Rake Lane (now Durning Road) and at 5 St James's Walk (now the site of the Anglican Cathedral) before moving in 1822 to a house in Lodge Lane, where he remained until his death in 1831. The affection in which he was held by his friends is demonstrated by their collection (without Roscoe's knowledge) of £2,500, which was invested in trusts for the benefit of himself and his family.

In 1824 Roscoe was devastated by the death of his beloved Jane, who had suffered several years of declining health. Even after forty years of married life Roscoe still wrote love poems to her:

Some forty years, or more, are fled,
Unless through age my memory falter,
Since Love our youthful footsteps led
And join'd our hands at Hymen's alter.

Through all the long succeeding scene,
Of sunshine days and stormy weather,
Where'er our changeful lot has been.
Our days have still roll'd on together.

And whilst to joys and sorrows past,
I turn with varying recollection,
O'er all one brighter tint is cast,
Of constant love and kind affection.[2]

We do not know a lot about Jane, but she appears to have been liked by all who knew her. On meeting the couple in 1813, the writer Maria Edgeworth remarked in a letter that 'Mrs Roscoe is an honest-faced, fat, *hearty*, good natured body, without the least pretensions to polish, but with a downright plain good understanding and uncommonly warm heart'. The affection the couple shared was clear to see: 'she seems to adore her husband, and to be so fond of her children'. Although she makes fun of Jane's 'broad Lancashire dialect', in a later letter she berates herself for being unkind and overly critical; 'It is true she is not polished and I was struck with it at the moment much more than I ought. She was most hospitable and kind to me, to all of us and the *real strong impression left upon my* mind was of her *goodness* – her openheartedness – her independence of spirit which treated Duke of Gloucester and Prince of Wales with less attention than the friends she loved.'[3] In a letter to Dr Wallich shortly after her death Roscoe speaks movingly of the happiness they had enjoyed and the comfort he was finding in his children. Roscoe's own health became increasingly precarious and prevented any return to the business world (which, perhaps surprisingly, he had contemplated), and the last eleven years of his life were mainly devoted to literary pursuits.

From his youth, Roscoe had been an admirer of the works

of Alexander Pope, who, like himself, lacked a formal education. Thus when he was approached in 1821 by a group of
London booksellers who designated themselves the
'Proprietors of Pope' to compile a new edition of Pope's works
to replace those now out of print (Warton, 1797 and Bowles,
1806), he had no hesitation in accepting the commission.
Originally scheduled to appear in the course of 1822 in order
to forestall a rival edition, Roscoe's ten-volume *Works of
Alexander Pope*, which included a *New Life of Pope*, was
finally published with many delays in July 1824. This edition
(the third major one in less than thirty years) came at a time
when the reputation of Augustan poets was undergoing a
serious crisis and that of Pope, in particular, had become the
centre of a vociferous, critical debate.[4] It was Roscoe's belief
that the main object of the new edition was a fuller and more
accurate life of Pope. He also felt that previous editors, in
particular Bowles, had been unfair to Pope, claiming that
Bowles appeared to have approached his task with strong feelings of prejudice against the character of Pope, whose
reputation has suffered more at his hands than at those of any
of his predecessors. However, Roscoe was equally prejudiced
in favour of his subject.

It was Pope's moral character as much as the merits of his
poetry that Roscoe enthusiastically set out to defend, and he
accepted that although he would find enjoyment in this task,
'it will not be possible to avoid a considerable share of controversy, which, however, I am fully prepared to meet'. In his
edition, Roscoe did not include every poem written by Pope
as he felt that the chief duty of an editor was 'to execute an
office which the author can no longer perform for himself ...
admitting nothing that he would himself have rejected, and
rejecting nothing that he would have admitted'.[5] Propriety, in
fact, played such an important role in Roscoe's thinking that
he had no qualms about omitting even major poems if he felt
that this was necessary for the sake of Pope's reputation. He

was determined 'to give such an edition as may once more be introduced to the Drawing Room and Toilette'.[6] He specifically excluded *Sober Advice from Horace*, *Three Hours after Marriage*, and the episode of the Double Mistress in the *Memoirs of Martin Scriblerus*. He professed to finding it 'unaccountable' that Warton and Bowles should ever have 'disgraced their editions' by printing these works.[7]

Roscoe used three letters written by Pope to Samuel Richardson to defend Pope against the charge that he 'had acknowledged himself an unbeliever in Christianity'. Roscoe asserted that 'Pope himself told us that he was neither Papist nor Protestant, but something between the two' and that 'he held in abhorrence the uncharitable doctrine, by whatever sect advanced, which pretends to limit within its own pale, the universal goodness of God'. These sentiments held much appeal to the Unitarian Roscoe.[8]

Although Roscoe's edition has fared badly over the years, contemporary critics were more favourable. The *Quarterly Review* declared that

> Mr Roscoe's selection from his predecessors is also copious and judicious ... His original criticism is not much, but is enlightened and liberal and the candour with which that and the life are written is quite refreshing after the blighting perversity of the preceding editors, whose misrepresentations and calumnies he had industriously examined and patiently refuted. Great industry is exhibited in the superior arrangement of his materials.

The critic suggests that there was an element of plagiarism in Roscoe's work: 'he has without ceremony taken much of what is valuable in Mr Bowles' book to add to the value of his own'.[9] This fact was probably responsible for some of the resentment that Bowles felt towards Roscoe. The accusation that Bowles had taken a malicious pleasure in vilifying Pope's character must have further added to this resentment, and a war of words broke out between the two men.

Not long after the publication of Roscoe's work, Bowles published a booklet entitled *A Final Appeal to the Literary Public, in Reply to certain Observations of Mr Roscoe in his Edition of the Works of Pope*. Roscoe's reply goaded Bowles into another publication, *Lessons in Criticism to William Roscoe Esq. F.R.S., Member of the Della Crusca Society of Florence F.R.S.L., in Answer to his Letter to the Rev. W.L. Bowles on the Character and Poetry of Pope*. Although Roscoe drafted a further letter in response, he opted for discretion and decided against sending, preferring to 'leave it to the public, if the public should yet interest themselves in a contest which has subsisted for a century, to decide between us'.[10]

Roscoe's interest in all gifted individuals regardless of their station in life was demonstrated in 1822 when he published a memoir of Richard Robert Jones, a destitute, self-taught linguist of Aberdaron. The fisherman, described as 'ragged as a colt', had taught himself Greek, Hebrew and Latin in addition to French and Italian. He could translate Latin into English or Welsh with ease. Although a prodigy, he appeared to lack any common sense and had no interest in personal hygiene or in his appearance. He had no permanent abode and carried a small library of books between his shirt and his skin. On first hearing about the young man, Roscoe had made him welcome at Allerton. In an interview with Dr Parr, a don at Oxford, Richard clearly had the upper hand and Parr 'rather precipitately retreated, leaving a token of liberality in the hands of the poor scholar'. When asked afterwards for his opinion on the learned doctor, Richard declared 'He is less ignorant than most men'.[11] Roscoe donated the proceeds of *A Story of Richard* to the young man and also wrote a sonnet in his honour. Although able to afford better clothes than before, Richard still travelled about with his small library stuffed inside them.[12]

Roscoe's friendship with Thomas Coke led him to become involved in the cataloguing of the manuscripts in Holkham's library. Coke's library was created by his ancestors Sir Edward Coke and Thomas Coke, first Earl of Leicester. Although 'properly arranged on their shelves in the library', the manuscripts were still in their original covers, and were rarely looked at.[13] Roscoe had first visited Holkham in 1814 after receiving several letters from his friend Sir James Smith alerting him to the treasures that were to be found there. In October 1814 Smith told him how on one visit he had discovered 'a most exquisite Boccacio, a very fine and old Dante, a Chronique de Henault ... a very fine collection of historical Italian Manuscripts fairly copied at Florence, Venice etc. for Lord Leicester ... [and] a complete copy of Burchard's Diary'.[14] Roscoe was unable to resist, and went to Holkham. He remained there until December 1814, and it was in Coke's library that he found one of the last volumes of Leonardo da Vinci's treatises on mechanics and a volume in Raphael's handwriting on Roman remains.[15] Roscoe was 'gratified beyond expression at the opportunity of examining at his leisure so rich and various a collection of literary treasures'. He persuaded Coke to have the manuscripts bound and offered to draw up a brief catalogue for them. In February 1815 Coke sent the first lot of manuscripts to Liverpool to be bound. Coke was very impressed by Roscoe, writing to Sir James Smith: 'the more I saw of him, the more I was delighted with the benevolence of his mind, the rectitude and liberality of his principles, as well as with his superior acquirements'.[16]

Coke was among the first to offer sympathy to Roscoe when the bank failed. He paid a large sum for five of Roscoe's pictures at the auction of Roscoe's effects, and was among the group of friends who purchased some of Roscoe's books and tried (unavailingly) to persuade Roscoe to accept them as a gift. At Roscoe's suggestion Coke bought a number of books for the library at Holkham, and one manuscript, which

Roscoe thought '*indispensable* to give a character of importance to any great collection'.[17]

Roscoe's business troubles precluded any serious work on
the manuscripts, but in 1820 he was persuaded by Coke to
return to Holkham to prepare the manuscript catalogue for
publication. Coke's intention was that this should not only be
a monument to his manuscripts but also a gesture of sympathy
to Roscoe, who was to receive the profits and whose portrait
was to be on the frontispiece.[18] Roscoe found the work difficult, telling his friend John McCreery that it was a task 'I
certainly should not have undertaken had I been aware of its
extent and difficulty'.[19] From 1820 until 1824 Roscoe worked
on the catalogue, visiting Holkham in the autumn of 1821 and
again in 1823. This was not the only call on his time in this
period. He was involved with his work on Pope, and in 1821
he was finishing his *Illustrations of the Life of Lorenzo*. He
was also considering editing a volume of Italian writers
(although this never came to fruition) and was writing on
penal reform.

The catalogue was beset by delays and finally Frederic
Madden was employed as co-adjutor. The relationship
between Roscoe and Madden (schooled in the Tower Record
Office) is illustrative of the gulf between the amateur and the
professional. Madden was ambitious and regarded the catalogue as a great opportunity to make his reputation and
advance his prospects at the British Museum. He arrived at
Holkham in March 1826, but Roscoe was unable to meet him
there due to ill-health. Madden was scathing about Roscoe's
work: 'I find Roscoe has committed so many blunders that
scarcely any manuscript is even *lettered* properly... Mr
Roscoe is perfectly ignorant of the *age* of manuscripts and
deceives himself completely in respect to the Homer'.[20]
Madden worked hard on the catalogue and sent it to Roscoe
in April 1826 with preliminary corrections. Although Roscoe
initially declared himself to be 'highly gratified' he soon came

to the conclusion that Madden had exceeded the original intention, which was to give an account that would be of interest to the public at large rather than to a circle of esoteric academics. Madden's version would also entail considerably higher expenditure than Coke and Roscoe had envisioned. Roscoe decided to halt the proceedings temporarily, a delay compounded when he became ill with paralysis. Madden was furious, as he considered himself to be a joint editor rather than an assistant, and he was tempted to refuse to finish the work. However, Coke used his influence to have him appointed sub-keeper of the manuscripts in the British Museum and Madden felt obliged to continue. By now, however, Coke's interest had waned and neither he nor Roscoe was prepared to send to press a catalogue so entirely different to their original conception. Eventually *Bibliotheca Holkhamensis* was bound in eight quarto volumes with its many facsimiles, engravings and specimens of colour prints, and sent to Holkham in 1829. It was placed in a room which Coke – in his early enthusiasm for the project – had adapted especially for the manuscripts, and adorned with a portrait of Roscoe.[21] Although it was an invaluable addition to the library, it had been a task beyond Roscoe's capabilities and had caused him many sleepless nights.

According to George Chandler, it was the monograph *Monandrian Plants of the Order Scitamineae* that was the 'most distinguished labour of Roscoe's old age'.[22] Although by this time he had suffered from several strokes, it is the book for which he is best known among botanists. He commissioned watercolour illustrations of the members of the ginger family as they came into flower, and also made use of drawings by unknown Chinese artists from the library of the thirteenth Earl of Derby. In addition he had considerable assistance from his daughter-in-law, Mrs Edward Roscoe. The completed work contained illustrations of 112 different species and varieties never previously collected in a single work. It was an early effort at imposing a 'natural system' of classification on a group that had previously been seen as an artificial assemblage defined by the flower's solitary anther. It also used lithography, an innovative method of reproducing illustrations that was just beginning to be adopted in Britain. The work appeared in fifteen parts between 1824 and 1828. It received excellent reviews, one stating that it was 'the most splendid work ever issued from a provincial press'.[23] Roscoe's contribution to the science of botany is still highly regarded today. In 2005 the University of Liverpool Art Gallery was the venue for the exhibition 'A Growing Concern: William Roscoe and Liverpool's first botanical garden'.

In 1827 Roscoe's friends and family grew increasingly concerned about his health. He suffered a stroke, losing the use of his right arm and suffering paralysis to the side of his face, which affected his speech. According to his physician Dr Traill, he recovered his faculties after being copiously bled, a treatment that Roscoe had a decided aversion to and had not submitted to since his youth. Roscoe's mental powers were unaffected and he was able to continue with his writings and to welcome friends old and new to his home in Lodge Lane.[24]

Among his visitors was J.J. Audubon, the American ornithologist and bird artist, who, having completed his portfolio of paintings and drawings for his *Birds of America* travelled to England from Louisiana in order to exhibit and publish them. He arrived in Liverpool in July 1826 with letters of introduction, including one to Richard Rathbone who suggested that Roscoe would be a valuable contact. Rathbone duly arranged a dinner party where the two men met, and the following day Audubon visited Roscoe at Lodge Lane. Audubon's drawings were exhibited at the Royal Institution, where he was allowed a room free of charge, initially for two hours a day for three days. In total he exhibited 235 drawings, with over 400 people attending on the last day. They excited so much interest that Audubon was persuaded to extend until September and also, very reluctantly, to charge an entry fee. He declared 'although I am poor enough, God knows ... I could not ... think it consistent to become a mere *showman* and give up the title of *J.J. Audubon, Naturalist'*. Interestingly, the man who persuaded him to change his opinion and clear his mind of what he described as the 'tormenting thought ' of the 'discredit' of exhibiting pictures for money was William Roscoe.[25] This is a clear illustration that Roscoe was not blind to the commercial aspects of art and that although he believed that artists should prove themselves worthy of patronage, those that did so should expect adequate recompense for their talents. Some years after his death, one of his fellow citizens recalled Roscoe's attitude to the arts; 'the late Mr Roscoe had spoken of the benefits derivable from their pursuit, even in a commercial point of view, and referred to the late Benjamin West, who by his skill, and a few weeks' industry, made a piece of canvas, which cost only a few shillings, sell for three thousand guineas'.[26]

The entrance fee was a shilling. Audubon earned £100 and in gratitude he gave the institution a large painting of a turkey-cock; William Roscoe received a drawing of a robin. He wrote to Roscoe on 8 September, 'My fate will force me Sunday morning to leave Liverpool and all the kind persons ... but I hope it will also be my good fortune to be enabled not to forget them as long as I live'.[27] From Liverpool, Audubon travelled to Manchester which he did not find as welcoming. He declared, 'the population appears denser and worse off than in Liverpool. The vast number of youth of both sexes, with shallow complexions, ragged apparel, and downcast looks made me feel they were not as happy as the slaves of Louisiana.'[28] At first he showed his paintings at the Manchester Exchange and was again granted the room free. Attendances were poor and after a fortnight he transferred it to a room in King Street. He left Manchester remarking sadly in his diary that he went away poorer than he had arrived.

Liverpool had proved a far more successful and friendly venue.[29]

A close friendship developed between the Italian Anthony Panizzi (1797–1879) and Roscoe. Panizzi fled to Liverpool after the 1821 revolution in Greece and earned a living teaching Italian. He soon came to the notice of Roscoe. The two men spent much time together and their relationship, according to Henry Roscoe, was similar to that of father and son. When Panizzi was appointed to the Professorship of Italian Literature at University College London, Roscoe felt the loss of his company deeply but took pleasure in giving him introductions to his friends. In 1831 Panizzi was appointed assistant librarian and later chief librarian at the British Museum where he undertook a new catalogue and designed the famous Reading Room. He was later knighted.[30]

Another visitor was the Indian religious reformer Rammohun Roy (1774–1833), who is often referred to as the father of modern India. Born in Bengal of high Brahman ancestry, he questioned his faith early. In 1820 he published *The Precepts of Jesus*, accepting the morality preached by Christ although rejecting his deity and miracles. He intended to recommend Christianity to his countrymen and set up a printing press in Calcutta (now Kolkata) at which his own work and other books designed to spread the Christian faith were published. Roscoe was intrigued by the book, as it mirrored some of the ideas that he had put forward in the book written in his youth, *Christian Morality as contained in the Precepts of the New Testament – In the Language of Jesus Christ*. Roscoe admired Rammohun Roy's concern for his people's welfare and his work in extending education in India, and he decided to contact him. He persuaded a young friend bound for India to take a letter and a selection of his writings to Rammohun Roy. However, before this reached India Rammohun Roy was on his way to Liverpool, where he attracted much attention. The two men were delighted to meet, Roscoe declaring: 'I bless God that I have been permitted to live to see this day', and Rammohun Roy claiming himself to be 'proud and happy to behold a man whose fame has extended not only over Europe but over the whole world'. Unfortunately, his stay in Liverpool was short as Roy wished to be present at the reading of the Reform Act and at debates on India. He left Liverpool with a letter of introduction to Lord Brougham, who took an interest in him.

Roscoe was delighted to receive a visit from the Liverpool-born poet Felicia Hemans (1793–1835). She is most remembered for her poem, *Casabianca*, which begins 'The boy stood on the burning deck'. (The poem captured the imagination of later generations of Liverpool children who chanted it in the schoolyard, albeit with a slight alteration of wording.)[31] She left a vivid description of Roscoe in his later years.

> He is a delightful old man, with a fine Roman style of head, which he had adorned with a green velvet cap to receive me in; because, as he playfully said, 'he knew I always admired him in it'. Altogether he put me in mind of one of Rembrandt's pictures; and as he sat in his quiet study, surrounded by busts, and books, and flowers, and with a beautiful cast of Canova's Psyche in the background, I thought that a painter, who wished to make old age look touching and venerable, could not have had a better subject.[32]

Shortly before his death, Roscoe was visited by the distinguished German art historian and museum curator, Johann David Passavant (1787–1861). As part of his research for his great work on Raphael (which finally appeared in 1839), Passavant had come to England searching for paintings, drawings and unpublished papers by his subject. He had heard (wrongly) that Roscoe had some original letters by Raphael and was also anxious to meet one of the few English art historians of the early nineteenth century. There were similarities in the lives of the two men; both had begun their careers in the business world and had devoted many years to improving the cultural infrastucture of their home town. However, unlike Roscoe, Passavant had freed himself from business commitments at a young age and spent four years studying in Paris and seven years studying in Italy. He was surprised to discover that Roscoe had never travelled outside Britain. Passavant had spent eight years researching his book on Raphael and the best part of nineteen years on its appendix volume, and has been described as the first serious art historian. He can be seen as representative of the new professional attitude towards historical studies that came to the fore in the nineteenth century, in contrast to Roscoe, whose broad intellectual interests marked him out as the last of the traditional eighteenth-century amateur historians. Despite their different approaches, Passavant was impressed by his host, writing: 'His memory will always be sacred to me, and I am only thankful that the opportunity was granted me of knowing one who inspired affection and respect alike to all who, whether intimately or remotely, enjoyed that privilege'.[33]

Roscoe appears to have been prepared for death and confided that

> he thanked God, the Almighty for having permitted him to pass a life of much happiness, which, though somewhat chequered by vicissitude, had been on the whole one of great enjoyment; and he trusted that he should be enabled cheerfully to resign it whenever it pleased God to call him... in this tranquil and happy frame of mind he continued to the last.[34]

When a severe outbreak of influenza hit Liverpool, the frail Roscoe fell victim and he died on 30 June 1831. He was interred in the burial ground of Renshaw Street Chapel on 7 July, his old friend William Shepherd conducting the funeral service. The chapel is no more but Roscoe's bones, uniquely, were allowed to remain in a corner of the small garden on Mount Pleasant. He was survived by six of his sons and two daughters. Liverpool was only too anxious to claim him as its own:

> The Learned of all countries have heard with surprise that Liverpool, once only known for its commercial wealth, and its local and political importance, has given birth to the most distinguished of the historians of Europe: and that, from this great mercantile city, as from a second Florence, have issued works which have shed light upon the most important era in the annals of Italy... Here he has lived and here he has died: here he commenced his literary labours, and pursued and perfected his historical researches.[35]

# Conclusion

> Scientific and Literary pursuits are not only consistent with our more serious associations, but ... have a direct and manifest tendency to promote the welfare and exalt the character of every community into which they have been introduced.[1]

Contemporary reports indicate that Liverpool's image underwent a transformation under the guiding hand of William Roscoe even if, as one jaundiced commentator remarked, 'In the opinion of strangers, Liverpool has acquired a character for literary pre-eminence which, on a more strict enquiry, would probably be found to rest on no very solid pretensions'.[2] But, as later citizens of Liverpool have found to their cost, whether this image was myth rather than reality is immaterial; it is the perceptions of the world at large that are important.

Liverpool's astute merchants were quick to recognize that cultural forms and practices were key in determining and reinforcing their social status. Although commerce remained their foremost driving force in eighteenth century this did not entirely preclude embryonic attempts to acquire some of the characteristics of civilized living. To view the town as a barren cultural wilderness and to accept a generalized view of the merchant community as cultural philistines would be a mistake. However, it has to be accepted that formal learned societies which required intellectual effort as well as monetary input were not well received and their lifespans were brief. By the last quarter of the eighteenth century, any cultural ambitions harboured by Liverpool appeared to be floundering. However, at the turn of the century there was a marked change. As with earlier initiatives, the need to construct a cultural profile consonant with the town's economic status played its part but it is also reasonable to suppose that the association of Liverpool's wealth with slavery added an extra dimension. The successful launch of some of Liverpool's lasting cultural institutions in this period supports Stobart's theory that the town may well have experienced not one urban renaissance but two.[3] Under the guidance of William Roscoe the merchant community appears to have rebranded not only the town's image but its own. For the essayist and critic William Hazlitt, it was Manchester rather than Liverpool that was unabashedly philistine. Drawing on his experience of life in both towns, and although he disliked both, he claimed to prefer Manchester, because there:

> You are oppressed only by the aristocracy of wealth; in the latter (Liverpool) by the aristocracy of wealth and letters by turns. You could not help feeling that some of their great men were authors among merchants and merchants among authors. Their bread was buttered on both sides and they had you at a disadvantage either way.[4]

This differentiation was further confirmed by an old stage-coachman who gravely described his 'insides' as 'a Liverpool gentleman, a Manchester man, a Bolton chap and a Wigan fellow'.[5]

The circumstances of the times certainly played their part in the flowering of Liverpool's intellectual life from the late 1790s but Liverpool was fortunate to have such a man as William Roscoe at that particular point in its history. Roscoe has sometimes been seen as something of a dreamer; just as he shut his eyes to some of the more unsavoury aspects of Lorenzo's rule, so too he may have shut his eyes to the reasons behind the merchants' support. However, it can be argued that he shared some of the traits of his fellow-citizens and he was far more of a realist and pragmatist than is generally supposed. He was prepared to accept the merchants' qualified support (and money) in the belief that the 'civilizing effects of the arts' would ultimately triumph. By allowing the merchants to identify with the princes of Renaissance Florence, Roscoe ensured not only his position as cultural leader, but also a permanent place in the pantheon of Liverpool's 'greats'.

Roscoe was one of the last of the great eighteenth-century amateurs, a generalist rather than a specialist. His personal reputation may have been enhanced had he chosen to concentrate on one of his many talents, but Liverpool, it can be argued, would have been the poorer. He encouraged every project that he believed was for the public good, and his loyalty to his family and his native town was second to none. Although a writer and a thinker, as David Alton rightly states, he was not 'simply long on words and short on actions'.[6] The Athenaeum remains in the city today and has many of Roscoe's books in its library. The societies inaugurated by Roscoe are no more, but his belief in the efficacy of such organizations inspired others to take their place.[7] Paintings from his collection hang in the Walker Art Gallery to be freely enjoyed by all of Liverpool's citizens. His support for the abolition of slavery and his vote for the Abolition Bill in the House of Commons told the world at large that not everyone in Liverpool was motivated solely by commercial considerations. Most importantly, Roscoe was a self-made man for whom earning a living to support his large family was a necessity rather than a choice. His ability to combine the worlds of business and culture made him a role model not only in Liverpool but in other commercial cities. Roscoe, it has been claimed, was always cited as an example to be followed by the Bristol merchant classes.[8]

It is true that part of Roscoe's success lay in the fact that he was simply the best man in the right place at the right time, but this should not detract from an appreciation of his many talents and the legacy that he left not only to his native town but to the wider world. Of course Roscoe had his imperfections. For him, the diffusion of the arts among his fellow citizens was essentially a moral quest, which tended to make him appear somewhat pompous and humourless. He was given to enthusiasms for his subjects which at times clouded his judgement, and he was reluctant to travel abroad, which meant relying on others for his primary research. He disliked being parted from his wife and family, which made him nervous and depressed during his early days in Parliament; he was overly sensitive to criticism, which made him turn away from his historical writings. His deep affection for his native town may have coloured his interpretation of Medici Florence, and he identified too closely with its ruler. Yet despite these reservations William Roscoe undoubtedly stands as a cultural linchpin in the development of Liverpool.

The fact that the city still celebrates Roscoe's life and achievements shows that his legacy has endured. The importance of Liverpool's selection as European capital of culture in boosting the city's image and economy is surely confirmation that we are witnessing a return to the cultural values of (and the value placed on culture by) William Roscoe. The historian of Liverpool James Picton is right to claim that 'no native resident of Liverpool has done more to elevate the character of the community, by uniting the successful pursuit of literature and the arts with the ordinary duties of the citizen and man of business'.[9] This belief in the union of commerce and culture was William Roscoe's greatest legacy to his native town.

# Notes

## Introduction

1  W. Irving, *Sketch of William Roscoe* (Liverpool, 1853), p. 14.

2  H. Roscoe, *The Life of William Roscoe by his Son Henry Roscoe* (London, 1833), vol. 1, p. 162.

3  Quoted in J. Willett, *Art in a City* (London, 1967), p. 24.

4  E. L. Griggs (ed.), *Unpublished Letters of Samuel Taylor Coleridge* (London, 1932), vol. 1, p. 149. Coleridge to Samuel Purkis, 29 July 1800.

5  J. Ramsay Muir, *A History of Liverpool* (Liverpool, 1907), p. 293.

6  D. Alton, 'William Roscoe: a true son of Liverpool', www.davidalton.co.uk/William Roscoe.

7  J. Belchem (ed.), *Liverpool 800: Culture, Character and History* (Liverpool, 2006), pp. 7–8, 16.

8  *Liverpool Town Book 1804–1815*, 6 April 1815, p. 503.

9  E. Morris, 'William Roscoe and Medici Florence', in P. Starkey (ed.), *Riches into Art: Liverpool Collectors 1770–1880* (Liverpool, 1993), p. 11.

10  J. Stobart, 'Culture versus commerce: societies and spaces for elites in eighteenth-century Liverpool', *Journal of Historical Geography*, 28, 4 (2002), pp. 473, 482.

## Chapter 1: Cometh the Hour, Cometh the Man

1  J. Wallace, *A General and Descriptive History of the Antient and Present State of the Town of Liverpool* (Liverpool, 1795), p. 191.

2  Belchem (ed.), *Liverpool 800*, p. 61.

3  D.J. Pope, 'Shipping and trade in the port of Liverpool 1783–1793', unpublished PhD thesis, University of Liverpool, 1970, pp. 1–5.

4   R.C. Jarvis, 'The head port of Chester; and Liverpool, its creek and member', *THSLC*, 102 (1951), p. 73.

5   Pope, 'Shipping and trade', p. 3.

6   Pope, 'Shipping and trade', p. 4.

7   C. Northcote Parkinson, *The Rise of the Port of Liverpool* (Liverpool, 1952), p. 42.

8   Parkinson, *The Rise of the Port*, p. 29.

9   G. Chandler, *Liverpool Under James 1st* (Liverpool, 1960), p. 9. The original streets were Water, Dale, Chapel, Tithebarn, Old Hall, Castle and High Street.

10   Parkinson, *The Rise of the Port*, p. 84.

11   W. Minchinton, 'The port of Bristol in the eighteenth century', in P. McGrath (ed.), *Bristol in the Eighteenth Century* (Newton Abbot, 1972), p. 134.

12   P. Marcy, 'Eighteenth century views of Bristol and Bristolians', in P. McGrath (ed.), *Bristol in the Eighteenth Century*, pp. 14–16.

13   W. Moss, *The Liverpool Guide; including a sketch of the environs; with a map of Liverpool* (Liverpool, 1796), p. 1

14   S. Marriner, *The Economic and Social Development of Merseyside* (London, 1982), p. 11.

15   T.C. Barker, 'Lancashire coal, Cheshire salt and the rise of Liverpool', *THSLC*, 103 (1952), p. 1.

16   Parkinson, *The Rise of the Port*, p. 2.

17   See D. Ascott, F. Lewis and M. Power, *Liverpool 1660–1750: People, Prosperity and Power* (Liverpool, 2006).

18   A.Wilson, 'Commerce and culture: Liverpool's merchant elite c.1790–1850', unpublished PhD thesis, University of Liverpool, 1996, p. 13.

19   T. Heywood (ed.), *The Moore Rental* (Manchester, 1847), p. 77.

20   *Gore's Liverpool Directory* (Liverpool, 1790).

21   T. Fletcher, *Autobiographical Memoirs of Thomas Fletcher of Liverpool (obit 1850); Written in the year 1843* (Liverpool, 1893), p. 33.

22   Quoted in Parkinson, *The Rise of the Port*, p. 75.

23   S. D. Behrendt, 'The captains in the British slave trade from 1785 to 1807', *THSLC*, 140 (1990), pp. 111–12.

24   G. Williams, *History of the Liverpool Privateers and Letters of Marque with an Account of the Liverpool Slave Trade* (London, 1897), p. 485.

25  M. J. Power, 'The growth of Liverpool', in J. Belchem (ed.), *Popular Politics, Riot and Labour: Essays in Liverpool History 1790–1940* (Liverpool, 1992), pp. 25–26; Pope, 'Shipping and trade', p. 451.

26  F. E. Sanderson, 'The structure of politics in Liverpool 1780–1807', *THSLC*, 127 (1978), p. 66.

27  S. G. Checkland, 'Economic attitudes in Liverpool 1793–1807', *Economic History Review*, 5 (1952–1953), p. 65.

28  Sanderson, 'The structure of politics', p. 67.

29  S. Drescher, 'The slaving capital of the world: Liverpool and national opinion in the age of abolition', *Slavery and Abolition*, 9, 2 (1988), p. 131.

30  Checkland, 'Economic attitudes', p. 58.

31  'State of society and manners in Liverpool, by Rev. William Shepherd', *Monthly Magazine*, 67, 1 January 1801, in *Holt and Gregson Papers: Materials towards a History of Liverpool Collected by John Holt and Matthew Gregson*, 5, LVRO, 942 HOL, Fq2091.

32  F. Hyde, *Liverpool and the Mersey: The Development of a Port 1700–1970* (Newton Abbot, 1971), p. 25.

33  P. Borsay, *The English Urban Renaissance: Culture and Society in the Provincial Towns 1660–1770* (Oxford, 1989).

34  J. Longmore, 'Civic Liverpool: 1680–1800', in Belchem (ed.), *Liverpool 800*, p. 140.

35  T. Troughton, *The History of Liverpool From the Earliest Authenticated Period Down to the Present Time* (Liverpool, c.1810), p. 286.

36  Quoted in J.R. Muir, *A History of Liverpool*, second ed. (London, 1907), p. 186.

37  R. Brooke, *Liverpool As It Was During the Last Quarter of the Eighteenth Century, 1775–1800* (Liverpool, 1853), pp. 86–88, 263–69.

38  W. Enfield, *Essay Towards the History of Liverpool* (Warrington, 1773), p. 21.

39  I. Taylor, 'Black spot on the Mersey: a study of environment and society in eighteenth and nineteenth century Liverpool', unpublished PhD thesis, University of Liverpool, 1976, pp. 29–36.

40  Moss, *The Liverpool Guide*, p.19.

41  Analysis from *Gore's Liverpool Directory, 1790*.

42  Enfield, *Essay*, p. 114.

43 Taylor, 'Black spot', p. 36.
44 J. Aikin, *A Description of the Country from Thirty to Forty Miles Round Manchester* (London, 1795; reprinted Newton Abbot, 1968), p. 331.
45 Aikin, *A Description*, p. 376.
46 T. Baines, *History of the Commerce and Town of Liverpool* (London, 1852), p. 475.
47 *Records Relating to Ye Ugly Face Club 1743–1757*, LVRO, 367/UGL Acc.502/1/1. See also E. Howell, *Ye Ugly Face Club, Leverpoole 1743–1757: A Verbatim Reprint From the Original Mss, in the Collection of the Late Joseph Mayer* (Liverpool, 1912).
48 *Liverpool Unanimous Society 1753–1778*, LVRO, 367/UNA/1. A full account of the club is given in Brooke, *Liverpool As It Was*, pp. 290–98.
49 Pope, 'Shipping and trade', p. 460.
50 P. Langford, *Public Life and the Propertied Englishman 1689–1798* (Oxford, 1991), pp. 218–19.
51 E. Horley, 'The Mock Corporation of Sefton', *THSLC*, 33 (1880–1881), pp. 233–246; 34 (1881–1882), pp. 25–38; E.B. Saxton, 'Early records of the Mock Corporation of Sefton', *THSLC*, 100 (1949), pp. 73–89.
52 Branches of the society appear to have existed in other towns, the most numerous being in London. *Peter Entwistle Collection of Materials for a History of Liverpool Potteries*, LVRO, 942 ENT/Fq 2572.
53 Pope, 'Shipping and trade', pp. 454–56.
54 *Holt and Gregson Papers*, p. 12.
55 N. McKendrick, J. Brewer and J.H. Plumb, *The Birth of a Consumer Society: The Commercialization of Eighteenth-century England* (London, 1982), p. 277.
56 See R. Porter, *English Society in the Eighteenth Century* (Harmondsworth, 1990), pp. 223–24.
57 J. Stonehouse, 'Dramatic places of amusement in Liverpool a century ago', *THSLC*, 5 (1852–1853), p. 194.
58 R.J. Broadbent, *Annals of the Liverpool Stage; From the Earliest Period to the Present Time* (Liverpool, 1908), p. 36.
59 Brooke, *Liverpool As It Was*, pp. 84–85.
60 Arthur C. Wardle, 'Liverpool's First Theatre Royal', *THSLC*, 90 (1939), pp. 207–09.

61 Broadbent, *Annals*, p. 55.
62 *Holt and Gregson Papers*, p. 24.
63 Brooke, *Liverpool As It Was*, pp. 270–73.
64 Troughton, *The History of Liverpool*, p. 326.
65 D. Wainwright, *Liverpool Gentlemen: A History of Liverpool College, an Independent Day School from 1840* (London, 1940), p. 20.
66 Quoted in Porter, *English Society*, p. 240.
67 T. Kelly, *Adult Education in Liverpool: A Narrative of Two Hundred Years* (Liverpool, 1960), pp. 9–10.
68 *Papers of William Heaton Wakefield (1861–1936)*, 5, LRO 942 WAK. acc.0137. T. Kelly, *Adult Education*, p. 12.
69 Kelly, *Adult Education*, p. 86.
70 Kelly, *Adult Education*, p. 90.
71 It also included five brewers, five drapers, four attorneys, one physician, three surgeons, four schoolmasters and seven gentlemen. S. Murphy, 'The Liverpool Library 1758–1941: its foundation, organisation and development', unpublished MA thesis, University of Sheffield, 1983, Appendix 1, pp. 90–92. In the 1781 Chamber of Commerce, half of the twenty positions were held by library members (Murphy, 'The Liverpool Library', p. 34).
72 *A Catalogue of the Present Collection of Books in the Liverpool Library: To Which is Prefixed a Copy of the Laws and a List of the Subscribers* (Liverpool, 1760), pp. 3–4.
73 H. Melville, *Redburn: His First Voyage: Being the Sailorboy Confessions and Reminiscences of the Son-of-a-Gentleman in the Merchant Service*, ed. H. Beaver (London, 1986), p. 285.
74 The others were Mrs Elizabeth Heywood, Mrs Elizabeth Lawrenson and Mrs Margaret Pettie.
75 Murphy, 'The Liverpool Library', pp. 38–39.
76 Kelly, *Adult Education*, pp. 7–8.
77 For example, 12 March 1782, 'On the Human Mind'; 3 April 1782, 'On Architecture'; 3 May 1782, 'On the Merits of Biography'. *Holt and Gregson Papers*, p. 10.
78 *Holt and Gregson Papers*, p. 10.
79 Kelly, *Adult Education*, p. 11.
80 *The Liverpolitan*, 6, 10 (October 1937), p. 9.
81 For a full account of the early art societies, see Chapter 5.
82 Wallace, *The Town of Liverpool*, pp. 283–84.

83  J.W. Hudson, *The History of Adult Education* (London, 1851), p. 96.

84  Drescher, 'The slaving capital', pp. 129–33.

85  Muir, *A History of Liverpool*, p. 193. Drescher, 'The slaving capital', p. 132.

86  Drescher, 'The slaving capital', p. 129.

87  David Samwell to Matthew Gregson, *Gregson Correspondence*, no date, 1788, LVRO, 920 GRE/17/41.

88  Quoted in E.A. Rathbone (ed.), *Records of the Rathbone Family* (Edinburgh, 1913), p. 36.

89  Muir, *A History of Liverpool*, p. 204.

90  Drescher, 'The slaving capital', pp. 133–40.

## Chapter 2: The Shaping of the Scholar

1   F. Espinasse, *Liverpool Worthies*, 2 vols (London, 1867), vol. 2, p. 274.

2   H. Roscoe, *The Life of William Roscoe*, 2 vols (Edinburgh, 1833), vol. 1, pp. 7–8.

3   *Roscoe Papers (RP)* 3925a. LVRO 920 ROS.

4   Roscoe, *Life*, vol. 1, p. 5.

5   *RP* 3925a.

6   Roscoe, *Life*, vol. 1, p. 76.

7   W. Roscoe, *The Life of Lorenzo de'Medici called the Magnificent*, tenth edition, revised by his son Thomas Roscoe (London, 1889), p. 21.

8   *RP* 3925a.

9   Roscoe, *Life*, vol. 2, p. 439.

10  C. Storey, 'Myths of the Medici: William Roscoe and Renaissance Historiography', unpublished PhD thesis, University of Oxford, 2003, p. 52.

11  *RP* 3925a.

12  *RP* 2025, 2054.

13  T. Roscoe, 'Memoir of the author', in Roscoe, *The Life of Lorenzo*, p. 24.

14  G. Chandler, *William Roscoe of Liverpool* (London, 1953), pp. 330–31.

15  *RP* 2054.

16  *RP* 2056.

17  G.E. Evans, *A History of Renshaw Street Chapel* (London, 1887), p. 5.

18 A. Holt, *Walking Together: A Study in Liverpool Noncon-formity, 1688–1938* (London, 1938), p. 128.

19 E. Glasgow, 'William Roscoe as a book collector', *Library Review*, 48, 8 (1999), p. 407.

20 Roscoe, *Life*, vol. 2, pp. 445–46.

21 D. Macnaughton, *Roscoe of Liverpool: His Life, Writings and Treasures* (Birkenhead, 1996), p. 9.

22 Roscoe, *Life*, vol. 1, pp. 33–34.

23 Further attestation to Roscoe's association with the academy is given by L. Aikin, *Memoir of John Aikin*, 2 vols (London, 1823), vol. 1, p. 300.

24 H. Bright, 'A historical sketch of Warrington Academy', *THSLC*, 13 (1861), pp. 14–15.

25 *RP* 1110.

26 H. McLachlan, *Warrington Academy, its History and Influence* (Manchester, 1943), p. 104.

27 H. McLachlan, 'Sport and recreation in nonconformist acade-mies' in *Essays and Addresses* (Manchester, 1950), pp. 199–200.

28 McLachlan, *Warrington Academy*, p. 85.

29 J. Aikin to J. Currie, 1 July 1794, *Manuscripts relating to James Currie, MD (1756–1805)*, LVRO, 920 Cur. acc. 209, 242.

30 Samuel Taylor Coleridge to Thomas Poole, 24 July 1800, in E.L. Griggs (ed.), *Unpublished Letters of Samuel Taylor Coleridge* (London, 1932).

31 W.W. Currie (ed.), *Memoir of the Life, Writing and Correspondence of James Currie, MD, FRS of Liverpool*, 2 vols (London, 1831), vol. 1, p. 500.

32 Checkland, 'Economic attitudes', pp. 69–74.

33 Currie (ed.), *Memoir of the Life*, p. 498

34 J.E. Graham, 'The political ideas and activities of William Roscoe, 1787–1801', unpublished MA thesis, University of Liverpool, 1970, p. xii.

35 F.E. Sanderson, 'The Liverpool abolitionists', in R. Anstey and P. Hair (eds), *Liverpool, the African Slave Trade and Abolition* (Chippenham, 1989), p. 204.

36 E. Gregg (ed.), *Reynolds-Rathbone Diaries and Letters 1753–1839* (printed for private circulation, 1905), p. 4.

37 Sanderson, 'The Liverpool abolitionists', p. 200.

38 *RP* 3998.

39 Sanderson, 'The Liverpool abolitionists', p. 205.

40  W. Roscoe to the Marquis of Lansdowne, n.d., c.1792, *RP* 2343.

41  Roscoe, *Life*, vol. 1, p. 57.

42  *RP* 3475.

43  Roscoe, *Life*, vol. 1, p. 48.

44  William Stanley (1782–1843), banker and later Sergeant-at-Mace to the Court of Passage at Liverpool; Edward (1785–1840), merchant; James (1787–1829); Robert (1789–1850), solicitor; Thomas (1791–1871), writer; Richard (1793–1864), doctor; Henry (1799–1839), barrister, father of the eminent chemist Sir Henry Enfield Roscoe; Mary Ann (1795–1845) writer; and Jane Elizabeth (1797–1853). A third daughter, Elizabeth, was born and died in 1783.

45  Chandler, *William Roscoe*, p. 382.

46  Rathbone (ed.), *Record*, pp. 114–15.

47  Roscoe, *Life*, vol. 1, pp. 203–06.

48  Roscoe, *Life*, vol. 1, p. 204.

49  *RP* 3051.

50  Roscoe, *Life*, vol. 1, p. 210.

51  *RP* 2284, 1335.

52  Roscoe, *Life*, vol. 1, p. 246.

53  Glasgow, 'William Roscoe', p. 406.

54  Chandler, *William Roscoe*, p. 108

55  Glasgow, 'William Roscoe', p.407.

56  See H. Stansfield, 'William Roscoe, Botanist, *Liverpool Bulletin*, 5 (November, 1955), p. 26.

57  Macnaughton, *Roscoe of Liverpool*, pp. 134–35.

58  R. Stewart Brown, *A History of the Manor and Township of Allerton* (Liverpool, 1911), pp. 64–65.

59  R. Pollard and N. Pevsner, *Lancashire: Liverpool and the South West* (New Haven and London, 2006), p. 392.

## Chapter 3: Roscoe the Littérateur

1  Roscoe, *The Life of Lorenzo*, p. 8.

2  G. Chandler, 'The published and unpublished poems of William Roscoe, 1753–1831', *Liverpool Bulletin*, 2, 1–2 (July and October 1953), p. 5.

3  Chandler, 'Published and unpublished poems', p. 7.

4  *RP* 1447.

5  Chandler, *William Roscoe*, p. 51.

6  P. Masson, *The Collected Writings of Thomas De Quincey*

(London, 1996), vol. 11, pp. 123–37.

7 Chandler, 'Published and unpublished poems', p. 5.

8 Chandler, *William Roscoe*, p. xxxi.

9 Roscoe, *Life*, 1, p.222.

10 Chandler, *William Roscoe*, p. 93.

11 Chandler, *William Roscoe*, p. xxxvi.

12 Roscoe, *The Life of Lorenzo*, p. 7.

13 Roscoe, *The Life of Lorenzo*, p. 14.

14 W. Roscoe to Lord Lansdowne, 23 December 1793, *RP* 2322.

15 Roscoe, *The Life of Lorenzo*, p. 9.

16 Roscoe, *The Life of Lorenzo*, p. 136.

17 Roscoe, *The Life of Lorenzo*, p. 15.

18 Roscoe, *The Life of Lorenzo*, p. 10.

19 J. Bullen, *The Myth of the Renaissance in Nineteenth Century Writing* (Oxford, 1994), p. 40.

20 W. Roscoe to Lord Lansdowne, n.d. (c.1795), *RP* 2327.

21 Roscoe, *Life*, vol. 1, p. 155.

22 Bullen, *The Myth of the Renaissance*, p. 42.

23 J. Hale, *England and the Italian Renaissance*, revised edition (London, 1963), p. 96.

24 Roscoe, *The Life of Lorenzo*, p. 14.

25 Macnaughton, *Roscoe of Liverpool*, p. 67.

26 Roscoe, *The Life of Lorenzo*, p. 205.

27 Storey, 'Myths of the Medici', p. 129.

28 Hale, *England and the Italian Renaissance*, p. 93.

29 Roscoe, *The Life of Lorenzo*, p. 10.

30 Bullen, *The Myth of the Renaissance*, pp. 52–53.

31 Roscoe, *Life*, vol. 2, p. 282.

32 In the preface to his book, Roscoe wrote of the difficulties of living in 'a remote part … deprived of many advantages peculiar to seats of learning'. Roscoe, *The Life of Lorenzo*, p. 13.

33 Sir Herbert Maxwell (ed.), *The Creevey Papers: A Selection from the Correspondence and Diaries of Thomas Creevey, MP, Born 1768 Died 1838*, 2 vols (London, 1904), vol. 2, pp. 256–57.

34 W. Irving, *Sketch of William Roscoe* (Liverpool, 1853), p. 6.

35 R. Story, 'Class and culture in Boston: the Athenaeum, 1807–1860', *American Quarterly*, 27, 2 (1975), p. 185. Roscoe's father may have been a butler at Allerton Hall prior to becoming an innkeeper. Stewart Brown, *A History*, p. 64.

36 Quoted in Roscoe, *Life*, vol. 1, p. 169.

37  Roscoe, *Life,* vol. 1, p. 152.
38  G. Murphy, *William Roscoe: His Early Ideals and Influence* (Liverpool, 1981), p. 26. See also *RP* 2320. P. McIntyre, 'Historical sketch of the Liverpool Library', *THSLC,* 9 (1857), p. 238.
39  For the growing assertiveness and competitiveness of provincial towns vis-à-vis London, see P.J. Corfield, *The Impact of English Towns 1700–1800* (Oxford, 1982), pp. 9–16.
40  See Introduction and Chapter 1.
41  Macnaughton, *Roscoe of Liverpool,* p. 92.
42  W. Roscoe, *The Life and Pontificate of Leo the Tenth,* 2 vols, 5th edition (London, 1846), Preface, p. x.
43  Roscoe, *The Life of Leo,* Preface, p. xi.
44  Roscoe, *Life,* vol. 1, p. 302.
45  T. Roscoe, 'Memoir of the author', in Roscoe, *The Life of Lorenzo,* p. 34.
46  Roscoe, *Life,* vol. 1, p. 330.
47  Roscoe, *The Life of Leo,* vol. 1, p. 395.
48  Macnaughton, *Roscoe of Liverpool,* pp. 103–05.
49  E. Baines, *The History of the County Palatine and Duchy of Lancaster,* 2 vols (London, 1870), vol. 2, p. 378.
50  Roscoe, *Life,* vol. 1, p. 350.
51  Storey, 'Myths of the Medici', p. 18.
52  Irving, *Sketch,* p. 9.

## Chapter 4: Liverpool's Cultural Icon

1  T. Baines, *Lancashire and Cheshire, Past and Present: A History and Description of the Palatine Counties of Lancashire and Cheshire,* 2 vols (Liverpool, 1868), vol. 2, p. 35.
2  J. Mayer, 'Roscoe and the influence of his writings on the Fine Arts', *THSLC,* 5 (1853), p. 143.
3  'Outlines of a plan for a library and newsroom', *Holt and Gregson Papers,* 8.
4  Fletcher, *Autobiographical Memoirs,* p. 67.
5  *Catalogue of the Athenaeum Library, Liverpool* (London, 1864), Preface, p. xiii.
6  J. Touzeau, *The Rise and Progress of Liverpool from 1551–1835,* 2 vols (London, 1910), vol. 2, p. 684.
7  F. Blair, *The Athenaeum, Liverpool* (Liverpool, 1947), p. 8.
8  *RP* 454.
9  R. Story, 'Class and culture in Boston: The Athenaeum, 1807–

1860', *American Quarterly*, 27 (1975), p. 186.

10 Story, 'Class and culture in Boston', p. 184.

11 Roscoe, *Life*, vol. 1, p. 230.

12 B.G. Orchard, *Liverpool's Legion of Honour* (Birkenhead, 1893), p. 54.

13 H. Stansfield, 'William Roscoe, botanist', *Liverpool Bulletin,* vol. 5 (1955), p. 25.

14 Roscoe, *Life*, 1, p. 254.

15 William Roscoe was the first president, and the committee included members of the town council (such as Thomas Earle) as well as members of the Roscoe circle (James Currie, William Clarke, John Yates and William Rathbone). Of the subscribers whose occupation is known, 102 were merchants or brokers; 9 were medical men; 6 were clergymen; 4 were bankers; 4 were attorneys; 2 were manufacturers; and 2 were sailmakers. By 1810 the number of subscribers had increased to 450.

16 'An address delivered before the proprietors of the Botanic Garden in Liverpool, previous to opening the garden', 3 May 1802 (Liverpool), p. 29.

17 Roscoe, *Life*, vol. 2, p. 455.

18 Roscoe, *Life*, vol. 1, p. 263.

19 J. Edmondson, *William Roscoe and Liverpool's First Botanical Garden* (Liverpool, 2005), p. 7.

20 *RP* 2398.

21 *Transactions of the Linnaen Society*, vol. 8, 1807, pp. 330–57.

22 Stansfield, 'William Roscoe', p. 38.

23 Edmondson, *William Roscoe*, p. 7.

24 For an account of this unusual expedition, see H. Stansfield, 'Plant collecting in Missouri: a Liverpool expedition, 1809–11', *Liverpool Bulletin*, vol. 1, October (1951).

25 'Spice of Life: Raffles and the Malay World', exhibition held in the Picton Reading Room, Central Library, Liverpool, 9 August–28 October 2007.

26 C. Colvin (ed.), *Maria Edgeworth: Letters from England 1813–1844* (Oxford, 1971), p. 416: Maria Edgeworth to Mrs Ruxton, 6 April 1813.

27 *RP* 176.

28 Troughton, *The History of Liverpool*, p. 208.

29 See Murphy, 'The Liverpool Library', p. 32.

30 See, for example, Kelly, *Adult Education*, p. 105; C.P. Darcy,

*The Encouragement of the Fine Arts in Lancashire and Cheshire 1760–1860* (Manchester, 1976), p. 95.

31  A. Thackray, 'Natural knowledge in a cultural context: the Manchester model', *The American Historical Review*, 79 (1974), pp. 672–709.

32  McLachlan, *Essays and Addresses*, pp. 67–68.

33  R. S. Watson, *The History of the Literary and Philosophical Society of Newcastle Upon Tyne (1793–1896)* (London, 1896), p. 36.

34  *Laws and Regulations of the Literary and Philosophical Society of Liverpool (1812)* (Liverpool, 1812 and 1815).

35  *Outlook: The University of Liverpool Bulletin of the Department of Extra-Mural Studies*, 3, 5 (winter, 1962), p. 2.

36  *Liverpool Literary and Philosophical Society Minute Book*, 1 (1 May 1812). LVRO, 060/Lit/1/2. The author is not named, but J. Hampden Jackson, *Liverpool Literary and Philosophical Society Centenary Roll 1812–1912*, LVRO, 060/Lit/3/1/2 ascribes it to William Shepherd. However, the *Kaleidoscope, or Literary and Scientific Mirror*, New Series 4 (1824), p. 188, cites the Quaker merchant Thomas Binns as the author.

37  Roscoe, *Life*, vol. 2, p. 55.

38  The accommodation granted gratis to the Lit. and Phil. by the Royal Institution was of great financial benefit to the society, negating the need to build or rent premises.

39  Roscoe, *Life*, vol. 2, p. 164.

40  The other four papers were: 'An Account of the Plymouth Institution' (1819); 'On the Principal Treasures of the MSS Library at Holkham' (1821); 'His Preface (before Publication) to the Author's Edition of Pope's Works' (1825); and 'The Holkham Library; An Account of its Foundation, and some of its Important MSS' (1829).

41  G. Kitteringham, 'Science in provincial society: the case of Liverpool on the early nineteenth century', *Annals of Science*, 39 (1982), pp. 335–36.

42  C.D. Watkinson, 'The Liberal Party on Merseyside in the nineteenth century', unpublished PhD thesis, University of Liverpool, 1968, pp. 48–49.

43  *Centenary Roll*, under William Rathbone's name.

44  *Lit. and Phil. Minute Book*, 2, 3 October 1817.

45  *Lit. and Phil. Minute Book*, 1, 1 October 1813.

46  Lit. and Phil. Minute Book, 1, 5 December 1817.

47  Minutes, 3 November 1824 to May 1825.

48  Darcy, The Encouragement of the Fine Arts, pp. 99–100.

49  Q. Hughes, Seaport: Architecture and Townscape in Liverpool (London, 1964), p. 44.

50  Hughes, Seaport, p. 116.

51  Hughes, Seaport, p. 144.

52  Outlook, p. 2.

53  Minute Book, 1. 6 May 1814.

54  Roscoe Club Minute Book, 1847–1850, July 1847.

55  J. Ramsay Muir, A History of Liverpool (London, 1907), p. 293.

56  Kelly, History of Adult Education, p. 114.

57  A.T. Brown, Some Account of the Royal Institution School Liverpool; With a Roll of Masters and Boys (1819–1892 AD), second edition (Liverpool, 1927), pp. 8–10.

58  Brown, Some Account, p. 22

59  John Foster to William Roscoe, 28 February 1815, RI Arch 50.23

60  Brown, Some Account, p. 12.

61  Brown, Some Account, p, 12.

62  Roscoe, Life, pp. 155–56.

63  W. Roscoe, On the Origin and Vicissitudes of Literature, Science and Art and their Influence on the Present State of Society; a Discourse, Delivered on the Opening of the Liverpool Royal Institution, 25th November, 1817 (Liverpool, 1817), p. 7.

64  Roscoe, On the Vicissitudes, p. 46.

65  Roscoe, On the Vicissitudes, p. 74.

66  Roscoe, On the Vicissitudes, p.4 4.

67  Blackwood's Edinburgh Magazine, ii (February 1818), pp. 537, 535.

68  T. Jefferson to W. Roscoe, 27 December 1820, RP 2207.

69  Roscoe, Life, vol. 2, p. 163.

70  J. Gladstone to T. Martin, 7 March 1822, RI Arch, 51.41.

71  S.G. Checkland, The Gladstones: A Family Biography 1764–1851 (Cambridge, 1971), p. 224.

72  Address delivered by B.A. Heywood, President, 13 February 1824. See also addresses of 27 February 1822 and 11 February 1825. 1822.

73  A School of Design was opened circa 1823, but it was under the auspices of the Academy of Art.

74  Resolutions, Reports and Byelaws of the Liverpool Royal

*Institution, March 1814 to 14 March 1820*, p. 9. G34.32(5), SJL.

75  H. Perkin, *The Origins of Modern English Society 1780–1880* (London, 1969), pp. 296–97.

76  The institution depended mainly on gifts to extend the collection, although some did come by way of exchange; for example with the Museum of the Zoological Society of London. H. Ormerod, *The Liverpool Royal Institution: A Record and a Retrospect* (Liverpool, 1953), pp. 36–37.

77  *Resolutions, Reports etc.*, 14 March 1820 (Liverpool, 1822).

78  *Resolutions, Reports, etc.*, 27 February 1822.

79  *Book for Inserting the Names and Places of Abode of Strangers, April 1822–1834*, RI Arch 19.

80  *Addresses Delivered at the Meetings of the Liverpool Royal Institution on the 27th February, 1822 & 13th February, 1824, by B.A. Heywood, Esq. President* (Liverpool, 1824), SJL R5 29.

81  *RP* 2300, 2302.

82  *Address delivered... on the 11th February 1825 by B.A. Heywood Esq. President*, SJL, S/DA690.L8.R.

83  Ormerod, *The Liverpool Royal Institution*, p. 18.

84  Ormerod, *The Liverpool Royal Institution*, p. 27.

85  Hudson, *The History of Adult Education*, p. 168.

86  J. Picton to T. Rathbone, 8 June 1850, *RI Arch* 53.

## Chapter 5: Art in the City

1  J. Richardson, *The Science of a Connoisseur* (1773) quoted in T. Fawcett, *The Rise of Provincial Art: Artists, Patrons and Institutions Outside London, 1800–1865* (Oxford, 1974), p. 5.

2  See Fawcett, *The Rise of Provincial Art*, pp. 4–8.

3  P. Oppé, 'Art', in G.M. Young (ed.), *Early Victorian England 1830–1865* (Oxford, 1951), p. 116.

4  Chandler, *William Roscoe*, p. 327.

5  Darcy, *The Encouragement of the Fine Arts*, pp. 26–27.

6  H.A. Taylor, 'Matthew Gregson and the Pursuit of Taste', *THSLC*, 110 (1958), p. 157.

7  H.C. Marillier, *The Liverpool School of Painters: An Account of the Liverpool Academy from 1810 to 1867, with Memoirs of the Principal Artists* (London, 1904), p. 5.

8  Marillier, *The Liverpool School*, p. 6.

9  J. Mayer, *Early Exhibitions Of Art in Liverpool* (Liverpool, 1876), p. 46.

10 H. Smithers, *Liverpool, its Commerce, Statistics and Institutions; with a History of the Cotton Trade* (Liverpool, 1825), p. 338.

11 Darcy, *The Encouragement of the Fine Arts*, p. 31.

12 Taylor, 'Matthew Gregson', p. 167.

13 Smithers, *Liverpool*, p. 338.

14 Taylor, 'Matthew Gregson', p. 157.

15 Taylor, 'Matthew Gregson', p. 175.

16 W.P. Carey, *Cursory Thoughts on the Present State of the Fine Arts Occasioned by the Founding of the Liverpool Academy* (Liverpool, 1810), p. 1.

17 Carey, *Cursory Thoughts*, p. 39.

18 Fawcett, *The Rise of Provincial Art*, p. 9.

19 B.H. Grindley, *History and Work of the Liverpool Academy of Arts* (Liverpool, 1875), p. 3.

20 Fawcett, *The Rise of Provincial Art*, p. 173.

21 *Liverpool Mercury*, 16 August 1811.

22 Grindley, *History*, p. 4.

23 Darcy, *The Encouragement of the Fine Arts*, p. 37.

24 With the exception of the exhibition of 1810, these were held in the union newsroom.

25 *Liverpool Academy of Arts Catalogue, 1910* (Liverpool, 1910), p. 45.

26 *Addresses Delivered at the Meetings of the Liverpool Royal Institution on the 27th February 1822 & 13th February 1824, by B.A. Heywood* (Liverpool, 1824).

27 *Liverpool Mercury*, 24 August 1824.

28 Grindley, *History*, p. 7.

29 Darcy, *The Encouragement of the Fine Arts*, p. 49.

30 *Liverpool Mercury*, 15 August 1828.

31 *The Albion, The Kaleidoscope*, the *Liverpool Mercury, Chronicle, Courier, Advertiser* and *Times*. Occasionally, reports from one newspaper would be copied in another.

32 Darcy, *The Encouragement of the Fine Arts*, p. 50.

33 *Catalogue of the Eighth Exhibition of the Liverpool Academy* (Liverpool, 1831). Of 56 occupations that can be traced, 43 were businessmen.

34 *Exhibition Catalogue*, 1910, pp. 47–48.

35 *Exhibition Catalogue*, 1831.

36 *Liverpool Academy of Arts Minute Book 1830–1848*, 10 April 1837.

37 This continued until about 1860. Grindley, *History*, p. 49.

38 *RP* 1664.

39 H. Macandrew, 'Henry Fuseli and William Roscoe', *Liverpool Bulletin*, 8 (1960), p. 20.

40 Macandrew, 'Henry Fuseli and William Roscoe', p. 16.

41 Macandrew, 'Henry Fuseli and William Roscoe', pp. 14–16.

42 Macandrew, 'Henry Fuseli and William Roscoe', p. 37.

43 Chandler, *Roscoe of Liverpool*, pp. xxx–xxxi.

44 Macandrew, 'Henry Fuseli and William Roscoe', p. 10.

45 Mrs Roscoe to W. Rathbone, 6 April 1791, *RP* 3509.

46 Macandrew, 'Henry Fuseli and William Roscoe', p. 31.

47 T. Cavanagh, *Public Sculpture in Liverpool* (Liverpool 1997), p. 252.

48 Fawcett, *The Rise of Provincial Art*, p. 51

49 Roscoe, *Life*, vol. 2, p. 143.

50 Cavanagh, *Public Sculpture*, p. xi.

51 B.R. Haydon, *Lectures on Painting and Design* (London, 1846), vol. 11, pp. 115–16.

52 Roscoe, *Life*, vol. 2, p. 128.

53 Fawcett, *The Rise of Provincial Art*, p. 96. See also M. Compton, 'William Roscoe and early collectors of Italian Primitives', *Liverpool Bulletin*, 9 (1961), pp. 27–51.

54 This picture was entirely the work of Aspertini; Colvin, *Maria Edgeworth*, p. 12.

55 M. Edgeworth to Mrs Ruxton, 6 April 1813, Colvin, *Maria Edgeworth*, p. 13.

56 E. Morris, 'The formation of the gallery of art in the Liverpool Royal Institution, 1816–1819', *THSLC*, 142 (1992), p. 91.

57 Darcy, *The Encouragement of the Fine Arts*, p. 126.

58 Roscoe, *Life*, vol. 1, pp. 125–28.

59 Compton, 'William Roscoe', p. 45.

60 Compton, 'William Roscoe', p. 27.

61 *Catalogue of a Series of Pictures Illustrating the Rise and Early Progress of 'The Art of Painting in Italy, Germany etc. Collected by William Roscoe Esq. and Now Deposited in the Liverpool Royal Institution* (Liverpool, 1819).

62 Quoted in Morris, 'William Roscoe and Medici Florence', p. 16.

63 Morris, 'William Roscoe and Medici Florence', pp. 13–15.

64 Fawcett, *The Rise of Provincial Art*, p. 98.

65 Darcy, *The Encouragement of the Fine Arts*, p. 60.

66 The merchants are listed as W. Ewart, G.P. Barclay, R. Benson, C. Tayleur, Jos. Sandars, Jos. Reynolds and B.A. Heywood. Morris, 'The formation of the gallery of art', p. 94.

67 Morris, 'William Roscoe and Medici Florence', pp. 19–20.

68 *A Catalogue of the Present Collection.*

## Chapter 6: Roscoe the Radical

1 Roscoe, *Life*, vol. 2, p. 448.

2 Sanderson, 'The Liverpool abolitionists', p. 196.

3 Northcote Parkinson, *The Rise of the Port*, p. 102.

4 G. Cameron and S. Cooke, *Liverpool: Capital of the Slave Trade* (Birkenhead, 1992), p. 56.

5 Sanderson, 'The Liverpool abolitionists', p. 198.

6 Chandler, *William Roscoe*, p. 349.

7 This group has mistakenly been described as a Liverpool branch committee of the society. See Sanderson, 'The Liverpool abolitionists', footnote 18, p. 232.

8 Sanderson, 'The Liverpool abolitionists', p. 229.

9 J. Trepp,'The Liverpool movement for the abolition of the slave trade', *The Journal of Negro History*, 13, 3 (July 1928), p. 272.

10 J. Aspinall, *Liverpool a Few Years Since by An Old Stager*, third edition (Liverpool, 1885), p. 64.

11 Quoted in D. Sam, *Liverpool and Slavery* (Liverpool, 1884), p. 8.

12 Sanderson, 'The structure of politics', p. 66.

13 R.V. Holt, *The Unitarian Contribution to Social Progress in England* (London, 1938), p. 135.

14 Sanderson, 'The structure of politics', p. 72.

15 Currie (ed.), *Memoir of the Life*, vol. 1, p. 500.

16 A. MacKenzie Grieve, *The Last Years of the English Slave Trade: Liverpool 1750–1850* (London, 1941), p. 23.

17 J. Barton to W. Roscoe, 27 March 1787, *RP* 243.

18 Sanderson, 'The Liverpool abolitionists', p. 207.

19 Currie (ed.), *Memoir of the Life*, vol. 1, pp. 112–26. Currie to Wilberforce, December 1787.

20 Graham, 'Political ideas and activities', p. 27.

21 *Minutes of the Common Council,* 4 June 1788.

22 Quoted in Sam, *Liverpool and Slavery*, p. 63.

23 H. Dannett, 'A Particular Examination of a Pamphlet Lately Published by the Rev. Raymond Harris' (London, 1788), p. ix.

24 Trepp, 'The Liverpool movement', p. 277.

25 Barton to Roscoe, 2 July 1788, *RP* 255.

26 F.E. Sanderson, 'The Liverpool delegates and Sir William Dolben's bill', *THSLC*, 124 (1973), p. 58.

27 Graham, pp. 42–44.

28 Currie, *Life*, 1, pp. 500–01.

29 Graham, 'Political ideas and activities', p. 50.

30 'Ode to the People of France, imitated from a Canzone of Petrarch', in Chandler, *William Roscoe*, p. 381.

31 Chandler, *Roscoe of Liverpool*, p. 70.

32 Mary Wollstonecraft (1759–1797) was a feminist polemicist who drew attention to the inequalities between the sexes in her *A Vindication of the Rights of Woman* (1792), an exposure of the double standards of the time. An unhappy love affair resulted in an illegitimate daughter and conservative critics linked her radical views with her 'disorderly' private life, and harshly criticized both. She married William Godwin in 1797, but died after giving birth to their daughter, the future Mary Shelley.

33 *The Life, Death, and Wonderful Achievements of Edmund Burke: A New Ballad, 1791*, in G. Chandler, *William Roscoe*, p. 390.

34 Graham, 'Political ideas and activities', p. 83.

35 *RP* 5330, 5328.

36 R.B. Rose, 'The "Jacobins" of Liverpool 1789–1793', *Liverpool Bulletin*, 9 (1960–1961), p. 38.

37 Rose, 'The "Jacobins" of Liverpool', p. 45.

38 Roscoe, *Life*, vol. 1, p. 110.

39 Roscoe, *Life*, vol. 1, p. 105.

40 The London Corresponding Society was founded in January 1792 by the radical Thomas Hardy to maintain a correspondence with other reformers, especially with other corresponding societies in the provinces, with the aim of achieving fair, equal and impartial representation of the people in Parliament. Its organizers and members were mainly artisans and working men.

41 *RP* 2322.

42 Roscoe, *Life*, vol. 1, p. 114; *RP* 22.

43 W. Roscoe to Lord Lansdowne, 23 December 1793. *RP* 2322.

44 Rathbone (ed.), *Record*, pp. 104–06.

45 Watkinson, 'The Liberal Party', pp. 18–19.

46 *Tarleton Papers* LVRO, 920 TAR, TA 65.

47 Rose, 'The "Jacobins" of Liverpool', p. 48.

48 Roscoe, *Life*, vol. 1, p. 110.

49 *RP* 2343. D. Read, *The English Provinces c.1760–1960: A Study in Influence*, (London, 1964), p. 50.

50 I. Sellers, 'William Roscoe, the Roscoe circle and radical politics in Liverpool 1787–1807', *THSLC*, 120, 1968, pp. 51–53.

51 Read, *The English Provinces*, p. 50.

52 W. Roscoe to D. Daulby, 23 February 1797, *RP* 1128.

53 Wright and Cruickshank, *A Compendium and Impartial Account of the Election at Liverpool Together with ... the Songs and Squibs ... and also a Correct List of the Freemen who Polled at the Late Election* (Liverpool, 1806), p. vi.

54 W. Rathbone to W. Roscoe, 29 October 1806. *Rathbone Family Papers* ii.1.169. pp. 237–38.

55 *An Impartial Collection of the Addresses, Songs, Squibs, etc, that were Published at Liverpool During the Election of Members of Parliament in November 1806*, (Dublin, 1806), pp. 21, 42.

56 J. Picton, *Memorials of Liverpool*, 2 vols (Liverpool, 1875), vol. 1, p. 271.

57 1806 election handbill, *Rathbone Family Papers* 11.4.16, p. 89.

58 Sanderson, 'The structure of politics', p. 77.

59 Wright and Cruickshank, *A Compendium*, p. ix.

60 *A Collection of Addresses, Songs, Squibs etc. Published at Liverpool during the Election for Members of Parliament in May 1807* (Isleman, 1807), p. 157.

61 Rathbone (ed.), *Record*, p. 131.

62 *Liverpool Chronicle*, 26 November and 3 December 1806.

63 *RP* 3054, 3058, 3059, 3060.

64 *RP* 2154.

65 Roscoe, *Life*, vol. 1, pp. 361–62.

66 Roscoe, *Life*, vol. 2, p. 316.

67 *RP* 4072, 3073.

68 Roscoe, *Life*, vol. 1, p. 362.

69 Roscoe, *Life*, vol. 1, pp. 364–75.

70 Rathbone (ed.), *Record*, p. 132.

71 Roscoe, *Life*, vol. 1, p. 367.

72 Roscoe, *Life*, vol. 1, p. 374.

73 Roscoe, *Life*, vol. 1, p. 375.

74 W. Rathbone to W. Roscoe, 19 April 1807, *Rathbone Family Papers* 11.1.157.

75 For an account of the riot, see E.A. Rathbone (ed.), *Record*, pp.

290–91.

76 Quoted in D. Ben Rees, *Local and Parliamentary Politics in Liverpool from 1800–1911* (Lampeter, 1999), p. 22.

77 *RP* 3883, 3886.

78 Sanderson, 'The Liverpool abolitionists', p. 227.

79 Sellers, 'William Roscoe', p. 61.

80 *RP* 1190, 1191.

81 Chandler, *William Roscoe*, p. 115.

82 *Liverpool Chronicle*, 8 July 1807.

83 I. Sellers, 'Liverpool nonconformity (1786–1914)', unpublished PhD thesis, University of Keele, 1969, pp. 282–83.

84 Sellers, 'Liverpool nonconformity', pp. 284–87.

85 D. Weinglass, 'The publishing history of William Roscoe's edition of the works of Alexander Pope Esq., 1824', unpublished PhD thesis, University of Kansas, 1969, p. 126.

86 *RP* 2480 and H. Roscoe, *Life*, vol. 1, p. 479.

87 K. Charlton, 'James Cropper and Liverpool's contribution to the anti-slavery movment', *THSLC*, 123 (1971), p. 60.

88 Roscoe, *Life*, vol. 2, pp. 193–95.

89 Roscoe, *Life*, vol. 2, p. 200.

90 Sanderson, 'The Liverpool abolitionists', p. 226.

## Chapter 7: Roscoe the Businessman

1 Porter, *English Society*, p. 76.

2 Sanderson, 'The Liverpool abolitionists', footnote 33, p. 232.

3 P.H. Williams, *A Gentleman's Calling – The Liverpool Attorney-at-law; On Behalf of the Incorporated Law Society of Liverpool* (Denbigh, 1980), p. 109.

4 *RP* 224, 226.

5 Williams, *A Gentleman's Calling*, p. 127.

6 *RP* 3520.

7 Quoted in Macnaughton, *Roscoe of Liverpool*, p. 38.

8 *Manchester Guardian*, 1 July 1931.

9 R. Enfield to W. Roscoe, 14 May 1791, *RP* 1446.

10 *RP* 4036, 3350.

11 *RP* 1758.

12 *RP* 1758, 857, 2479.

13 Roscoe, *Life*, vol. 1, pp. 247–48.

14 B.L. Anderson, 'Financial institutions and the capital market on Merseyside in the eighteenth and nineteenth centuries', in

B.L. Anderson and P.J.M. Stoney, *Commerce, Industry and Transport: Studies in Economic Change on Merseyside* (Liverpool, 1983), p. 32.

15 J. Hughes, *Liverpool Banks and Bankers 1760–1837* (London, 1906), p. 63.

16 Hughes, *Liverpool Banks*, p. 65.

17 *RP* 3079.

18 Roscoe, *Life*, vol. 2, p. 113.

19 Glasgow, 'William Roscoe', pp. 2–3.

20 Hughes, *Liverpool Banks*, p. 72.

21 X. Brooke, 'The Blundells of Ince Blundell Hall as collectors', unpublished paper read before the Historic Society of Lancashire and Cheshire, 19 October 2006.

22 Roscoe, *Life*, vol. 2, p. 313.

23 Roscoe, *Life*, vol. 2, pp. 251–52.

24 Hughes, *Liverpool Banks*, p. 81.

## Chapter 8: Towards Immortality

1 Letter to W. Smith, 29 January 1795, in R.B. McDowell (ed.), *The Correspondence of Edmund Burke*, vol. 8 (Cambridge, 1969).

2 Roscoe, *Life*, vol. 2, p. 317.

3 M. Edgeworth to Mrs Ruxton, 6 April 1813. M. Edgeworth to C. Sneyd Edgeworth, 1 May 1813. Colvin, *Maria Edgeworth*, pp. 10–11, 48.

4 Weinglass, 'The publishing history', abstract.

5 Roscoe, *Life*, vol. 2, pp. 335–41.

6 *RP* 687.

7 Quoted in Weinglass, 'The publishing history', p. 686.

8 Macnaughton, *Roscoe of Liverpool*, pp. 126–27.

9 *Quarterly Review*, October 1825, pp. 276–77.

10 Roscoe, *Life*, vol. 2, pp. 344–45.

11 Macnaughton, *Roscoe of Liverpool*, p. 43.

12 *Liverpool Echo*, 2 July 1931.

13 J.E. Graham, 'The cataloguing of the Holkham Manuscripts', *Transactions of the Cambridge Bibliographical Society*, 4, 2 (1965), p. 128.

14 Roscoe, *Life*, vol. 2, p. 83.

15 Chandler, *William Roscoe*, p. xviii.

16 Roscoe, *Life*, vol. 2, p. 95.

17  Graham, 'Holkham Manuscripts', p. 131.
18  Graham, 'Holkham Manuscripts', p. 129.
19  Roscoe, *Life*, vol. 2, p. 264.
20  Quoted in Graham, 'Holkham Manuscripts', p. 144.
21  Graham, 'Holkham Manuscripts', p. 129.
22  Chandler, *William Roscoe*, p. 132.
23  Edmondson, *William Roscoe*, p. 11.
24  Roscoe, *Life*, vol. 2, p. 376.
25  D.S. Bland, *John James Audubon in Liverpool, 1826–1827* (Liverpool, 1977), p. 6.
26  Quoted in Wilson, 'Commerce and culture', pp. 174–75.
27  Chandler, *William Roscoe*, p. xvii.
28  M. Audubon, *Audubon and his Journals* (Massachussetts, 1972), p. 117.
29  Fawcett, *The Rise of Provincial Art*, p. 69.
30  Roscoe, *Life*, vol. 2, p. 407.
31  'The boy stood on the burning deck, the captain blew the hooter, around the corner who should come, but … on a scooter.' This is a mild version; others are considerably more risqué.
32  Espinasse, *Liverpool Worthies*, pp. 283–84.
33  Morris, 'William Roscoe and Medici Florence', pp. 7–10.
34  Roscoe, *Life*, vol. 2, p. 420.
35  Quoted in Roscoe, *Life*, vol. 2, pp. 477–78.

## Conclusion

1   Roscoe, *On the Viccissitudes*, p. 9
2   *Holt and Gregson Papers*, LVRO, 942/HOL/5.
3   Stobart, 'Culture versus commerce', p. 481.
4   Quoted in P.J. Waller, *Democracy and Sectarianism: A Political and Social History of Liverpool, 1868–1939* (Liverpool, 1981), pp. 13–14.
5   D. Read, 'Review article: Manchester men and Liverpool gentlemen', *Northern History*, 7 (1972).
6   Alton, 'William Roscoe', p. 2.
7   For example, The Historic Society of Lancashire and Cheshire, founded in 1848.
8   M. Neve, 'Science in a commercial city: Bristol 1820–60', in I. Inkster and J. Morrell (eds), *Metropolis and Province: Science in British Culture, 1780–1850* (London, 1983), p. 202.
9   J.A. Picton, *Memorials of Liverpool* (London, 1873), vol. 1, p. 505.

# Bibliography

**Non–Printed Primary Sources and Manuscript Collections**

Gregson, M., *A Collection of printed records, catalogues and circulars, original correspondence and manuscript notes, relating to Gregson's activities as a founder and proprietor of the Liverpool Royal Institution, 1814–1823, with a typed list of contents*, SJL GR1.2(3).

*Historical Collections of William Heaton Wakefield*, LVRO, 942WAK.

*Holt and Gregson Papers; Materials towards a History of Liverpool collected by John Holt and Matthew Gregson*, LVRO, 942HOL 1–32.

*Liverpool Academy of Art Exhibition Catalogues, 1810–1814; 1822–1830*, LVRO, Hq706.4 CAT.

*Liverpool Philomathic Society Archive*, SJL.

*Liverpool Unanimous Society Records, 1753–1778*, LVRO, 367/UNA/1.

*Manuscript Collection of Matthew Gregson*, LVRO, G20 GRE.

*Manuscripts Relating to James Currie MD (1756–1805)*, LVRO,. 920CUR 1–24, 126.

Ormerod, H.A., *Correspondence, notes and papers c.1950*, SJL.

*Papers relating to the Botanic Garden opened 1802*, LVRO, 580 BOT.

*Peter Entwistle Collection of materials for a history of the Liverpool Potteries*, LVRO, 942ENT 1–37.

*Rathbone Family Papers*, SJL. 11.1.168.9.

*Records of the Literary and Philosophical Society of Liverpool 1812–1955*, LVRO, 060LIT 1–12.

*Records of the Liverpool Library, Lyceum, 1769–1955*, LVRO, 027LYC 1–19.

*Records of the Liverpool Society of Fine Arts*, LVRO, 706FIN

*Records Relating to the Liverpool Academy of Art*, Walker Art Gallery.

*Records Relating to Ye Ugly Face Club, Leverpool, 1743–1757*, LVRO, 367/UGL.

*Records of Sefton Mock Corporation*, 1753–1829, L.VRO, 367SEF.

*Roscoe Letters and Papers*, LVRO, 920ROS.

*Royal Institution Archive*, SJL.

*Tarleton Papers*, LVRO, 920TAR.

Veitch, George Stead, *Personal Papers as Professor of History 1909–1914*, SJL.

## Secondary and Printed Sources

Adams, John, *An Impartial Collection of the Addresses, Songs, Squibs, etc, that were Published at Liverpool during the Election of Members of Parliament in November 1806* (Dublin, 1806).

Aikin, J., *A Description of the Country from Thirty to Forty Miles round Manchester* (London, 1795, reprinted Newton Abbot, 1986).

Aikin, L., *Memoir of John Aikin* (London, 1823).

*An Address Delivered before the Proprietors of the Botanic Garden in Liverpool Previous to the Opening of the Garden, May 3 1802* (Liverpool, 1802).

Anderson, B. and Stoney, P. (eds), *Commerce, Industry and Transport: Studies in Economic Change on Merseyside* (Liverpool, 1983).

Anstey, R. and Hair, P.E.H. (eds), *Liverpool, the African Slave Trade and Abolition: Essays to Illustrate Current Knowledge and Research* (Chippenham, 1989).

Arkle, A.H., 'The early coffee houses of Liverpool', *THSLC*, 64 (1912).

Aspinall, J., *Liverpool A Few Years Since: By an Old Stager*, third ed. (Liverpool, 1885).

Baines, E., *The History of the County Palatine and Duchy of Lancaster*, 2 vols. (London, 1870).

Baines, T., *History of the Commerce and Town of Liverpool* (London, 1852).

Baines, T., *Liverpool in 1859, With a Plan* (London, 1859).

Barker, T.C., 'Lancashire coal, Cheshire salt and the rise of Liverpool', *THSLC*, 103 (1952).

Behrendt, S.D., 'The captains in the British Slave Trade from 1785 to 1807', *THSLC*,140 (1990).

Belchem, J. (ed.), *Popular Politics, Riot and Labour: Essays in Liverpool History* (Liverpool, 1992).

Belchem, J. (ed.), *Liverpool 800* (Liverpool, 2006).

Ben Rees, D., *Local and Parliamentary Politics in Liverpool from 1800–1911* (Lampeter, 1999).

Blair, F.G., *The Athenaeum Library, Liverpool* (Liverpool, 1947).

Borsay, P., *The English Urban Renaissance: Culture and Society in the Provincial Towns 1660–1770* (Oxford, 1989).

Bright, H., 'A historical sketch of Warrington Academy', *THSLC*, 13 (1861).

Broadbent, R., *Annals of the Liverpool Stage: From the Earliest Period to the Present Time* (Liverpool, 1908).

Brooke, R., *Liverpool as it was During the Last Quarter of the Eighteenth Century 1775–1800* (Liverpool, 1853).

Brown, A.T., *Some Account of the Royal Institution School Liverpool: With a Roll of Masters and Boys (1819–1892 AD)* (Liverpool, 1927).

Bullen, J.B., *The Myth of the Renaissance in Nineteenth-Century Writing* (Oxford, 1994).

Butler, K.T.B., 'A "petty" professor of modern history: William Smyth (1765–1849)', *Cambridge Historical Journal*, 9, 2 (1948).

Cameron, G. and Cooke, S., *Liverpool – Capital of the Slave Trade* (Liverpool, 1992).

Carey, W.P., *Cursory Thoughts on the Present State of the Fine Arts Occasioned by the Founding of the Liverpool Academy* (Liverpool, 1810).

*Catalogue of the Athenaeum Library, Liverpool* (London, 1864).

*Catalogue of the Liverpool Library, to Which are Affixed the Laws of the Institution and a List of Proprietors* (Liverpool, 1901).

*Catalogue of the Present Collection of Books in the Liverpool Library: To Which is Prefixed a Copy of the Laws and a List of the Subscribers* (Liverpool, 1760)

Chandler, G., 'The published and unpublished poems of William Roscoe, 1753–1831', *Liverpool Bulletin*, 2, 1–2 (July–October 1952).

Chandler, G., *William Roscoe of Liverpool* (London, 1953).

Chandler, G., *Liverpool* (London, 1957).

Chandler, G., *Liverpool under James 1st* (Liverpool, 1960).

Charlton, K., 'James Cropper and Liverpool's contribution to the anti-slavery movement', *THSLC*, 123 (1971).

Checkland, S.G. 'Economic attitudes in Liverpool, 1793–1807', *The Economic History Review*, 5, 1 (1952).

Checkland, S.G., *The Gladstones: A Family Biography 1764–1851* (Cambridge, 1971).

Clemens, P., 'The rise of Liverpool 1650–1750', *Economic History Review*, 29 (1976).

Coleridge, H., *Lives of Northern Worthies* (London, 1852).

Colvin, C. (ed.), *Maria Edgeworth: Letters from England 1813–1844* (Oxford, 1971).

Compton, M., 'William Roscoe and early collectors of Italian Primitives', *Liverpool Bulletin*, 9 (1960–1961).

Currie, W.W., *Memoir of the Life, Writing and Correspondence of James Currie, MD, FRS of Liverpool*, 2 vols (London, 1831).

Dannett, H., *A Particular Examination of a Pamphlet Lately Published by the Rev. Raymond Harris* (London, 1788).

Darcy, C.P., *The Encouragement of the Fine Arts in Lancashire, 1760–1860* (Manchester, 1976).

Derrick, S., *Letters Written from Leverpoole, Chester, Corke, the Lake of Killarney, Dublin, Tunbridge Wells, Bath*, 2 vols (London, 1767).

Drescher, S., 'The slaving capital of the world: Liverpool and national opinion in the age of abolition', *Slavery and Abolition*, 9, 2 (1988).

Dunston, F.W., *Roscoeana, Being Some Account of the Kinsfolk of William Roscoe of Liverpool and Jane (née Griffies) his Wife* (privately printed, 1905).

Edmonson, J., *William Roscoe and Liverpool's First Botanical Garden* (Liverpool, 2005).

Enfield, W., *Essay Towards the History of Liverpool* (Warrington, 1773).

Espinasse, F., *Liverpool Worthies* (London, 1867).

Evans, G.E., *A History of Renshaw Street Chapel, Liverpool, and its Institutions with some Account of the Former Chapel in Castle Hey and Benn's Garden* (London, 1887).

Fawcett, T., *The Rise of English Provincial Art: Artists, Patrons and Institutions outside London* (Oxford, 1974).

Fletcher, T., *Autobiographical Memoirs of Thomas Fletcher of Liverpool (Obit 1850); Written in the Year 1843* (Liverpool,

1893).

Glasgow, E., 'William Roscoe as a book collector', *Library Review*, 48, 8 (1999).

*Gore's Liverpool Directories*

Graham, J.E., 'The Cataloguing of the Holkham Manuscripts', reprinted from *Transactions of the Cambridge Bibliographical Society*, 4, 2 (1965).

Gregg, E. (ed.), *Reynolds–Rathbones Diaries and Letters 1753–1839* (printed privately, 1905).

Gregson, M., *Portfolio of Fragments Relative to the History and Antiquaries of the County Palatine and Duchy of Lancaster* (Liverpool, 1817 and 1824).

Griggs, E.L. (ed.), *Unpublished Letters of Samuel Taylor Coleridge* (London, 1932).

Grindley, B.H., *History and Work of the Liverpool Academy* (Liverpool, 1875).

Hale, J., *England and the Italian Renaissance*, revised edition (London, 1963).

Haydon, B.R., *Lectures on Painting and Design* (London, 1846).

Herring, J., *A Collection of Addresses, Songs, Squibs etc. Published at Liverpool During the Election for Members of Parliament in May 1807* (Isleman, 1807).

Heywood, T. (ed.), *The Moore Rental* (Manchester, 1847).

Hibbert, C., *The Rise and Fall of the House of Medici* (London, 1974).

Holt, A., *Walking Together: A Study in Liverpool Nonconformity* (London, 1938).

Holt, Raymond, V., *The Unitarian Contribution to Social Progress in England* (London, 1938).

Howell, E., *Ye Ugly Face Club, Leverpoole 1743–1757, A Verbatim Reprint from the Original Mss, in the Collection of the Late Joseph Mayer* (Liverpool, 1912).

Hudson, J.W., *The History of Adult Education* (London, 1851).

Hughes, J., *Liverpool Banks and Bankers* (London, 1906).

Hunt, T., *Building Jerusalem: The Rise and Fall of the Victorian City* (London, 2004).

Hyde, F., *Liverpool and the Mersey: An Economic History of a Port 1700–1970* (Newton Abbot, 1971).

Inkster, I and Morrell, J. (eds), *Metropolis and Province: Science in British Culture, 1780–1850* (London, 1983).

Irving, W., *Sketch of William Roscoe* (Liverpool, 1853).

Jarvis,R., 'The head port of Chester; and Liverpool, its creek and member', *THSLC* 102 (1951).

Kelly, T., *Adult Education in Liverpool: A Narrative of Two Hundred Years* (Liverpool, 1960).

Kelly, T., *A History of Adult Education in Great Britain* (Liverpool, 1970).

Kitteringham, G., 'Science in provincial society: the case of Liverpool in the early nineteenth century', *Annals of Science*, 39 (1982).

Langford, P., *Public Life and the Propertied Englishman 1689–1798* (Oxford, 1991).

Macandrew, H., 'Henry Fuseli and William Roscoe', *Liverpool Bulletin*, 8 (1959–1860).

McGrath, P. (ed.), *Bristol in the Eighteenth Century* (Newton Abbot, 1972).

Macintyre, P., 'Historical sketch of the Liverpool Library', *THSLC*, 9 (1987).

McKendrick, N., Brewer, J. and Plumb, J., *The Birth of a Consumer Society: The Commercialization of Eighteenth-century England* (London, 1982).

MacKenzie Grieve, A., *The Last Years of the English Slave Trade; Liverpool 1750–1807* (London, 1941).

McLachlan, H., *Warrington Academy, Its History and Influence* (Manchester, 1943).

Macnaughton, D., *Roscoe of Liverpool* (Birkenhead, 1996).

Marillier, H.C., *The Liverpool School of Painters: An Account of the Liverpool Academy from 1810–1867, With Memoirs of the Principal Artists* (London, 1904).

Marriner, S., *The Economic and Social Development of Merseyside* (London, 1982).

Masson, P., *The Collected Writings of Thomas De Quincey* (London, 1996).

Mathews, G.W., *William Roscoe, A Memoir* (London, 1931).

Maxwell, Sir H. (ed.), *The Creevey Papers: A Selection from the Correspondence and Diaries of Thomas Creevey MP* 2 vols (London, 1904).

Mayer, J., 'Roscoe and the influence of his writings on the Fine Arts', *THSLC*, 5 (1853).

Mayer, J., *Early Exhibitions of Art in Liverpool* (Liverpool, 1876).

Melville, H. and Beaver, H. (ed.), *Redburn* (London, 1986).

Menzies, E., 'The freeman voter in Liverpool 1802–1835', *THSLC*, 124 (1973).

Morris, E., 'The formation of the gallery of art in the Liverpool Royal Institution, 1816–1819', *THSLC*, 142 (1992).

Moss, W., *The Liverpool Guide: Including a Sketch of the Environs; with a Map of Liverpool* (Liverpool, 1796).

Muir, J.R., *A History of Liverpool*, second ed. (London, 1907).

Murphy, G., *William Roscoe, His Early Ideals and Influence* (Liverpool, 1981).

Ormerod, H., *The Liverpool Royal Institution: A Record and a Retrospect* (Liverpool, 1853).

Northcote Parkinson, C., *The Rise of the Port of Liverpool* (Liverpool, 1952).

Perkin, H., *The Origins of Modern English Society 1780–1880* (London, 1969).

Picton, J.A., *Memorials of Liverpool, Historical and Topographical, Including a History of the Dock Estate* (London, 1873).

Picton, J.A., *Municipal Archives and Records*, 2 vols (Liverpool, 1883–1886).

Pollard, R. and Pevsner, N., *The Buildings of England: Lancashire: Liverpool and the South West* (New Haven and London, 2006).

Porter, R., *English Society in the Eighteenth Century* (Harmondsworth, 1990).

Rathbone, E.A. (ed.), *Records of the Rathbone Family* (Edinburgh, 1913).

Roscoe, H., *The Life of William Roscoe*, 2 vols (Edinburgh, 1833).

Roscoe, W., *The Life and Pontificate of Leo X* (London, 1805).

Roscoe, W., *On the Origins and Vicissitudes of Literature, Science and Art and their Influence on the Present State of Society: A Discourse Delivered on the Opening of the Liverpool Royal Institution, 25th November 1817* (Liverpool, 1817).

Roscoe, W., *Catalogue of a Series of Pictures Illustrating the Rise and Early Progress of the Art of Painting in Italy, Germany etc.* (Liverpool, 1819).

Roscoe, W., *The Life of Lorenzo de'Medici, Called the Magnificent* seventh ed., (London, 1846).

Rose, R.B., 'The "Jacobins" of Liverpool 1789–1793', *Liverpool Bulletin*, 9 (1960–1961).

Ross Williamson, H. *Lorenzo the Magnificent* (London, 1974).

Sanderson, F.E., 'The Liverpool delegates and Sir William Dolben's

Bill', *THSLC*, 124 (1973).

Sanderson, F.E., 'The Structure of Politics in Liverpool 1780–1807', *THSLC*, 127 (1978).

Sellers, I., 'William Roscoe, the Roscoe circle and radical politics in Liverpool 1787–1807', *THSLC*, 120, 1968.

Shaw, G., *History of The Athenaeum Liverpool, 1798–1898* (Liverpool, 1898).

Smithers, H., *Liverpool, its Commerce, Statistics and Institutions; with a History of the Cotton Trade* (Liverpool, 1825).

Stansfield, H., 'William Roscoe, botanist', *Liverpool Bulletin*, 5 (November 1955).

Starkey, P. (ed.), *Riches into Art: Liverpool Collectors 1770–1880* (Liverpool, 1993).

Stewart-Brown, R., *A History of the Manor and Township of Allerton* (Liverpool, 1911).

Stobart, J., 'Culture versus commerce: societies and spaces for elites in eighteenth-century Liverpool', *Journal of Historical Geography*, 28, 4 (2002).

Stonehouse, J., 'Dramatic places of amusement in Liverpool a century ago', *THSLC*, 5 (1852–1853).

Story, R., 'Class and culture in Boston: The Athenaeum, 1807–1860', *American Quarterly*, 27 (1975).

Sweet, R., *The English Town, 1680–1840: Government, Society and Culture* (Harlow, 1999).

Taylor, F.H., *Liverpool and the Athenaeum* (Liverpool, 1965).

Taylor, H.A., 'Matthew Gregson and the pursuit of taste', *THSLC*, 110 (1958).

Thackray, A. 'Natural knowledge in a cultural context: the Manchester model', *The American Historical Review*, 79 (1974).

Thomson, D.m *The Stranger's Vade Mecum or Liverpool Described* (Liverpool, 1854).

Touzeau, J., *The Rise and Progress of Liverpool from 1551–1835*, 2 vols (Liverpool, 1910).

Traill, T.S., *Memoir of William Roscoe* (Liverpool, 1853).

Trepp, J., 'The Liverpool movement for the abolition of the slave trade', *The Journal of Negro History*, 13, 3 (July 1928).

Troughton, T., *The History of Liverpool from the Earliest Authenticated Period down to the Present Time* (Liverpool, c.1810).

Wainwright, D., *Liverpool Gentlemen: A History of Liverpool*

*College; An Independent Day School from 1840* (London, 1940).

Wallace, J., *A General and Descriptive History of the Antient and Present State of the Town of Liverpool* (Liverpool, 1797).

Waller, P.J., *Democracy and Sectarianism: A Political and Social History of Liverpool 1868–1939* (Liverpool, 1981).

Wardle, A., 'Liverpool's first Theatre Royal', *THSLC*, 90 (1939).

Watson, R.S., *The History of the Literary and Philosophical Society of Newcastle Upon Tyne (1793–1896)* (London, 1896).

Whale, J., 'The making of a city of culture; William Roscoe's Liverpool', *Eighteenth Century Life* 29, 2 (spring 2005).

Williams, G., *History of the Liverpool Privateers and Letters of Marque with an Account of the Liverpool Slave Trade* (London and Liverpool, 1897).

Williams, P.H., *A Gentleman's Calling: The Liverpool Attorney-at-law; On Behalf of the Incorporated Law Society of Liverpool* (Denbigh, 1980).

Wright and Cruikshank, *A Compendium and Impartial Account of the Election at Liverpool ... together with ... the Songs and Squibs ... and also a Correct List of the Freemen who Polled at the Late Election* (Liverpool, 1806).

Young, G.M. (ed.), *Early Victorian England 1830–1865* (Oxford, 1951).

## Unpublished Theses

Graham, J.E., 'The political ideas and activities of William Roscoe, 1787–1801', unpublished MA thesis, University of Liverpool, 1970.

Murphy, S., 'The Liverpool Library 1758–1941: its foundation, organisation and development', unpublished MA thesis, University of Sheffield, 1983.

Pope, D.J., 'Shipping and trade in the port of Liverpool 1783–1793', unpublished PhD thesis, University of Liverpool, 1970.

Sellers, I., 'Liverpool nonconformity 1786–1914', unpublished PhD thesis, University of Keele, 1969.

Storey, C., ' Myths of the Medici: William Roscoe and Renaissance historiography', unpublished PhD thesis, University of Oxford, 2003.

Taylor, I., 'Black spot on the Mersey: a study of environment and society in eighteenth and nineteenth century Liverpool', unpublished PhD thesis, University of Liverpool, 1976.

Watkinson, C.D., 'The Liberal Party on Merseyside in the nineteenth century', unpublished PhD thesis, University of Liverpool, 1968.

Weinglass, D., 'The publishing history of William Roscoe's edition of the works of Alexander Pope Esq., 1824', unpublished PhD thesis, University of Kansas, 1969.

Wilson, A., 'Culture and commerce: Liverpool's merchant elite c.1790–1850', unpublished PhD thesis, University of Liverpool, 1996.

# Index